TRUE NORTH

GARY INRIG

TRUE NORTH

DISCOVERING GOD'S WAY *in a* CHANGING WORLD

DISCOVERY HOUSE

PUBLISHERS®

Requests for permission to quote from this book should be directed to: Permissions Department, Discovery House Publishers, P.O. Box 3566, Grand Rapids, MI 49501, or contact us by e-mail at permissionsdept@dhp.org

All Scripture quotations, unless otherwise indicated, are taken from the Holy Bible, New International Version®, NIV®. Copyright © 1973, 1978, 1984 by Biblica, Inc.™ Used by permission of Zondervan. All rights reserved worldwide. www.zondervan.com

Interior design: Nicholas Richardson

ISBN 978-157293-076-6

Printed in the United States of America

Third printing in 2013

To Stephen and Jula
with the prayer that as you navigate together
you might live to the glory of God
and the good of others.

Contents

Acknowledgments

Leonard Sweet first planted in my mind the metaphor of navigational skills. He has developed that picture in terms of church leadership in a book entitled *Aqua Church*. It is appropriate for me to acknowledge my indebtedness to him.

The family of believers at Trinity Church in Redlands has been a wonderful blessing in my life. They were the first to hear much of this material, and I am profoundly grateful for their warm response and their continual encouragement.

My wife, Elizabeth, is not only a wonderful sailing companion on the seas of life; she is also a constant example of one who navigates life well, to the glory of her Lord. I thank my God for her.

INTRODUCTION

The images will never leave our minds. The stunning news that a plane had flown into one of the towers of New York City's World Trade Center on September 11, 2001, seemed at first like a terrible accident. When, shortly thereafter, another plane flew into the second tower, followed by an attack on the Pentagon and a thwarted attack on an unknown target, it became evident that these were horrific acts of terrorism. As we heard the news and watched those massive buildings collapse, thinking of the thousands of innocent people trapped inside, we all felt a bewildering mixture of stunned disbelief, intense grief, and deep anger. In moments, two famous landmarks of the world's greatest nation were reduced to "Ground Zero." In an act of incomprehensible evil, thousands of lives were cut short, families were torn apart, and everything changed in a multitude of ways, large and small. The world and the way we deal with it changed on 9–11, 2001.

Suddenly, leaders faced situations for which there were no contingency plans. How could emergency planners possibly have conceived of such diabolical willingness to sacrifice one's own life and take so much innocent life? The situation was complicated by the obvious sophistication of the terrorists' plans and compounded by rumors, uncertainties, and further terrorist attacks via mail laced with anthrax. Experts could turn to no developed maps or plans. They had no previously designed scenarios to follow.

We would love to believe that we live in a world where human brilliance can imagine all eventualities. But you cannot imagine the unimaginable. Government leaders at all levels found themselves navigating their way through a horrendous storm, using all the skills they had learned over the years in many different contexts and applying them to new and very fluid situations. They were sailing off the map, trying to steer a course through waters the nation had never previously traveled.

Those fallen towers may well become the symbol of the new millennium into which we are moving. Hopefully, the trauma of September 11 will never be repeated. But it is not the only way in which seemingly immoveable landmarks are removed from our culture. When Daniel Moynihan retired in 2000 as United States senator from New York, he was asked what had been the biggest change in his forty years of public service. His response is worth pondering: "The biggest change, in my judgment, is that the family structure has come apart all over the North Atlantic world. [It has happened] in an historical instant. Something that was not imaginable forty years ago has happened."[1]

I am personally convinced that the slow but sure collapse of the family is having even greater long-term effects on our lives and culture than Osama bin Laden's terrorist attacks. Coupled with that collapse is a massive shift toward a pluralism and relativism that undermines our understanding of truth, spiritual reality, and moral values.

Our local paper recently printed a poignant letter from a teacher who had returned to the classroom after a twenty-year absence. Nervously she approached her seventh-grade class, worrying about how she would begin. In her earlier years, she had begun the school day with the greeting, "Good morning, students," to which they would reply, "Good morning, Miss Jones." Deciding to repeat what was familiar, she walked into the classroom, put her books on the desk, wrote her name on the board, and then turned to face the class. "Good morning, students," she began. A loud voice in the front row responded, "Shut up, _____," and the class erupted in laughter. In her letter to the editor she asked, "What happened in America between 'Good morning, students,' and 'Shut up, _____,' and who is going to do something about it?"

The world has changed, and the old maps no longer match reality. We live in a fast-changing, unpredictable, highly fluid world from which many of the familiar landmarks have vanished. In past times, people talked about sailing or marching off the edge of their maps. That is where we are in our new world.

Maps are helpful if they accurately reflect the landscape. But when maps fail us, we need to know how to navigate. The heart of this book is the conviction that God has given us both the tools and the skills to navigate our world, so that we will safely and successfully arrive at the destination to which He is calling us.

In the thirteenth century, the world changed dramatically because a simple new device, called the compass, arrived on the scene. The compass opened up the world for exploration, trade, and discovery by freeing sailors from the coastlands. One scholar describes the impact of this most basic navigational tool: "The compass was the first instrument that allowed navigators, at sea, on land, and—much later—in the air, to determine their direction quickly and accurately at any time of the day or night and under almost any conditions. This allowed goods to be transported efficiently and reliably across the seas and opened up the world to maritime exploration. The earth would never be seen the same way again. The compass was therefore the most important technological invention since the wheel."[2]

The compass was a revolutionary device that changed the way people related to the natural world. But the Lord Jesus has given His people something even greater: navigational tools that transform our relationship to His world, as well as to our own rapidly changing world. The idea that we are called to navigate life actively by using God-given tools has been a tremendous help to me in thinking about how we are called to live as followers of Christ in a fluid world. In the chapters that follow, we will try to think about what it takes to navigate life successfully by using the tools, developing the skills, and following the examples the Lord has given.

Chapter One

OCEAN BOUND

When Ferdinand Magellan finally emerged from the tumultuous straits at the southern tip of South America that now bear his name, he wept for joy. For months, he had searched the coastline to find a passage to the west. The one he found proved to be difficult beyond imagining. For thirty-eight days, he and his men had battled a treacherous, unexplored body of water that even today is not an easy place for ships. The modern pilot manual warns sailing ships that it is "both difficult and dangerous, because of incomplete surveys, the lack of aids to navigation, the great distances between anchorages, the strong current, and the narrow limits for the maneuvering of vessels."[1] Imagine what it was like for the very first to attempt the journey! "Only Magellan's iron courage against the elements and his deft mastery of men kept him going."[2]

Magellan's tears were tears of joy for a victory hard won and a goal about to be realized. When he was told that his men had seen the cape and the open sea and had tasted the salty water, he "called that cape, Cape Dezeado [Desire], for we have been desiring it for a long time."[3] As

Magellan wept, his men sang hymns, the gunners fired their cannons, and the flag of Spain was unfurled. Charles V, the king of Spain, had commissioned Magellan to find a passage around South America to what Balboa had called the Mar del Sur, the Southern Sea. He was then to sail westward to the Spice Islands, which we know as the Moluccas, part of modern Indonesia. When Magellan broke through to the Pacific on November 28, 1520, he had already been underway for fourteen months. But he felt sure that the worst was behind him. His maps told him that within a few days, or at the most a few weeks, he would reach the Spice Islands and become the first to circumnavigate the world. He had already sailed to the Spice Islands from the east.

Little did Magellan know that his information was tragically in error. The problem was that no one had developed a reliable way to measure longitude. As a result, even the best estimates available to him underestimated the size of the Pacific Ocean by 80 percent. The most popular globe of the world showed Japan about one hundred miles off the coast of Mexico. "For Magellan, the extent of the Pacific was an excruciating surprise! Of course, it would also be his greatest and his most unwilling discovery."[4]

No one suspected that they were headed for tragedy as they sailed to the north. The sea was calm, the air balmy, and the winds consistent. For their whole journey, they did not experience a single storm, which seemed to confirm the name they had given this ocean, Pacific. But if they didn't encounter storms, neither did they encounter land. Week followed week, and the shortage of supplies became desperate. Six weeks out of the straits, men began to die.

> Such food as the three ships carried began to rot under the soggy tropical airs. The penguins and seals they had killed and salted in Patagonia started to turn putrid; maggots raged through the

ship, eating clothes and supplies and rigging; water supplies turned scummy and rank. Men began to develop the classic symptoms of scurvy—their teeth loosened in their gums, their breath began to smell horribly sour, huge boils erupted from their shrunken frames, they sank into inconsolable melancholia.[5]

Conditions only got worse. The crew was reduced to eating rats, ox hides soaked in the sea, and, finally, sawdust. Even Magellan broke under the strain. In a fit of rage, he threw all his charts overboard, shouting, "With the pardon of the cartographers, the Moluccas are not to be found in their appointed place!" It wasn't until March 6, 1521, that the ships made landfall at Guam. The voyage that was supposed to have taken four or five days had taken three months and twenty days and cost the lives of nineteen men and the debilitation of the entire crew. By the time the expedition was over, only eighteen of the original 238 remained. Magellan himself was killed when he was caught in the middle of tribal warfare in the Philippines.

When our maps are accurate, they enable us to navigate unfamiliar terrain with confidence and skill. But when our maps are inaccurate or out of date, they become at best a nuisance and at worst a terrible danger. As Magellan ventured into uncharted territory, wrong maps were far worse than no maps. They gave him false expectations, which endangered the lives of all his men. His situation was made worse by navigational devices that could not answer his most urgent questions.

Our modern world resembles a vast, uncharted ocean. We are no longer in familiar territory. Huge changes are sweeping across our world, which have made our maps obsolete. We have never been here before. A fundamental fact of life in the third millennium is that nothing is as permanent as change. Some people claim that the twentieth century experienced more change than all previous human history; and the 1990s, more changes than the previous ninety years. It isn't possible to prove such claims, but there can be no doubt that the rate of change in our world is not only high but also accelerating exponentially. Rapid change is an inescapable reality in every sphere of life, not just in obvious areas such as technology and demographics. Change is not only continual; it is discontinuous. That is, it is not just the past being recycled in new forms; it is old landmarks being dismantled, and a new order of things coming into being, which no one can truly predict. This creates a world of continual, discontinuous, unpredictable, accelerating change—and this is the context in which modern Christ-followers are called to live out their commitment to the Lord Jesus Christ.

The technological changes that are reshaping modern life confront us every day. We daily take for granted things that were nonexistent a few years ago or were reserved for the favored few. I am a computer novice, bravely trying to find my way in a strange new world. But, even at the level of my incompetence, I am amazed at the amount of information placed at my fingertips and my instant ability to be in contact with the other side of the world at the click of a mouse. Who hasn't marveled or given thanks for advances in the field of medicine that save the lives of loved ones or allow us to survive once hopeless problems? Laborsaving devices enable us to enjoy lifestyles earlier generations never imagined. The list of such changes is endless, and each one subtly but surely shapes our view of life.

As I write, I am flying from my home in Southern California to my childhood home city of Vancouver, Canada. Both areas profoundly illustrate our changing world. One of the men in our congregation in California runs a translation agency. He tells me that he has provided translation services in an astonishing 120 different languages. The world truly has come to Southern California, and there is no longer a majority ethnic group. In Vancouver, the beauty of the mountains and the ocean makes me feel instantly at home. Yet my parents' home is gone, replaced by a larger one, and Chinese has become the predominant language on my elementary school playground. Parts of the city resemble Hong Kong more than they do the very British city of my youth. Other areas feel like India.

Globalization is a fact, one that affects us in many subtle ways. For example, in the 1960s, futurologists boldly declared that the average worker would work fewer than thirty hours a week by the year 2000. Reality is very different. The workweek is longer than it was in 1965, not shorter, and families fight hard to carve out time for things that matter. One factor is the global economy, which has increased competition and intensified pressure. The same technological innovations that make some things easier also raise expectations and make it harder to get away from our work. Technology is often a two-edged sword.

At a less visible but more important level, Western culture has profoundly changed. A major culture shift has taken place, radically redefining concepts of truth, morality, and spirituality. "Postmodernism" is a term most of us would have trouble defining. In some ways, it is a mindset rather than a coherent philosophy. Nevertheless, it has blanketed our culture like smog slowly creeping up the Los Angeles basin. We live in a postmodern world, and the Christian consensus has been displaced. The assumption that our society should honor, at least officially, Judeo-Christian values, is no longer operative. Diversity rules, tolerance is supreme, and relativism is the only absolute. Sexual morality has given way to sexual preferences; the family has been replaced by a bewildering variety of families. Out-of-wedlock births have soared to tragically high rates, along with the number of absentee fathers. Religion is out; spirituality is in. But spirituality often amounts to little more than a pursuit of spiritual experiences, a journey into one's inner self or personal truth, which makes the living God irrelevant. It is also no longer clear when a person uses the word *God* that he means anything resembling the God of Scripture.

My purpose is not to induce cynicism or pessimism. Instead it is to point out that we are living in uncharted territory. The familiar landmarks have vanished, and the old cultural maps are outdated. So we need to think not so much of maps as of navigational skills, not so much of travel guides as of principles that will help us find our way through the fluid, complex, fast-changing ocean on which we have to navigate. That is the purpose of this book, and it is built on the conviction that God, in His Word, has given us exactly what we need to navigate life well in the twenty-first century.

The changes we are experiencing are indeed massive and unpredictable. The future, whatever it is, will not be the logical extension of the past. We truly are in uncharted territory. But no matter how extensive these changes prove to be, they will not surpass the changes experienced by the first followers of the Lord Jesus Christ. Before they met Him, their lives were relatively predictable. They were simple working people whose world had narrow and clearly defined boundaries. Their land was small; their opportunities were few; their education was limited; their ambitions were meager; their vision was narrow. For the most part they expected to live, love, work, and rear a family in Galilee, with occasional visits to Jerusalem, where they would reaffirm their intention to live and die within the familiar boundaries of Judaism. In many ways, their future was like the lake by which they lived and on which some of them made their livings—small, familiar, but subject to occasional storms. Then they met Jesus and began to follow Him as Lord. They had no idea that they were going to leave their little lake, literally and symbolically, and venture onto the ocean of God's purposes. Men whose world had been small and familiar would be led by their Lord to places they had never imagined going, to do things they had never imagined doing. In the process, God used them to launch a world-engaging, world-transforming movement under the banner of their Lord. It is tremendously encouraging to me to recognize that the first disciples had none of the natural abilities we would expect in such people. Seeing how these first Christians learned to navigate the uncharted waters of their new world provides an example for us.

The disciples didn't need to learn to navigate the Lake of Galilee. They had spent their lives on its waters and around its shores. Everything was familiar, and at their furthest from shore, they were never out of sight of land. But the Lord used a morning on that lake to begin to plant the idea that He had a mission for them greater than their wildest imagination. The story is told in Luke 5:1–11.

> One day as Jesus was standing by the Lake of Gennesaret, with the people crowding around him and listening to the word of God, he saw at the water's edge two boats, left there by the fishermen, who were washing their nets. He got into one of the boats, the one belonging to Simon, and asked him to put out a little from shore. Then he sat down and taught the people from the boat.
>
> When he had finished speaking, he said to Simon, "Put out into deep water, and let down the nets for a catch."
>
> Simon answered, "Master, we've worked hard all night and haven't caught anything. But because you say so, I will let down the nets."
>
> When they had done so, they caught such a large number of fish that their nets began to break. So they signaled their partners in the other boat to come and help them, and they came and filled both boats so full that they began to sink.
>
> When Simon Peter saw this, he fell at Jesus' knees and said,

"Go away from me, Lord; I am a sinful man!" For he and all his companions were astonished at the catch of fish they had taken, and so were James and John, the sons of Zebedee, Simon's partners.

Then Jesus said to Simon, "Don't be afraid; from now on you will catch men." So they pulled their boats up on shore, left everything and followed him.

Lawrence Peter once wrote a book that humorously described something we have all experienced. He called it *The Peter Principle* and stated it in these words: "In a hierarchy, people tend to rise to the level of their incompetence." His insights began when he mailed all the documents required to obtain a teaching certificate to the required agency, only to receive the package back a few weeks later. An explanatory letter accompanied the material: "New regulations require that such forms cannot be accepted by the Department of Education unless they have been registered at the Post Office to ensure safe delivery. Will you please re-mail the forms to the department, making sure to register them this time." The logic of returning safely delivered mail to ensure safe delivery epitomizes the Peter Principle. Unfortunately, sometimes it seems like official government policy.

In the gospel, we find something very different at work, beautifully illustrated in the life of the apostle Peter. We could call it the Peter Paradigm: "In Christ, people can rise to the level of their God-given potential." The Lord saw in Peter what no one else saw, and the Lord's presence in Peter's life meant that Peter experienced a continually expanding sphere of competence and influence. That process is evident in this encounter, which becomes almost a pattern of the way the Lord works in the lives of His followers.

Shallow Water: The Lord Uses My Boat

One Sabbath day, the Lord Jesus visited the synagogue in His hometown of Nazareth and claimed the words of Isaiah 61:1–2 as a description of himself:

"The Spirit of the Lord is on me, because he has anointed me to preach good news to the poor. He has sent me to proclaim freedom for the prisoners and recovery of sight for the blind, to release the oppressed, to proclaim the year of the Lord's favor." (Luke 4:18–19)

The Lord was not only declaring that He was the fulfillment of prophecy; He was declaring His kingdom manifesto. This was the pattern of His life, a ministry of bringing broken people to wholeness. Luke describes the ministry of the Lord Jesus as He moved through Galilee, a part of Palestine notorious for its spiritual darkness and its cultural diversity, healing and teaching. It was a ministry of transformation within those who became His followers, and His priority was clear: "I must preach the good news of the kingdom of God to the other towns also, because that is why I was sent" (Luke 4:43).

Then, in Luke 5, we find another fundamental principle of His ministry: He comes to bring transformation not only within His people but also through His people. He enlists ordinary human beings to become agents of His kingdom in the sphere of influence where they are and then to enlarge that sphere of influence, as He directs. This is not only a first-century phenomenon. This is the way the Lord works in the lives of His followers in every time and place, and the pattern given in these early verses of Luke 5 is one He provides for His people in the third millennium as well. "As the Father has sent me, I am sending you" (John 20:21).

We would misread Luke 5, however, if we saw this as the original encounter of these men with Jesus. In the previous chapter, we are told that Jesus had spent time in the home of Simon (that is, Peter) and that the Lord had healed Peter's mother-in-law. The gospel of John fills in more details. It describes Peter's initial meeting with the Lord Jesus and the Lord's words: "You are Simon son of John. You will be called Cephas" (John 1:42). It is clear that Peter, at that point, became a disciple, although his knowledge of Jesus was rudimentary, and John describes the other disciples accompanying Jesus as He moved through Judea and Galilee.

But Peter remained a fisherman, making his living on Lake Galilee, or, as it was also known, the Lake of Gennesaret. And on this particular morning, he and his companions were doing typical fishermen's chores, washing and mending their nets after a night's fishing. This was business as usual, made different only by the presence of Jesus, who was accompanied by a large crowd listening to His teaching. Luke mentions the crowd, but that's not where his interest is. He focuses our attention on the interaction between Peter and his Lord.

At some point, Jesus moved close enough to get into Peter's boat, and asked him to push out from shore. This was not a major request, and it made sense. People could more easily see and hear the Lord if He was a few feet offshore. But it was an interruption of Peter's activities, and the boat was relatively sizable. A typical first-century Galilean fishing boat, according to archaeological discovery, measured about twenty-eight feet in length and eight feet in width. Pushing a boat of that size out into the water required special effort. It also meant pulling in the nets and storing them in their proper place in the boat. Peter did not object, and there is no suggestion that he felt anything but a sense of privilege in serving his Lord. He granted the Lord's request and pushed out from shore, far enough for the water to act as a natural acoustic system. I can imagine his sense of satisfaction as he sat there, watching the Lord teach and instruct the crowds. He had allowed his resources to be used in the furtherance of the kingdom, and that was deeply satisfying. Peter valued Jesus and he loved fishing, and now the two were being linked in an exciting way. I think the Lord often does that, recruiting us into kingdom ministry at entry level. The first stage is to become a Christ-follower, experiencing the joy of a life-changing relationship with the Lord Jesus. Stage two is when we realize that the Lord wants to use something we possess as a means of furthering the kingdom. It may be a skill or ability. It may be a position of influence. Perhaps it is a physical possession or monetary resources. Whatever our boat is, the Lord asks to use it, tells us to put out from shore, and allows us to watch as He uses our boat in a way that furthers His purposes. It is a thrilling experience when the Lord chooses to use something that we own to make a permanent difference in the lives of other people.

But consider this fair warning. The Lord isn't content just to use our boat. He has a disconcerting way of taking it over, as Peter soon discovered.

PUSHING DEEPER: THE LORD TAKES OVER MY BOAT

The Lord finished His message and suddenly turned to Peter. His next words came as a command, not a request: "Put out into deep water, and let down the nets for a catch" (Luke 5:4). This is something different. The Lord is not merely using the boat; He is taking over. This whole episode takes place at His initiative, and His demand is a significant one. Setting out the nets was not only considerable work in itself; it meant repeating all the work of washing and refolding them. To what purpose? Any novice fisherman on Lake Galilee knew that midmorning was not the time for fishing. And this doesn't involve Peter alone. The Lord's first command, "Put out into deep water," is singular, addressed to Peter as the master of the boat. The second command is plural: "[You, plural], let down the nets." Peter's crew is to be involved in this apparently useless activity. Some of them might have wondered, Why is a carpenter giving orders to fishermen?

Peter's response is intriguing: "Master, we've worked hard all night and haven't caught anything. But because you say so, I will let down the nets" (Luke 5:5). Peter begins with respect (the term *Master* obviously acknowledges Jesus' authority) and ends with submission. But he is reluctant. For good reason. After all, Peter is the expert on fishing. He has spent all his life on the lake, and he knows it like the back of his hand. First, it is the wrong time for fishing. Deep-water fishing took place at night and early morning, and the men had just returned from a futile night of hard work. Second, it is the wrong place. For whatever reason, the fishing is bad. I wonder if Peter thought what I often feel: "It's okay for the Lord to use my boat for religious purposes. But not for fishing. That's where I'm the expert!" Sometimes it is harder to trust the Lord in the areas of our strengths than in the areas of our weaknesses.

Scholars discuss whether this is a miracle of knowledge (Jesus knew the fish were there) or of power (He brought them there). What does it matter? It is undeniably a miracle. The catch overwhelms the capacity of the nets, the boats, and the fishermen. Even when help comes, the catch is so large that it endangers both boats. The Lord is making a point: When our expertise is surrendered to His directions, we become effective beyond our imagining. He knows our business even better than we do.

This becomes a defining moment for Peter. It isn't the catch that impresses him but the Lord. He abandons the frantic activity of trying to save the catch and the boats and falls at Jesus' knees. "Go away from me, Lord; I am a sinful man!" (Luke 5:8). Peter has a new respect for Jesus, indicated by the new term he uses to describe him: "Lord." Moments before he had called Him "Master," a clear term of respect. Now he calls Him "Lord." This is not just a stylistic difference. Peter is beginning to understand that Jesus is no mere man, but something far more. He is beginning to realize that Jesus belongs in a very different category from that shared by ordinary sinful humans. Over the course of time, Peter would come to realize that Jesus held that title *Lord* in the highest sense. At a crowning moment in his own life, Peter would declare, "You are the Christ, the Son of the living God" (Matthew 16:16). In his second epistle, he would describe Him as "our Lord and Savior Jesus Christ" (2 Peter 1:11), which is why in his first epistle he exhorted Christ-followers: "in your hearts set apart Christ as Lord" (1 Peter 3:15). On his knees before Jesus in a sinking boat full of wriggling fish, that is what Peter was beginning to do.

Peter not only recognizes Jesus for who He is (Lord) but also sees himself for who he is, a sinner. In the light of the Lord's greatness, he feels unworthy and overwhelmed. He recognizes his immaturity and inadequacy, not because the Lord has revealed his shortcomings but because He has revealed His own glory. A few minutes earlier, Peter had pushed his boat out in what he was convinced was a futile effort in an empty lake. By obeying the Lord, he had not only made the catch of a lifetime, but had also experienced a revolution in the way he saw all of life, himself included. Little did he know the journey had barely begun!

Ocean Bound: The Lord Expands My Horizon

The Lord makes it clear that this is a defining moment, a turning point: "Don't be afraid; from now on you will catch men" (Luke 5:10). Until this moment, Peter's world was not much bigger than the lake he fished. He had seen his future as one of catching and selling fish. But from now on, nothing would be the same. He had been spoiled for little things, because he had seen Jesus through the eyes of faith.

The Lord had a purpose for Peter that was deeper and richer than anything he could imagine: "You will keep on catching people." I don't know what Peter imagined that meant, and the Lord makes no attempt to explain it to him. Peter had no possibility of knowing what the future held: where he would go, what he would do, who he would become. In fact, had he known, he would have been overwhelmed and afraid. He only knew that in some way the Lord was inviting him to join in an adventure that would indelibly affect not only his life but also the lives of many others. He knew that he needed and longed to follow Jesus.

Peter wasn't alone. His friends and partners, James and John, had been watching carefully. Suddenly, the greatest catch of their lives, the kind fishermen talk and dream about, had no power to hold them. "So they pulled their boats up on shore, left everything and followed him" (Luke 5:11). As the missionary statesman E. Stanley Jones once put it: "I looked into His face and was forever spoiled for anything unlike Him." It was a following that was going to catapult them away from their little lake into the ocean of God's purposes.

This is an actual event in the life of our Lord. It speaks to us on the level of history. It also speaks on another level, and that is one of pattern. Luke is concerned in his gospel and in the book of Acts to tell us not only what the gospel is but also how it reaches out to the ends of the earth. The gospel of Luke is the story of all that Jesus began to do in His earthly life (Acts 1:1); Acts is the story of all that He continues to do through His people. Here, in the beginning of his story, Luke reports an episode that establishes a pattern the Lord will follow. He brings transformation in His people and then through His people. He keeps pushing us into deeper water until we find ourselves out of our depths, navigating uncharted waters, as agents of his kingdom. This picture helps me think more clearly about what it means to be a Christ-follower in the third millennium.

A Christ-follower allows the Lord to establish the destination. Navigators must be able to answer two crucial questions: Where do I want to go? Where am I now? If we don't have the answer to those questions, we may be cruising or we may be drifting, but we aren't navigating. We spend a lot of time thinking about where we are now; we spend much less time considering where we are going. Many try to use the obvious markers of success to chart their course: money, comfort, fame, pleasure, power, status. These things may be good and valuable as resources, but they are dangerous as goals.

Fast Company is a business magazine that chronicles the fast-paced businesses of the new economy. One insightful issue addressed the question: How much is enough? The editor began with this observation:

> People who are winning at the gaming tables of the new econ-omy must ask this perplexing question: How Much is Enough?
> . . . Ceaseless striving is indelibly stamped on the American character. The American Dream . . . says that we can have it all. The American Reality whispers that when you do get it all, you'll only want more.[6]

The fact is that no human harbor can satisfy the heart. We need to know what the Lord's goal is for us and to set sail for it. Wise navigators make sure that they know where they are headed.

A Christ-follower practices celestial navigation. Wise navigators also make sure that they know where they are. Following Jesus was radically different from following a normal Jewish rabbi. If Peter had set out to follow a rabbi, he would have received an elaborately detailed map and accompanying handbook that answered every question and addressed every situation. There would have been codes of conduct for every situation. But those would never have taken Peter where the Lord intended him to go, into the uncharted waters of the Gentile world to build a church for all peoples. The Lord didn't give His people maps; He taught them to navigate. Those navigational principles are as relevant to the twenty-first century as they were to the first. There are navigational fixed points (the North Star), navigational tools (sextants, compasses, chronometers), and navigational skills. All of these have their spiritual counterparts, as we shall see in the following chapters. The crucial thing is to recognize that the postmodern world is too complex and fluid for maps. We must learn to navigate.

However, it is difficult to navigate a sinking ship, so we also must know how to keep the water out of the boat.

A Christ-follower cares about seaworthiness. Wise Christians care about character, about what our condition is below the waterline, where no one else can see. Long before the Lord did something through Peter, He did something in Peter. That is always the Lord's way, and so we will take time to do some careful evaluation of our seaworthiness in the chapters that follow. We will also track the lives of others who have gone before us to learn from their successes and failures. We don't have man-made maps to chart our way into the new world. We have something much better—a living Lord, His eternal navigational instruments, and His indwelling Spirit.

Chapter Two

FINDING TRUE NORTH

When Ernest Shackleton and his six companions jumped into a little boat and pushed off from a barren, desolate beach on Elephant Island, deep in the southern ocean, there was virtually no chance that they would ever again see the twenty-one men they were leaving behind. It was amazing that they had survived this long. It was Monday, April 24, 1916. Fifteen months before, as they attempted to become the first expedition to cross Antarctica, their ship had become icebound. Under the careful leadership of Shackleton, they had survived through a brutal Antarctic winter and a harsh summer. But, finally, the relentless pressure of the ice had crushed and sunk their ship. They had managed to scramble onto the ice and salvage what they could, but the ice was a treacherous home. So they had been forced to make a desperate escape in their salvaged lifeboats to a bleak rocky island, where they were on solid ground but where no human life could survive for long. To stay where they were would mean certain death, whether by freezing or by starvation. No one would come to their rescue. Nobody knew where they were, and no ships ever came willingly into such dangerous waters.[1]

Their only hope was to be found on South Georgia Island, eight hundred miles away, across some of the stormiest waters on earth, in the middle of winter. They would encounter bitter cold, icebergs, waves up to seventy feet high, and eighty-mile-an-hour winds. With virtually no navigational devices, they would have to hit their target precisely, or they would be swept out into three thousand miles of empty ocean. Only fools or desperate men would try such a venture. As experienced sailors, Shackleton and his crew knew their task was virtually hopeless. But there were no other options. There was only one small boat capable of making the trip, and so the lives of twenty-seven men would be in the hands of six men, led by Shackleton.

Pushing off the beach of Elephant Island during a break in the storm was difficult enough. Dealing with the elements was worse. But their greatest problem was navigating. The weather was gloomy, and in seventeen days they saw the sun only four times. At night the stars were nearly always invisible.

Frank Worsley, who acted as the navigator, later recalled his efforts: "Dead reckoning or DR—the seaman's calculation of courses and distance—had become a merry jest of guesswork. Once, perhaps twice, a week the sun smiled a sudden wintry flicker through storm-torn clouds. If ready for it, and smart, I caught it."[2]

But those brief moments when they could see the heavens proved to be enough. They were able to get their bearings, and in one of the greatest feats of seamanship in history, Shackleton and his men reached South Georgia Island through the heart of a hurricane that sank larger vessels. From there, he returned to rescue all of his men alive from Elephant Island.

The only hope a sailor has of surviving a storm and navigating an ocean is to have a fixed reference point that enables him to discover where he is and where he is heading. The first navigators kept in sight of land, using familiar landmarks. When mariners dared to push beyond the sight of land, they still needed to find a fixed point of reference. So they looked to the heavens. As knowledge grew and celestial navigation developed, the primary reference point for navigators in the Northern Hemisphere became the North Star, Polaris. Modern technology has changed the process. Sextants and compasses have given way to electronic navigation and the Global Positioning System (GPS). But the principle remains the same. The fixed reference points for GPS are a system of twenty-four satellites that send out signals, which a receiver then uses to compute latitude, longitude, and even altitude. Those satellites have precisely fixed locations.

The North Star for navigating life is the triune God revealed in the Lord Jesus Christ. This is true whether we are in relatively familiar waters with old landmarks comfortably in sight, or far out in uncharted waters with nothing on the horizon. It is our focus on Christ that will keep us on course. That can easily sound like a pious platitude, but in the middle of a storm it becomes an urgent necessity. Few places in the Bible illustrate that as well as the compelling story of Job. Although the story has a profound depth that demands careful attention, my goal is more modest. We are going to look at some of the book's essential themes, which provide several important navigation principles.

LIFE'S STORMS MAY HIT THE MOST UNEXPECTED PEOPLE

Whatever else is true of Job, he is not an ordinary man, and his is not an ordinary life. As we read his story, we must recognize that he is an exception, not the norm. This is not the way things usually happen. And profound as the book is, it does not attempt to answer all of our questions about the mystery of evil. But its opening words introduce us to a life well lived and a man whom God marked out for his upright character.

In the land of Uz there lived a man whose name was Job. This man was blameless and upright; he feared God and shunned evil. He had seven sons and three daughters, and he owned seven thousand sheep, three thousand camels, five hundred yoke of oxen and five hundred donkeys, and had a large number of servants. He was the greatest man among all the people of the East.

His sons used to take turns holding feasts in their homes, and they would invite their three sisters to eat and drink with them. When a period of feasting had run its course, Job would send and have them purified. Early in the morning he would sacrifice a burnt offering for each of them, thinking, "Perhaps my children have sinned and cursed God in their hearts." This was Job's regular custom. (Job 1:1–5)

There is much that we do not know about Job. We are not told when he lived, and we have only a general idea of where (northern Saudi Arabia or southern Jordan). We are unsure about his relation, if any, to the people of Israel. Who wrote the book and when also remain unanswerable questions. But the message that the Holy Spirit intends us to learn from Job's story does not depend on these things. It does, however, require us to consider carefully the information we are given about the man described in these first few verses.

Job is a person of impeccable character, a man of integrity, "blameless and upright." This is not just the human author's opinion. Remarkably, it is the opinion of God, who challenges Satan with Job's character: "Have you considered my servant Job? There is no one on earth like him; he is blameless and upright, a man who fears God and shuns evil" (Job 1:8). No higher affirmation can be imagined. "The fear of the Lord—that is wisdom, and to shun evil is understanding" (Job 28:28). Job is a sinful human being, but he towers above his contemporaries in the integrity of his inner life.

Job is also a person of substance. The description of his wealth doesn't immediately strike us as making him worthy of inclusion on a list of the world's wealthiest men, especially in a culture that seems to make people billionaires overnight on the stock market and instant millionaires on game shows. But Job, in the currency of his day, was a successful and prosperous man. Family was considered wealth, and a man with seven sons was rich indeed. Seven thousand sheep, three hundred camels, five hundred working teams of oxen, five hundred donkeys, a large retinue of servants—these were all marks of power and prominence. Job was a man to be reckoned with, a man who was not only personally prosperous but also wielded great economic influence in his region. He was not merely successful; he was "the greatest man among all the people of the East."

A third thing we are told about Job is that he was a man with a vigorous and authentic spiritual life, combined with a deep concern for his family. His wealth had not made him self-indulgent or self-sufficient. He was a man of prayer and upheld his childen before the Lord. His sons and daughters loved to party. We are not told exactly what these parties involved, but they apparently troubled Job enough for him to be concerned about his children's spiritual and moral well-being. To that end, he made sure that all of these feasts were followed by some kind of ritual purification for his children. Then he would offer sacrifices for each of them, with a prayerful concern for their relation to God and their inner lives: "Perhaps my children have sinned and cursed God in their hearts." The precise details of this process are obscure to us; the larger meaning is not. Job did not take his wealth for granted and forget God. Nor did he believe his children were entitled to live the good life, indifferent to God.

We therefore begin with a clear picture of the man who is at the center of the action. Job is a pillar of moral integrity, a model of spiritual authenticity, and a recognized and respected success. In every sphere of life, Job flourished. He was the kind of person people admired and God marked out as special.

Then, suddenly, unpredictably, everything changes. Job's life is torn apart, and he has no way of knowing why. He is living at ground level as one disaster after another tears apart his carefully constructed life. As readers, we are given the advantage of seeing Job's life from a heavenly perspective. But as we live our own lives, we live where Job did, at ground level, unable to see things from above. And that is the heart of the life of faith—trusting when and where we do not see or understand.

Round one begins with the sudden arrival of a report from one of his servants:

> One day when Job's sons and daughters were feasting and drink-ing wine at the oldest brother's house, a messenger came to Job and said, "The oxen were plowing and the donkeys were grazing nearby, and the Sabeans attacked and carried them off. They put the servants to the sword, and I am the only one who has escaped to tell you!" (Job 1:13–15)

It isn't clear whether this is an act of war or a brutal robbery, but it is an act that combines terror with massive financial and personal losses. Job probably grieved far more for his lost servants than for his lost oxen and sheep. But the avalanche of troubles is only beginning.

> While he was still speaking, another messenger came and said, "The fire of God fell from the sky and burned up the sheep and the servants, and I am the only one who has escaped to tell you!" (Job 1:16)

Job barely has time to catch his breath when the second blow falls. This time it is some kind of natural disaster, perhaps a massive lightning strike that causes a fire that destroys his sheep and his shepherds. But once again, Job has no time for the bad news to sink in:

> While he was still speaking, another messenger came and said, "The Chaldeans formed three raiding parties and swept down on your camels and carried them off. They put the servants to the sword, and I am the only one who has escaped to tell you!" (Job 1:17)

This time the troubles are again human in origin. The raiding parties of the Chaldeans have swept down, stolen Job's camels, and killed his herdsmen. He must have wondered whether some strange alliance of tribal groups had targeted him. But, once again, he has no opportunity to process the information. Another messenger arrives with far worse news. For the third time we have the phrase "while he was still speaking." These messengers are almost falling over one another in their urgency to bring the bad news:

> While he was still speaking, yet another messenger came and said, "Your sons and daughters were feasting and drinking wine at the oldest brother's house, when suddenly a mighty wind swept in from the desert and struck the four corners of the house. It collapsed on them and they are dead, and I am the only one who has escaped to tell you!" (Job 1:18–19)

Of all the news Job has received, none is worse than this. A tornado-like wind has taken the lives of all who are most precious to him. Combined with the other messages, this becomes a waking nightmare for Job. His prosperity, his security, his lifestyle, his social standing, and his family have vanished in a moment's time. Within minutes, he has been transformed from the greatest man of the East to the most desolate man on earth. Harsh as Job's nightmare day is, however, this is only round one. Round two will target Job's personal health and well-being:

> So Satan went out from the presence of the LORD and afflicted Job with painful sores from the soles of his feet to the top of his head. Then Job took a piece of broken pottery and scraped himself with it as he sat among the ashes.
>
> His wife said to him, "Are you still holding on to your integrity? Curse God and die!" (Job 2:7–9)

The specifics of Job's disease aren't clear, but his condition was extremely painful and socially isolating. He was reduced to a beggar-like existence, sitting on a garbage heap, surrounded by broken pottery and the ashes of burned-out fires. He had lost everything of value to him: family, health, property, social standing. Even his wife, traumatized by her grief, is in no condition to give him support. In fact, she holds God and perhaps Job responsible for what has happened. Nothing in life makes sense to Job at that moment, although something of value does remain and that is his view of God. It has been threatened, but it has not been lost. In fact, as we shall see, it is Job's focus on God as the North Star that enables him to navigate the storm.

Few, if any, human beings have experienced what Job did. But we can identify with the feeling of being far out at sea in a life-threatening storm with no familiar landmarks in sight. As I write this, I am about to visit a young woman whose husband suddenly collapsed during a workout, leaving her a widow with two small children. Her clearly envisioned future has come to a sudden and painful end. How does she go on? That becomes the fundamental question when we are faced with situations we can hardly imagine but cannot change.

The book of Job is intended to help us answer that question, but not in a theoretical way. Although the book confronts us with the problem of evil, it does not intend to give us a philosophical resolution. Instead it challenges us, in the face of unexplained and unexplainable tragedies, to fix our eyes on God. The first two acts of Job's tragedy unfold on earth. Now we are invited to view the events of his life from another perspective, one that involves a fundamental mystery of human life.

An Unseen Cause Behind the "Seen" of Life

God claims every inch of the universe, and that claim is attacked and challenged by Satan. Behind the "seen" of human history and our lives is a cosmic conflict between God and the evil one. It is not an even contest. Satan is in no way God's equal or even His rival, although he bitterly opposes all that God does. We are rarely aware of how that invisible war touches our lives, but the truth is that our lives are part of a story bigger than we can imagine. And the unique thing the book of Job does is to allow us to stand in the heavenlies and understand the heavenly prelude to earthly events. We are able to see what Job never sees and to know what he is never told. The story unfolds in dramatic form, and we need to be careful about pressing the details in a way Scripture doesn't intend. It does, however, make it clear that our world is the focus of an enduring conflict between God and Satan, and our lives are part of that bigger story. It also calls us to recognize the mystery of life, and reminds us that many of the explanations we attempt to give are profoundly shortsighted.

One day the angels came to present themselves before the

LORD, and Satan also came with them. The LORD said to Satan, "Where have you come from?"

Satan answered the LORD, "From roaming through the earth and going back and forth in it."

Then the LORD said to Satan, "Have you considered my servant Job? There is no one on earth like him; he is blameless and upright, a man who fears God and shuns evil."

"Does Job fear God for nothing?" Satan replied. "Have you not put a hedge around him and his household and everything he has? You have blessed the work of his hands, so that his flocks and herds are spread throughout the land. But stretch out your hand and strike everything he has, and he will surely curse you to your face."

The LORD said to Satan, "Very well, then, everything he has is in your hands, but on the man himself do not lay a finger."

Then Satan went out from the presence of the LORD. (Job 1:6–12)

While we are told very little in the Bible about how the world of the heavenlies operates, Job does present us with a remarkable glimpse behind the scenes. The angelic beings come into God's presence, and Satan is with them—but not as one who is loyal to God. Elsewhere in Scripture we meet Satan as "the accuser of our brothers, who accuses them before our God day and night" (Revelation 12:10). That same passage tells us that he will be cast out of heaven just before the final events of the tribulation period. It seems, until then, that Satan has access to the presence of God, where he opposes God's work by attacking and accusing God's people. Why God permits this we are not told. However, it is in such a setting that God takes the initiative by issuing a challenge to Satan: "Where have you come from?" The Lord is not asking for information; he is calling Satan to account. Satan's response is ambiguous: "I've been wandering around the earth, everywhere in general and nowhere in particular." This is met by the Lord's direct challenge, which takes the form of an amazing affirmation of Job: "Have you considered my servant Job? There is no one on earth like him; he is blameless and upright, a man who fears God and shuns evil."

We should not pass over this too quickly, for there is a profound fact about human existence found in these words. God's purpose is to magnify His worth and glory in and through His people. Of all the features of His creation He could have used to shame Satan, the Lord chose a believer. The importance of this for every single Christ-follower cannot be exaggerated. We bear the name and reputation of our God, not only before the world but also before the principalities and powers (Ephesians 3:10). The chief end of man truly is to glorify God and to enjoy Him forever, and when we do, Satan is defeated and God is exalted.

If God's purpose is to magnify His glory, Satan's purpose is to defame God and to deface His glory. His counterchallenge strikes at the heart of a believer's relation to God. You can hear the sneer of contempt in his words:

> "Does Job fear God for nothing? . . . Have you not put a hedge around him and his household and everything he has? You have blessed the work of his hands, so that his flocks and herds are spread throughout the land. But stretch out your hand and strike everything he has, and he will surely curse you to your face." (Job 1:9–11)

Satan's words are a tremendous insult to God. In effect he is saying that God is not worth serving simply on the basis of who He is. Instead, He needs to buy the loyalty of Job and the rest of mankind. Satan implies that the only reason anyone chooses to worship God is out of self-interest. And Satan understands self-interest. It is his basic philosophy. That is one of the reasons the Lord Jesus is such a mystery to him. How can Satan understand Someone who, "being in very nature God, did not consider equality with God something to be grasped, but made himself nothing" (Philippians 2:6–7)? He cannot, just as he cannot understand a Christ-follower who loves God for who He is and not merely what He gives.

This is the central question of the book of Job: not, Why do the righteous suffer? but, Why do the righteous serve God? Human beings are sinful, and the corrupt motives of people say more about us than about God. Nevertheless, Satan raises an issue that every Christian must deal with: Why do I follow Christ? Some forms of preaching that promise health, wealth, and prosperity to "the King's kids" appeal to the worst instincts within us. Do I love God for His gifts or for himself? Would I still love Him if He called me to walk the path of suffering and sacrifice? Warren Wiersbe sums up this essential issue well:

> Satan's accusation cuts at the very heart of worship and virtue. Is God worthy to be loved and obeyed even if He does not bless us materially and protect us from pain? Can God win the heart of man totally apart from His gifts? In other words, the very *character of God* is what is at stake in this struggle.[3]

The Lord could have dismissed Satan's insolence with the contempt it richly deserved: "I don't need to prove anything to you or to anyone else." But He doesn't. Instead, He allows Job to become a test case: "Very well, then, everything he has is in your hands, but on the man himself do not lay a finger" (Job 1:12). Job now becomes the latest front in the invisible war, the place where Satan will seek to demean God's worth and God's glory.

We have no way of knowing whether this precise scenario has ever played itself out in the lives of other believers. But, whatever our circumstances, God's glory is at stake in the way we respond to situations that enter our lives. The issues we face are often far bigger than our own peace and happiness.

The second act of the heavenly drama is a virtual rerun of the first, only this time Job himself, rather than his family or possessions, becomes the object of attack. When God points out that Job "still maintains his integrity," Satan demands direct access to Job:

> On another day the angels came to present themselves before the LORD, and Satan also came with them to present himself before him. And the LORD said to Satan, "Where have you come from?"
>
> Satan answered the LORD, "From roaming through the earth and going back and forth in it."
>
> Then the LORD said to Satan, "Have you considered my servant Job? There is no one on earth like him; he is blameless and upright, a man who fears God and shuns evil. And he still maintains his integrity, though you incited me against him to ruin him without any reason."
>
> "Skin for skin!" Satan replied. "A man will give all he has for his own life. But stretch out your hand and strike his flesh and bones, and he will surely curse you to your face."
>
> The LORD said to Satan, "Very well, then, he is in your hands; but you must spare his life." (Job 2:1–6)

That permission triggers Satan's onslaught on Job's health. Job is reduced to a pain-wracked outcast, scraping his sores with shards of pottery, vainly seeking relief from his pain.

At this point, the onslaught of catastrophes comes to an end, but this is not the end of the story. After all, we have only reached the second chapter of a forty-two-chapter book. As Winston Churchill said of the first Allied victory in World War II, "Now this is not the end. It is not even the beginning of the end. But it is, perhaps, the end of the beginning." Satan disappears from view. His part has only been a prelude to the core of the book, which tells of Job's encounter with God at a level more intense and profound than anything he has known before.

Although these dramatic events are considered the prologue, they do have an enduring message. Job's experiences remind us that *our storms and sufferings are part of a larger struggle.* In ways that we cannot see as we live life at ground level, we are part of a larger cosmic struggle. We have not been promised exemption from life's challenges, and the way we respond in the storm has direct bearing on whether we reach the goal of bringing glory to God.

We also need to recognize that *suffering falls within the sweep of God's sovereignty.* How a sovereign, all-powerful God relates to the sufferings and evils of a fallen world can be an enormous mystery. Yet, as we will see, Job did not make the mistake of assuming that if he could not understand it, God must not have anything to do with it. Job did not sacrifice the truth of God's ultimate sovereignty on the altar of his frail understanding. Neither must we. Satan does what he does, but not outside the boundaries of God's control. Even the evil one is not free to act autonomously. He could touch Job only with God's permission. As he complains, "Have you not put a hedge around him?" Our God remains sovereign even in the inexplicable events of life.

Job's story also reminds us that *there is such a thing as undeserved suffering.* Perhaps our society, with its frail sense of sin and guilt, needs to hear the opposite message: there is a God who must and will punish sin. Some suffering is due to God's punishment or to the consequences of sin in our lives. Nevertheless, not all suffering is the result of personal sin.

That is a concept Job's friends utterly fail to grasp in the central section of the book. Their theology is as clear as ice and twice as cold: Whatever a person reaps, he has sown. They are sure that Job must have committed some deep, hidden sin to experience such dire consequences, and they are relentless in their accusations. But they are also wrong.

God makes it clear that Job's sufferings occur not because he is sinful but because he is righteous. There is mystery here, and that is precisely the point. We are not in possession of all the facts, and we need to be humble before claiming to know the mind of God. The *why* of his suffering remains a mystery to Job, as ours often does to us. I do not know why my colon suddenly ruptured or why my retina detached, permanently damaging my eyesight. I do not know why my wife contracted cancer or, even more mysteriously, why she survived while other wonderfully godly friends died of the same disease. But I am sure of two things. First, suffering is not always a consequence of direct personal sin, but it is always the result of living in a fallen world. None of us are exempt from the effects of that fallenness. Second, suffering may be undeserved, but it is never purposeless. Job says it beautifully: "He knows the way that I take; when he has tested me, I will come forth as gold" (Job 23:10). God uses even undeserved suffering to refine us and to produce in us a growing likeness to Jesus for the glory of God and for the good of others.

Suffering presents us with mystery. As Job pours out his feelings and thoughts, it becomes clear that he thinks God is, for some unexplained reason, angry with him (Job 3–31). He is wrong. In fact, God is proud of him. Throughout their discourse, Job and his friends see his situation as a problem that must be solved. Only in the end does Job realize that it is a mystery that must be surrendered to an all-wise, all-powerful God.

It has helped me immeasurably to realize that my fundamental concern in such times must not be, How can I get out of this? but, What can I get out of this? That is not a stance of passive resignation. Job struggles mightily to understand and barrages heaven with his questions. God approves his desperate quest for answers even as He rebukes the rigid orthodoxy of Job's friends: "You have not spoken of me what is right, as my servant Job has" (Job 42:7). But in the end Job is reduced to silence before the mystery of God's sovereign purposes.

And what is Job's response to the sufferings that have befallen him? Job holds course, even in the midst of catastrophic storms. The reason is clear. He has a North Star, and he takes his bearings from a reference point that is fixed and certain.

WE NEED A CLEAR SIGHT OF THE TRIUNE GOD TO CHART OUR COURSE

Job's immediate recourse is to the sovereign, gracious control of God. Job does not come to these crises unequipped. He knows God. You may deepen your knowledge of God in a crisis, but it is a poor time to try to find Him. Job draws upon a lifetime of worshiping and walking with God. When Job's nightmare day comes to an end and he finds himself stripped of everything he valued, he speaks words that are profoundly moving:

> At this, Job got up and tore his robe and shaved his head. Then he fell to the ground in worship and said:
>
> > "Naked I came from my mother's womb,
> >   and naked I will depart.
> > The LORD gave and the LORD has taken away;
> >   may the name of the LORD be praised."
>
> In all this, Job did not sin by charging God with wrongdoing.
> (Job 1:20–22)

It is impossible not to be moved by Job's response. He makes no effort to choke off his emotions. Yet, through tears, he maintains his focus on the Lord. His response of worship is not empty ritual but the practiced response of a man who has learned to walk with his God. Job feels the storm in all its intensity, but he chooses to focus on the Star, not the storm, to see above the horizon to the living God. He is deeply aware of God's grace ("the Lord gave") and His sovereignty ("the Lord has taken away"), and he chooses to praise God, even in the midst of his pain. These are not trite words; they are not pious words he is expected to say. This is the resolve of his deepest being.

The second round of testing ends in a remarkably similar way. This time Job's focus is revealed in an encounter with his wife:

> His wife said to him, "Are you still holding on to your integrity? Curse God and die!"
> He replied, "You are talking like a foolish woman. Shall we accept good from God, and not trouble?"
> In all this, Job did not sin in what he said. (Job 2:9–10)

At first glance, this may seem like fatalistic resignation. That is not the case. As chapters 3 to 31 reveal, Job has a passionate trust in God. But he quickly enters the crucible of grief, and these chapters describe the depth of his struggle to maintain his confidence in God's goodness, as well as His control.

If Job's immediate recourse was confidence in God's control, his ultimate resolution was trust in the character of God. In the powerful conclusion of the book, Job meets the living God (Job 38–42). He receives no explanations for what has happened or why. Instead he meets God and is overpowered by His wisdom, His power, His grace, and His care. Job's ultimate answer is not philosophical or theological but personal. He finds himself humbled and repentant before the God of glory and grace: "My ears had heard of you but now my eyes have seen you. Therefore I despise myself and repent in dust and ashes" (Job 42:5–6). In God's presence, Job's view of God and himself has changed. There is much that has not taken place. God has not explained Job's pain; He has not answered his questions; He has not defended His actions; He has not unraveled the mystery of evil. But He has revealed himself and called for Job's trust. The Lord is more concerned to enlarge Job's trust than to satisfy his curiosity.

God can always be trusted, even when we do not understand what He is doing. He is unchanging in His character, the only fixed point in a changing world.

God has a right to do what He does: He is sovereign. God has a reason for what He does: He is good and wise. God has a goal in all He does: He is fair and gracious.

The story of Job drives home a powerful truth. We need to fill our minds with thoughts of God that are worthy of Him. All unworthy ideas get us dangerously off course. At the heart of his ordeal, Job cries out in words of faith and hope:

> I know that my Redeemer lives,
>   And that in the end he will stand upon the earth.
> And after my skin has been destroyed,
>   Yet in my flesh I will see God;
> I myself will see him,
>   With my own eyes—I, and not another.
> How my heart yearns within me! (Job 19:25–27)

What a powerful example for us. For the truth is, we know so much more of God than Job did. Our vision of Him is far more compelling.

Our North Star is the triune God revealed in the Lord Jesus Christ. We know the Word become flesh. We possess the words and works of Jesus. We see in His person the incarnate truth about God. We stand at the cross and wonder at the depth of His love. We stand before the open tomb and recognize His power. We have His Spirit living within to personalize His presence. We possess His Word of truth, in which we can hear His voice. He is the fixed point, the North Star, or, to use His description of himself, "the bright Morning Star" (Revelation 22:16). He is the indispensable constant to enable us to live life well. If He is not the fixed reference point by which we constantly determine our location and direction, we are doomed to flounder.

Chapter Three

"Don't Leave Home Without It"

My university years bring back an unusual memory—the plaintive sound of a foghorn warning ships of danger nearby. The University of British Columbia is located on a beautiful peninsula that leads into Vancouver's harbor, one of the busiest on the Pacific. But winter fogs can blanket the area, making it impossible to discern the presence of dangerous rocks. So the foghorns sound their warnings for freighters and pleasure craft alike.

Early in the eighteenth century, a British admiral with the imposing name of Sir Clowdisley Shovell found himself enveloped in a blanket of fog that did not lift for twelve days. He was leading home a fleet of five British warships that had engaged the French fleet near Gibraltar and had won a series of battles, although they had failed to gain the intended prize of the fortress of Toulon. But now they were in grave danger. Somewhere in the fog were the Scilly Isles, and if they did not turn east at the proper time, they would be wrecked on their rocky shores. But how could they determine their position? Eighteenth-century naviga-tors knew how to calculate latitude, but longitude remained an unsolved mystery, and the fog made visual sighting impossible.

Sir Clowdisley's navigators conferred and announced their conclu-sion: they were safely west of any major trouble. The news brought a feeling of great relief to the sailors on board, but one of the crew mem-bers approached the admiral with a dissenting opinion. He had been keeping his own navigational journal, and he was convinced the officers were wrong. If their location was what he thought it was, they were in great peril. This sailor's act was one of considerable courage. In the rigid class system of the Royal Navy, such private navigation was considered subversive. Officers, not humble crewmen, did such work. Yet if the man was right, the fleet was in imminent danger.

Sir Clowdisley was not amused, or convinced. He ordered the man hung for mutiny on the spot.

He should have listened. Within hours, four of the five ships were wrecked on the Scillies, taking two thousand men to a watery grave. As Dava Sobel observes,

> The demise of Sir Clowdisley's fleet capped a long saga of sea-faring in the days before sailors could find their longitude. Page after page from this miserable history relates quintessential hor-ror stories of death by scurvy and thirst, of ghosts in the rigging, and of landfalls in the form of shipwrecks, with hulls dashed on rocks and heaps of drowned corpses fouling the beaches. In literally hundreds of instances, a vessel's ignorance of their lon-gitude led swiftly to her destruction.[1]

For centuries, sailors struggled to discover ways to determine their true position at sea. The first rule was to follow the coast. Keep in sight of land. But what if land was nowhere to be seen? Sailors devised increasingly complex means to sight the sun and stars and calculate latitude. A block of wood, tied by a string to the mast, could give a surprising amount of help to a skilled practitioner. Later generations developed the cross-staff, a T-shaped device whose base was held up to the eye; the astrolabe, a refinement that prevented blindness by allowing the navigator to turn his back to the sun; and the sextant, a device invented in 1731 that allowed navigators to determine latitude within a mile or two. These all did the same thing with differing degrees of accuracy: they enabled a person to sight the stars and bring that position down to the horizon.

Longitude proved to be a more vexing problem. In fact, in 1714 the British Parliament passed the Longitude Act, offering an award equal to millions of dollars in modern currency to the first person who could devise a practical and useful way to determine longitude. It was the equivalent of *Who Wants to Be a Millionaire?* as scientists raced to win the prize and, with it, scientific fame. The honor finally settled on an English watchmaker named John Harrison, who invented a clock that would keep precise time at sea. This allowed navigators to calculate their distance from the arbitrary fixed point of Greenwich, England, and so calculate their precise longitude.

These newer methods were not merely technological improvements. For sailors at sea, they were life-and-death matters. As Sobel observes:

> For lack of a practical method of determining longitude, every great captain in the Age of Exploration became lost at sea despite the best available charts and compasses. From Vasco da Gama to Vasco Nunez de Balboa, from Ferdinand Magellan to Sir Francis Drake—they all got where they were going willy-nilly, by forces attributed to good luck or the grace of God. . . .
> Launched on a mix of bravery and greed, the sea captains

of the fifteenth, sixteenth, and seventeenth centuries relied on "dead reckoning" to gauge their distance east or west of home port. The captain would throw a log overboard and observe how quickly the ship receded from this temporary guidepost. He noted the crude speedometer reading in his ship's log-book, along with the direction of travel, which he took from the stars or a compass, and the length of time on a particular course, counted with a sandglass or a pocket watch. Factoring in the effects of ocean currents, fickle winds, and errors in judgment, he then determined his longitude. He routinely missed the mark, of course—searching in vain for the island where he had hoped to find fresh water, or even the continent which was his destination. Too often the technique of dead reckoning marked him for a dead man.[2]

All of this sounds dry and uninteresting in the age of the Global Positioning System (GPS). Modern technology has made the older methods obsolete. In fact, the Naval Academy no longer requires its students to learn celestial navigation. Yet the principles of navigation remain the same, whether the method is electronic or celestial. You must be able to locate your position when no landmarks are in sight. Navigational tools are not a useful luxury but an indispensable requirement. Don't leave home without them, if you want to get home again!

As we have said, living life in the modern world is like trying to navigate an uncharted, rapidly changing, unpredictable ocean. We have sailed off the edge of our maps. The first need is to have a fixed, unchanging reference point. That North Star is our triune God, made known in the Lord Jesus Christ. Navigation, however, requires much more than a fixed reference point. I know how to find the North Star in the night skies. I don't have the slightest idea how to find my location by using it. Even if

I did, I would need the appropriate tool to enable me to bring the North Star down to my horizon. A Christian knows that the Bible, the written Word of God, is the God-given navigational tool to enable us to reach our God-intended destination, which is likeness to Jesus, for the glory of God and the good of others. But I need more than knowledge that the Bible is my spiritual sextant. I need to know how to use it properly. The great example of the proper attitude toward and use of Scripture is found in the Lord Jesus. That being so, the attitude of the Lord Jesus Christ to Scripture must shape my use of and attitude to God's Word.

One of the constant themes of the gospels is the centrality of Scripture in the life of the Lord. The Bible filled His teaching, directed His choices, and foretold His sufferings. He steered His life by Scripture, and that is never more clearly seen than in His encounter with Satan at the outset of His public ministry. Luke gives us the account in chapter 4 of his gospel:

> Jesus, full of the Holy Spirit, returned from the Jordan and was led by the Spirit in the desert, where for forty days he was tempted by the devil. He ate nothing during those days, and at the end of them he was hungry.
>
> The devil said to him, "If you are the Son of God, tell this stone to become bread."
>
> Jesus answered, "It is written: 'Man does not live on bread alone.'"
>
> The devil led him up to a high place and showed him in an instant all the kingdoms of the world. And he said to him, "I will give you all their authority and splendor, for it has been given to me, and I can give it to anyone I want to. So if you worship me, it will all be yours."
>
> Jesus answered, "It is written: 'Worship the Lord your God and serve him only.'"

The devil led him to Jerusalem and had him stand on the highest point of the temple. "If you are the Son of God," he said, "throw yourself down from here. For it is written: '"He will command his angels concerning you to guard you carefully; they will lift you up in their hands, so that you will not strike your foot against a stone.'"

Jesus answered, "It says: 'Do not put the Lord your God to the test.'"

When the devil had finished all this tempting, he left him until an opportune time. (Luke 4:1–13)

The greatest privilege of life is to become a Christ-follower, a person living by faith in Jesus Christ as Lord and Savior. The greatest purpose in life is to become like Christ, living a fully developing, fully human life, imitating Christ. There are many ways in which we cannot become like the Lord Jesus, for He is the God-man, and the temptation of Christ reveals His unique nature as the Son of God. At the same time, the temptation was possible only because the Lord Jesus had taken an authentic human nature, and in His victory over temptation He employed the same resource we, His followers, possess—the Word of God.

The Temptation of the Lord Jesus Reveals His Unique Person

There were no human witnesses to this remarkable confrontation, which is recorded in the gospels of Matthew, Mark, and Luke. The Lord Jesus must have told this story to His disciples to enable them to see His uniqueness more clearly. The striking thing is that this is not a surprise attack by Satan. Luke tells us that the Spirit led Jesus in the desert. Matthew is even more specific: "Then Jesus was led by the Spirit into the desert to be tempted by the devil" (Matthew 4:1). This encounter was not an ambush, sprung by Satan on an unsuspecting Jesus. It was a demonstration, engineered by the living God. Satan's intention in his attack was the destruction and disqualification of the Lord Jesus. Were He to succumb, Jesus could not become our Savior. So Satan put Jesus under relentless, shrewd, calculated pressure. God's purpose was entirely different. The steadfastness of Jesus under Satan's most intense attacks vindicated and validated Him. His true nature as the perfect man, proven under testing, qualified Him to be the Substitute for His people and the High Priest who identifies and sympathizes with His tempted people. In the Lord's case, temptation didn't cause His failure; it exposed His remarkable character.

The conditions of the temptation Christ endured are significant. The place is the desert, where God's people Israel had failed so deeply centuries before, when the Lord brought them out of Egypt. Adam, by contrast, had failed under temptation in a perfect environment. Jesus will demonstrate that He is all that Adam and Israel should have been and failed to be. The process is a forty-day ordeal in which the Lord goes without food. Apparently several temptations occurred during that period, but the Gospels point us only to the final three, which come at a time when Jesus is physically at His weakest and most depleted. Socially, He is isolated, utterly without an earthly support system.

Round one of Satan's attack directly addresses the Lord's obvious physical condition. "If you are the Son of God, tell this stone to become bread." Satan begins with the subtle smoothness of the skilled seducer. He does not begin by attacking or doubting Jesus' claim to be the Son of God. In fact, he accepts it for the sake of argument: "If you are the Son of God (and I'll assume that you are . . .)." The essence of the attack is in the suggestion: "tell this stone to become bread." On the basic level, this is an enticement to a hungry man to satisfy his hunger. The Lord Jesus' body did not differ from ours in its physical needs. What could be more powerful than an invitation to eat after forty days of denial? By a simple act, He would not only satisfy His hunger, but would also demonstrate His special powers to the enemy.

But this temptation operates at an even deeper level, which shows the subtlety of the tempter. As God the Son, Jesus had exercised His divine attributes for all eternity in perfect agreement with the Father. Now, as He lived His life as the God-man, He had submitted himself to His Father's will. Satan's inducement is for Jesus to live by self-gratification, using His powers autonomously, serving His own agenda, and doing His own thing.

It is not wrong in itself to satisfy a physical need such as hunger. It is not wrong to do a miracle, turning stones into bread. But Satan's appeal was for Jesus to take a shortcut, to cut His Father out of the equation and to set His needs above everything else. This is one of Satan's favorite ploys. "Your needs, your desires are the priority. Satisfy them. Serve yourself." Sex, food, marriage, money, pleasure, possessions—these are good in themselves. They are to be enjoyed fully within the boundaries of the will of God, boundaries that are set for our well-being. But when these things become the priority, when we indulge our desires autonomously, we are falling into the trap of the evil one. This is the old lie he used with Eve: "You will be like God, knowing good and evil." The point wasn't just that Eve would have intellectual knowledge of good and evil but that she would *define* good and evil, determining for herself what was right or wrong. This is the essence of sin: we usurp the place of the sovereign God.

The Lord's response is brief but direct: "It is written: 'Man does not live on bread alone, but on every word that comes from the mouth of the Lord.'" He is saying, emphatically, "I eat at the direction of my Father, not at the urging of my stomach." Luke gives a shorter version of the quotation than Matthew does, but the message is the same: food (or, my body and its needs and desires) doesn't have the priority. God does. He is Lord. The Lord Jesus could have asserted His authority, but He rests His response upon written Scripture (Deuteronomy 8:3). He is not only responding to Satan; He is declaring the fundamental principle by which He navigates life: *obeying God is the supreme priority of life.*

Round two of Satan's attack on the Lord begins with a physical change of location. Satan transports Jesus to a high place from which he shows Him "in an instant all the kingdoms of the world." Since there is no physical location where that would be possible, this is obviously some kind of visionary experience. Satan's claim is breathtaking in its audacity: "I will give you all their authority and splendor, for it has been given to me, and I can give it to anyone I want to." The claim is delusional, like a child with someone else's toy: "I have it. It's mine." The sovereign God has not ceded authority of any part of His creation to the enemy. When the Lord Jesus describes Satan as "the prince of this world" in John 14:30, He is not suggesting that the devil has any legitimate authority over the world. The "world" in that context is the evil world system, in rebellion against God and composed of those in rebellion against God. It is this Satan offers: "Take it. It's yours. I won't fight you for it. All you need to do is bow down and worship me."

The offer must have been enticing. The kingdoms of the world rightfully belong to the Lord Jesus. Were He to accept Satan's offer, He could reclaim His property and avoid the cross. Success without suffering. What a concept! He could take the easy way and detour around the cross. If we have any idea of how costly the cross was to the Lord, we can understand how attractive Satan thought this offer might be to Jesus. Modern Christ-followers know the same temptation in another form: avoid suffering and enjoy the world. Just serve another king.

The Lord's response is clear and direct. He could have debated Satan's claim. He does not. He could have attacked Satan's audacity. He does not. He could have mocked Satan's credibility. He does not. Instead, once again He quotes God's Word, again from the book of Deuteronomy: "It is written: 'Worship the Lord your God and serve him only,'" establishing a second nonnegotiable principle by which He navigates life: *worshiping God is life's supreme priority.* Any rival claims must be rejected. Only the eternal God is worthy of our reverence.

Round three, as Luke records the events, involves another change of location, this time to the temple in Jerusalem. Luke probably has placed this encounter as the climax because it mirrors the flow of events in his gospel.[3] In fact, Luke 9:51 depicts the Lord resolutely setting out for Jerusalem, where He confronts the final attack of Satan in the events that lead to the cross (Luke 19 ff.). This, then, becomes a kind of preview of that final encounter, waged on "the highest point of the temple." This was probably a place on the walls of the temple area, which dropped off more than four hundred feet to the Kidron Valley below. The devil's suggestion is clear: "If you are the Son of God," he said, "throw yourself down from here," although it is not clear whether this was meant to be a public act, seen by many, or a private one, witnessed only by Satan.

This time there is an added twist from Satan, who attempts to buttress his temptation by quoting the Bible. If Jesus uses the Scriptures, so will he! "For it is written: 'He will command his angels concerning you to guard you carefully; they will lift you up in their hands, so that you will not strike your foot against a stone'" (see Psalm 91:11–12). Satan quotes the Scripture accurately but devilishly, tearing it out of its intended context and using it to try to turn Jesus away from His Father, not toward Him. This is extremely important for us to remember: There is a way of using the Word of God that transmutes it into the voice of Satan. It isn't enough just to use the Bible. We must use it in a way that honors and respects Scripture for what it truly is: God's Word written.

Satan's temptation here is a subtle one: "You claim to believe the Bible. Here's a promise. Step out in faith; take a risk. God will bail you out." We live in an age that collects experiences, even spiritual ones. Sometimes ideas are presented as if the whole thing is about us, about our success, our prosperity, or our happiness. "Name it and claim it," we're told. Bible verses are wrenched out of context to justify a self-indulgent lifestyle. God becomes our servant, catering to our whims. And we can prove it from the Bible!

The Lord's response is again direct: "It says: 'Do not put the Lord your God to the test.'" And again He goes to Deuteronomy (6:16). Testing the Lord is not trusting Him. Scripture is not supreme; God is. Please don't misunderstand. The Bible is God's inspired authoritative Word. But it must be used under His authority, consistent with His character and purpose.

Thus, this third navigational principle is consistent with the previous two: *trusting God is life's supreme priority.* The three join inseparably together: obeying God, worshiping God, trusting God.

The Lord Jesus is unique, and His victorious resistance over Satan's temptation demonstrates His uniqueness and His supremacy. But the account of the temptation also points to the abiding navigational principles that guided His life and should also guide ours.

THE EXAMPLE OF THE LORD JESUS REVEALS OUR INDISPENSABLE RESOURCE: THE WORD OF GOD

The account of the Lord's victory over Satan's seduction is rich with lessons for every Christ-follower. But there are three of special significance when it comes to navigating life in a fluid, unpredictable world.

First, *navigating life requires a deep confidence in the Word of God.* The Lord Jesus obviously had an authority not possessed by any human being.

In the Sermon on the Mount, He proclaims authoritatively, "You have heard it said . . . but I say to you. . . ." His is not the authority of a learned rabbi or the voice of tradition or official position. He speaks as the Son of God, possessing unique power and authority over Satan and every other created being. But He does not argue His case or even declare the truth in His own name. Rather, His continued response is to quote Scripture. "It is written," He declares, and He repeats God's Word in simplicity and brevity. Nothing could be clearer than the fact that, for Jesus, Scripture is the final court of appeal. What Scripture says, God says. Just as significantly, Satan makes no effort to dispute the Bible. He may misuse it, but he never counters the Lord's response when Jesus stands upon the authority of the Bible.

Few things are more important for a Christ-follower to consider than the attitude of the Lord Jesus Christ to the Word of God and His profound respect for its authority. At every major point in His ministry, the Word of God is there. He defines His ministry by quoting the words of Isaiah 61 as His personal manifesto (Luke 4:16–21). He builds His most famous sermon around a clarification of the true meaning of Scripture (Matthew 5–7). He condemns the Jewish leaders, not because they value Scripture too highly but because they are ignorant of its clear message (John 5:39–40, 46) or because they have encrusted it with layers of tradition that cover its true meaning (Matthew 15:1–9). He declares that the Bible is of enduring authority, an authority that reaches to its smallest part:

> "Do not think that I have come to abolish the Law or the Prophets; I have not come to abolish them but to fulfill them. I tell you the truth, until heaven and earth disappear, not the smallest letter, not the least stroke of a pen, will by any means disappear from the Law until everything is accomplished.

Anyone who breaks one of the least of these commandments and
teaches others to do the same will be called least in the kingdom
of heaven, but whoever practices and teaches these commands
will be called great in the kingdom of heaven. For I tell you that
unless your righteousness surpasses that of the Pharisees and
the teachers of the law, you will certainly not enter the kingdom
of heaven. (Matthew 5:17–20)

Indeed, "the Scripture cannot be broken" (John 10:35). Jesus saw the
events of His life as the fulfillment of Scripture, since "the Scriptures
must be fulfilled" (Mark 14:49). Even on the cross His mind was full
of God's Word (John 19:28); and after the resurrection, one of His priorities was to open the Scriptures for His followers and explain "all the
things concerning himself" (Luke 24:27, 32). The Lord Jesus lived God's
Word, loved God's Word, and was loyal to God's Word. Scripture was
His guidebook for His life, His protection in His spiritual warfare, His
authority in His public teaching, and His directive for His God-given
ministry. He obeyed its commands with His actions, and He honored
its meaning with His teaching.

The implications are obvious and essential. If our Lord and Savior
shaped His life by Scripture, how could we imagine we need it less than
He did? If we call Him Lord and Teacher, how can we have a lower view
of Scripture than He did? If we are His followers, how can we rely on it
less than He did? We are no match for the wiles and seductions of Satan,
but God's Word retains its power as the sword of the Spirit, able to put
our enemy on the defensive.

It is foolish for a navigator to trust his own instincts, to rely on his
intuitions, and to ignore his instruments. When John Kennedy Jr.'s plane
crashed into the Atlantic, experts were virtually unanimous regarding
the probable cause. As a relative novice flying in night conditions beyond

his experience, Kennedy had been unable to locate the horizon and had relied on his instincts rather than his flight instruments. He had become disoriented and flown his plane into the ocean.

One of the first lessons a pilot is taught is, "Rely on your instruments." Christ-followers need to learn the same lesson from the Lord Jesus. Our instincts, our intuitions, our desires speak to us loudly. It is tempting to do our own thing, to steer by the moral seat of our pants. But such a lifestyle is not only foolish; it is disloyal to our Lord. A Christ-follower imitates his Master by living out a solid confidence in Scripture as God's written Word. He views the Bible as an indispensable navigational tool for making the daily choices of life. Changing the imagery somewhat, John Stott rightly says, "Christ rules his church through the Scriptures. Scripture is the scepter through which King Jesus reigns,"[4] in His church and in each of us, His people.

A closely related principle follows. *Navigating life requires a working knowledge of God's Word.* The Lord Jesus not only valued Scripture but also knew it and used it. The passages He quotes from the book of Deuteronomy show His deep familiarity with the text of Scripture. Obviously He was a student of the Bible. His respect for the Word is also shown by His refusal to allow Satan to misuse the Bible. Scripture has a meaning intended by its divine Author; therefore, the text must be handled properly, allowing God to speak and not manipulating it to speak our truths rather than God's truth. So He prays for us as His people: "Sanctify them by the truth; your word is truth" (John 17:17).

The great need is for Christ-followers to know God's Word and to handle it properly. It is impossible to be deeply affected by what you do not know. Are you able to think your way through the Bible's basic story line? Do you know the great biblical passages that describe most clearly the central Christian truths about the nature and character of God, the way of salvation, the fundamental moral and ethical principles that shape Christian behavior, and the basics of prayer? Have you mastered the truths of God's revelation of His heart and mind?

Somewhere in my reading I came across the story of the prince of Grenada, the heir to the Spanish throne in a past era. He was sentenced to a life of solitary confinement in an ancient prison in Madrid, a dreadful, dirty, dreary place from which no one emerged alive. He was given one book to read, a Bible. For thirty-three years it was his cherished possession, and he read it hundreds of times. After his death, when his keepers cleaned out his cell, they found notes he had written, based on his study, etched on the soft stone of the prison walls. The following are typical: Psalm 118:8 is the middle verse of the Bible; Ezra 7:21 has all the letters of the alphabet except J; Esther 8:9 is the longest verse in the Bible. Thirty-three years of exposure to the truth of God, and all he apparently collected was trivia!

We also must handle God's Word with the respect it deserves. As Paul exhorts Timothy, "Do your best to present yourself to God as one approved, a workman who does not need to be ashamed and who correctly interprets the word of truth" (2 Timothy 2:15). A navigator who tries to manipulate his instruments into giving him a reading he desires rather than the reading that reflects reality is a fool. It has become fashionable to read the Scripture with only one question in mind: What does this mean to me? The question is mistimed. The first question must always be, What does this passage mean? What is the author really saying, under the inspiration of the Holy Spirit? Then, and only then, when I am confident that I have faithfully understood the meaning of the text, should I ask, What does this then mean to me? The meaning of Scripture must always determine its significance to my life. Otherwise I shift the authority to me, and I merely use the Bible to validate my opinions. Wise Christians work hard to develop good skills of Bible interpretation, just as a navigator trains himself to use his instruments carefully. For in the final analysis, lives depend on it.

The third principle, then, follows naturally. *Navigating life requires a lifestyle of obedience to the Word of God.* The goal of confidence in the Bible as God's Word and of knowledge of the Bible is conformity to the truths of the Bible. It does no good to have accurate navigational instruments and readings that you do not follow. The Lord Jesus declared His life principle in these pithy words: "My food is to do the will of him who sent me and to finish his work" (John 4:34). "I have come down from heaven not to do my will but the will of him who sent me" (John 6:38). "I have brought you glory on earth by completing the work you gave me to do" (John 17:4). At every point, His life was shaped and directed by the will of His Father. He navigated life by His Father's guidance.

The Bible is the Christian's sextant. It takes the fixed point of the triune God, the North Star, and brings it down to the horizon to locate us in time and space. It spells out for me, sometimes in direct commands but more often in overarching principles, what it means to live as a follower of Christ. It reveals where I am, often with painful precision, by convicting me of sin. It points me where I need to go by showing me the marriage to which I need to aspire, the character I need to pursue, the behaviors I need to avoid, the habits I need to develop. It holds before me my ultimate destination, which makes the whole journey worthwhile, and inspires me to keep on keeping on. "All Scripture is God-breathed and is useful for teaching, rebuking, correcting and training in righteousness, so that the man of God may be thoroughly equipped for every good work" (2 Timothy 3:16–17).

But it is not enough to possess it; we need to steer by it. The Bible does its God-appointed work only as it becomes the active navigational tool in our lives. Only a fool would carefully calculate his headings and then throw them overboard and do what comes naturally. That is why the Lord's brother, James, warns us: "Do not merely listen to the word, and so deceive yourselves. Do what it says" (James 1:22).

The expression "Don't leave home without it" has been made famous by a certain credit card company. For Christians intent on navigating a chaotic world successfully, the term takes on new meaning. The indispensable navigational tool for life is God's Word, the Bible.

> How can a young man keep his way pure?
> By living according to your word. . . .
> I have hidden your word in my heart
> that I might not sin against you. (Psalm 119:9, 11)

Do not let this Book of the Law depart from your mouth; meditate on it day and night, so that you may be careful to do everything that is written in it. Then you will be prosperous and successful. (Joshua 1:8)

Chapter Four

SPIRITUAL BALLAST

Michael Plant loved the sea. So, when he announced his intention in 1992 to make a solo crossing of the North Atlantic from the East Coast of the United States to France, none of his friends were especially concerned. They knew the dangers of such a crossing, especially in the fall, when violent storms could sweep across his intended course. But they also knew that Plant was an experienced sailor who had sailed around the world more than once. Furthermore, his sailboat, the *Coyote*, was designed with just such a voyage in mind.

The *Coyote* was thoroughly modern. Its design, materials, and navigational technology were all cutting edge. Plant also had equipped it with an emergency location device, an Epirb radio, which would transmit a signal to a satellite in case of sudden trouble. Ground stations would be able to detect the signals, fix his location, and dispatch help instantly. As Gordon MacDonald observes, "One couldn't say that Plant didn't have everything—the best of expertise, experience, and equipment—when he unfurled his sails and put out to sea for Europe. That explains the prevailing assumption of Plant and his friends: nothing will go wrong."[1]

What exactly did go wrong will never be known for sure. Eleven days out to sea, locators lost radio contact with the *Coyote*. At first, Plant's friends were convinced that he was too busy battling the difficult weather into which he had sailed to make contact. Besides, there had been no reports of distress signals, either from the Epirb tracking stations or from ships in the area. But when the silence continued for a few days, alarm began to mount. A search began, but there were no reports of sightings or signals.

Then the crew of a freighter reported finding the *Coyote* floating upside down, with no sign of Plant. Perhaps he had abandoned ship and was drifting in the emergency raft. But those hopes were dashed when the *Coyote* was pulled from the water and the raft was discovered partially inflated inside the cabin. Whatever had happened, Plant was no longer alive.

The clue to the tragedy was that the hull of the sailboat had been found floating upside down. Sailboats are designed on a fundamental principle: there must be more weight below the waterline than above it. Because of this, even in the most violent of storms and winds, the ship will right itself. As long as the weight of the keel is attached, the boat will not turn turtle and remain upside down. The *Coyote* was designed with a ballast of eight thousand pounds attached to the keel. But when she was found, the ballast had broken away. There was no way to determine whether this was caused by a collision with some ocean debris or by a manufacturing flaw. But whatever had occurred, the fundamental principle of stability had been violated. Without her ballast, the *Coyote* and Michael Plant were helpless victims of the wind and the waves. The end had come so quickly that Plant had not been able to send any kind of emergency signal.

There must be more weight below the waterline than above it. MacDonald rightly points out that this is not only a law of sailing; it is a law of life. A sailboat without ballast is safe only when it is tied to the dock, in a peaceful harbor. People without ballast are stable only in life's safe harbors. But most of life isn't lived in safe harbors. We often find ourselves in stormy seas. So ballast isn't an option. It's a necessity.

When it comes to navigating life, prayer is our spiritual ballast. The Bible may be God's compass that points us in the right direction. But only a living relationship with our Lord, nurtured and deepened by prayer, will keep us upright in the storm. One of the Bible's great passages on prayer is found in Hebrews 4. It takes us into a world different from ours, a world of priests and sacrifices and rituals. But while the culture may be different, the need isn't, and in these words we are given promises that enable us to make sure that our lives have spiritual ballast.

> Therefore, since we have a great high priest who has gone through the heavens, Jesus the Son of God, let us hold firmly to the faith we profess. For we do not have a high priest who is unable to sympathize with our weaknesses, but we have one who has been tempted in every way, just as we are—yet was without sin. Let us then approach the throne of grace with confidence, so that we may receive mercy and find grace to help us in our time of need. (Hebrews 4:14–16)

Several years ago, a persistent pain in my stomach sent me to the emergency room at our local hospital. Hours of testing followed, and the surgeon finally told me that he thought I had an atypical appendicitis and should be operated on immediately. He also suggested several other things he thought the problem might be, none of which I took very seriously. When I woke up from emergency surgery, I discovered that I was now the proud owner of a colostomy. My problem had been far more serious than was suspected: my colon had ruptured. At first I was too ill to be anything but grateful, but as I regained strength, I realized that I now had to deal with something I had never even imagined. My doctor and nurses explained to me how a colostomy functioned, and a gracious and competent woman walked me through the regimen that would dominate my life until the procedure could be reversed. Although I tried to project an image of calm acceptance on the outside, inside I was afraid, intimidated, and more than a little embarrassed. Would I ever be able to live normally again?

Then someone I knew and respected wrote me a letter telling me something I had never suspected. She had had a colostomy years earlier and referred to it as her "friend." What a difference that made. The experts had given me all the right answers. Nothing they told me differed from what she said. But she had lived what they had only studied. Somebody else had been where I was, understood what I felt, and was living a normal life. She couldn't change my situation, but she could fully identify with it, and in that I found hope.

Most of us have times in life like that, times when we are fighting a battle that feels beyond us. We respect experts, but we long for someone who has been there, who can identify inside out. That is what makes this passage on prayer so powerful. It reminds us that when we pray, we pray to the living God, who has become like us. The Lord Jesus identifies with us, because He has known human life inside out. Yet, because He is the God-man, He is able not only to understand and identify with us but also to care for us, to empower us, and to intervene on our behalf. We are given three great encouragements to come to Him in prayer, because He is our completely capable High Priest.

WE CAN PRAY WITH CONFIDENCE BECAUSE WE HAVE AN EXALTED HIGH PRIEST

To fully understand what the Scripture is saying here, we need to understand two things: the situation of these people and the background against which these words are written. We will return to the first question in more detail later in this book, as we devote our attention to the great truths of Hebrews 11. For the present, we need to know that the unknown writer of the book of Hebrews is writing to a group of Hebrew Christians. He is sure that the vast majority of them truly belong to Christ. But he is concerned that some in the community have been carried along by the enthusiasm of the group and may not have experienced the reality of God's grace in their lives. The community is under great pressure. Their Jewish friends and family are anything but enthusiastic that they have left Judaism to become followers of Christ, and are continually pointing out the things they have left behind: the sacrificial system, the temple, the priesthood of Israel. These Christians are experiencing the pressures and persecutions of Gentile society as well. In addition to these external pressures, there are the internal battles that all Christians fight against sin in their lives and in the lives of others. Christians may be forgiven, but they are far from perfect, and it is easy for them to become disillusioned with the weakness of their lives and their status on the margins of society. Some are tempted to turn back and to try to find an easier way.

Their life setting is significantly different from ours, but the essential issues are the same. Any Christian who is seeking to live for Christ knows what it is to feel like he or she is swimming upstream against the current of the culture. Often it would seem so much easier to give in and go with the flow. How, if we truly know Christ, can we be so weak and fragile? And our churches! All too often they seem to contradict almost everything about the message they proclaim. We are tempted to give up and quietly drift away.

Their greatest need, and ours, the writer of Hebrews tells us, is to know who their great high priest truly is. For us in the twenty-first century, that seems a strange way to put it. But not for these people. They were Hebrews, people who had lived in a system given them by God that centered on a place of worship (the tabernacle and then the temple), a pattern of worship (the sacrifices and rituals of the Old Testament), and personnel of worship (supremely, the high priest). They knew that system inside out, having lived with it all their lives until they realized that it was all designed to point them to the Lord Jesus Christ, who fulfilled and superseded the old system.

To fully understand these words, we need to consider a particular event in the Jewish calendar. Called Yom Kippur, or the Day of Atonement, it was the most significant day in the life of the nation of Israel in terms of sustaining its relation to God. One part of the temple was called the Holy of Holies, or the Most Holy Place. That was where God's special glory was on display, His holy presence, and since no human was worthy of being in His presence, no one was allowed in that place, ever—with one exception. On the Day of Atonement, when the high priest would offer a sacrifice to cleanse himself and the people from their sins, he would enter the Holy of Holies and sprinkle the blood of the sacrifice on a special piece of furniture known as the mercy seat. The high priest entered the Holy of Holies as the representative of the people, making possible their acceptance by a holy and righteous God.

All of this is a picture of the Lord Jesus Christ. As the sinless One, He had no need to offer a sacrifice for himself. He is the perfect sacrifice for our sins, and He is also the High Priest, who represents us before God. As Jesus, the Man, He is fully qualified to represent us. As the Son of God, He is fully qualified to enter God's presence. And He doesn't enter into a symbolic Holy of Holies located on earth; He enters into the presence of God in heaven. That is what the writer of Hebrews has in mind when he says, "We have a great high priest who has gone through the heavens, Jesus the Son of God." The Lord Jesus has ended the need for an earthly temple. God demonstrated this at the time of the crucifixion, when "the curtain of the temple was torn in two from top to bottom" (Matthew 27:51). This curtain was the barrier between the Holy Place, which priests entered on a daily basis, and the Most Holy Place, which could be entered only once a year by one man, the high priest. This curtain was sixty feet by thirty feet, as thick as a man's hand. It took three hundred men to handle it. Yet, when Christ died, God split it open, from top to bottom, to show that our great High Priest, Jesus the Son of God, had opened a new way into God's presence. Later in Hebrews the writer describes this in these words: "Therefore, brothers, since we have confidence to enter the Most Holy Place by the blood of Jesus, by a new and living way opened for us through the curtain, that is, his body, and since we have a great priest over the house of God, let us draw near to God" (Hebrews 10:19–22).

These Hebrew Christians, who had been taught to value their earthly temple and their human high priest, needed to remember that they had "a great high priest" whose person and works dwarfed anything else. If they remembered who Jesus was, they would hold firmly to their faith.

The high priest offered continual sacrifices for the sins of the people; the great High Priest offered one perfect and final sacrifice for sins at the cross. The high priest represented the people because he was identified with them as a fellow Hebrew; the Lord Jesus perfectly represents us, having fully identified with our humanity by taking human nature himself. The high priest was the mediator for the people, because he heard their confessions and prayers to God; the great High Priest is the one perfect Mediator, who knows our sins and failings firsthand and is the perfect advocate with His Father in heaven.

Alexander Whyte, a great Scottish preacher of the nineteenth century, described the perfection of our Lord in these terms: "Jesus Christ, regarded as the High Priest, meets the deepest needs of every heart and fits every human need. He is the answer to all our questions, the satisfaction of all our wants, the bread for all our hunger, the light for all our darkness, the strength for our weakness, the medicine for our sickness, the life for our death."

If these Hebrews forgot who the Lord Jesus was, they would put themselves in great danger. They had a Priest who had done everything necessary to bring them into God's presence. To lose sight of the supremacy and finality of Christ's work was to lose the heart of the gospel. The Reformation found its core in these same truths: that there is no priest but Christ, no sacrifice but Calvary, and no confessional but the throne of grace.

We, too, need this deep-seated confidence in the Lord Jesus if we are going to pray effectively. We must pray in His name. That does not mean simply ending our prayers with "in Jesus' name, Amen." It means that we approach God on the basis of who the Lord Jesus is and what He has done on our behalf. God does not respond to our prayers but to us, because we are His children. Prayer isn't about a technique, about saying the right words. Prayer is about a relationship with God, established through the Lord Jesus. We can pray with confidence because we are represented in the presence of the Father by His Son, who is our great High Priest. If we remember who He is, we will stand firm in faith, no matter how wild the sea. He is our spiritual ballast.

WE CAN PRAY WITH CONFIDENCE BECAUSE WE HAVE AN UNDERSTANDING HIGH PRIEST

It is one thing to know that the Lord is able to represent us because He is "Jesus, the Son of God"; it is quite another to know that He is able to understand us as He represents us before the Father. The pagans worshiped gods who were seen as remote and detached, indifferent to human need. The Jews knew the truth of a majestic and holy God who involved himself in the affairs of His people, but they had come to see God as so majestic in His glory that they avoided even the use of His name. It is hard to pour out your heart to gods who are indifferent, or to a God whose name you cannot use. But the Lord Jesus shows us that the heart of God is open to His people.

Hebrews 4:15 phrases it negatively to heighten the contrast: "For we do not have a high priest who is unable to sympathize with our weaknesses." The writer could just as easily have said, "We have a high priest who is able to sympathize with our weaknesses." The fact is that when the Lord Jesus took on human nature, He took on human weakness. The writer clarifies that in the next phrase by reminding us that He is "without sin." But we must not miss his point. The Lord Jesus was not Superman, wearing a suit of clothes over a superhuman body. He took a full human nature, a fact the writer of Hebrews is careful to emphasize: "Since the children have flesh and blood, he too shared in their humanity.... For this reason he had to be made like his brothers in every way, in order that he might become a merciful and faithful high priest" (Hebrews 2:14, 17). "During the days of Jesus' life on earth, he offered up prayers and petitions with loud cries and tears to the one who could save him from death, and he was heard because of his reverent submission" (Hebrews 5:7).

Jesus' weaknesses involved the frailties of human nature. Physically, He experienced pain, exhaustion, and hunger. Emotionally, He knew what it was to go through times of grief, fear, shame, rejection, aloneness, misunderstanding and opposition, mistreatment and misrepresentation, adulation and animosity. He lived a fully human life under a foreign oppressor and under a corrupt local government and religious establishment. He apparently experienced the premature death of a father and conflicts within His family. He knew what it was to put in a long day at work, to work at a craft, and presumably to haggle with buyers and sellers over the fair prices of commodities He wanted to sell or needed to buy. He knew what it was to be homeless and what it was to be a refugee in a foreign country.

All of this means that the Lord Jesus is able to sympathize with our weaknesses. He is not just able to imagine what they are like, as a White House official or a royal family member might do when he visits a place of severe human need, only to retreat to a luxurious hotel room to prepare a report. I do not say this to disparage such visits. They are important ways in which people in positions of privilege and power stay in touch with some of the rawer realities of life in a fallen world. But their experience is very different from that of someone who lives through those conditions and has no place to escape or retreat. That is the wonder of the Incarnation. God became man. He, who was rich, became poor for our sakes. He entered into our context, so that He could not only feel for us but also identify with us. He cares; He doesn't condone. He helps; He doesn't hurt. He shares our experiences of weakness, but He shares as someone who is able to do more than share our pain. He is able to meet our need.

The Lord Jesus had experienced temptation. This is the second time the author of Hebrews makes this point. In Hebrews 2:18 he writes, "Because he himself suffered when he was tempted, he is able to help those who are being tempted." Now he adds, "We have [a high priest] who has been tempted in every way, just as we are—yet without sin" (4:15). The writer does not mean that the Lord Jesus was tempted with every specific sin that we are tempted with. He was not tempted to view pornography on the Internet, or to break speed limits on the highway, or to engage in fraud by using someone else's credit cards. None of those temptations existed in His time. But He was tempted by Satan and by sinful people, exactly as we are. He experienced the attacks of the evil one and He felt the pressures and appeals of the culture around Him. His temptations came in all the forms and outward pressures we know:

criticism, opportunity, praise and flattery, threats and hostility. He also knew temptations from within. As the God-man, everything about the cross was repulsive to Him. As a human, His inner self revolted against the pain, humiliation, and finality of death. As God, the thought of becoming the Sinbearer, of experiencing the wrath and judgment of His Father, contradicted all that He was. The intensity of His inward struggle must have been overwhelming, and in the Garden of Gethsemane we are given a brief glimpse as to what that involved. His whole life was one of testing, at levels of intensity far greater than we will ever know.

When I sense I am in a spiritual battle and the evil one is stalking me like a determined lion, I know that the Lord Jesus understands. When I know the pressures of people and the culture around me, I know that He understands. Whether it is the undeserved hostility of people in prominence, the criticisms of family members, the betrayal of professed friends, the incompetence and unreliability of supposed friends, or the appeal of success and popularity, I know that He has been in all of those places. When I battle inward forces that seem too strong to control, I know that He understands because He knew what it was to have everything within Him calling out to do something different from the will of God, yet He did not yield. Truly He is able to sympathize with my weakness.

But I need more than sympathy and understanding. People who sympathize with me may merely be affirming my weakness, rather than giving me a model of victory. That is not the case with the Lord Jesus. He was tempted in every way, as I am, "yet he was without sin." He resisted whatever was thrown at Him. He not only fought the battles I fight; He won them. He not only faced weakness and temptation; He endured them triumphantly.

That confidence, that we have not only an exalted and sympathetic High Priest, but also a victorious one, brings us to the third truth about prayer in this passage.

WE PRAY WITH CONFIDENCE BECAUSE
WE HAVE A GRACIOUS HIGH PRIEST

It does little good to have such a High Priest if we do not take advantage of who He is. "Let us then approach the throne of grace with confidence." The original text is even more encouraging: "Let us keep on drawing near." This is a constant privilege for the people of God. The old temple system allowed only the priests to enter the Holy Place and only the high priest to enter the Holy of Holies once a year. But the invitation of the New Covenant is to all believers—to "us." When the veil was torn and the work of Christ on our behalf was completed, every child of God was granted the right and privilege to keep entering the presence of God. Here it is described as the "throne of grace." We are invited to the center of the divine sovereignty, the control room of creation, where God dwells in His glory. It is called the throne of grace because grace characterizes the One who sits on the throne. Grace is the basis of our access there, and grace is what we receive. Nothing about prayer is based on our merit. From first to last, it is about the grace of God. And we are to approach the throne of grace "with confidence."

My son once worked as part of the concierge staff at an exclusive hotel. Some of the guests were members of the royal families of Middle Eastern nations. When the staff came into the presence of the princess, they were required to get down on their faces and wait until they were given permission to approach the royal presence. Even in our democracy, we know that we cannot approach the president at will. But we are told that we can approach the King of glory with confidence. The word *confidence* does not describe the emotions we feel, so much as the rights we possess. In Greek the word described the rights of a citizen in Greek society, the right to speak in the public assembly, the right to remark on anything that concerned you. In Hebrews 10:19, the writer returns to the same idea: "We have confidence to enter the Most Holy Place by the blood of Jesus." The Lord Jesus has made it possible for us to come into God's presence with our needs and concerns, because we stand fully accepted in Him. It is the right of a family member to enter when and where no one else would dare to come.

The privilege of access to a holy and righteous God is infinitely precious. It is the heart of prayer. Wherever I am and whatever I am doing, I have access to the throne of God. Prayer is not a carefully structured and elaborately ritualized religious activity to be carried out in special places in special ways. It does not require carefully constructed phrases that use all the right words. The word *confidence* means that we have instant access and the opportunity to pour out our hearts freely to God.

There are many reasons for prayer. We may pray to pour out our hearts in worship. We may pray to draw close to God and share a sense of spiritual intimacy. We may pray to confess our sins or to declare our gratitude. We may pray because we are overwhelmed by a need in someone else's life or because we are dealing with issues in our own hearts. We may pray for timely help, for God's response to situations that overwhelm us. But because we are needy people, one of the major reasons we pray is to "receive mercy and find grace to help us in our time of need."

Mercy is God's provision for our sins and failures. Mercy sees us in the misery of our shortcomings and responds with forgiveness and cleansing. And God's response is always one of grace. He does not respond to our merit but to our need. Donald Bloesch puts it well: "Our hope depends not on the right technique or the proper phrase or gesture, which borders on magic, but on the promise of God to look with favor on those who throw themselves on his mercy and who acknowledge the efficacy of the atoning sacrifice of his Son, Jesus Christ, for their redemption."[2]

Effective prayer relies upon the willing power of God. We have a confidence inspired by the work of the Lord Jesus, representing us before the throne of grace. God's enabling help flows to those who, on the basis of their relation to the Lord Jesus, are God-dependent, not self-sufficient.

When we pray, we come to the throne of grace with our need and find a Father who responds in mercy and grace. When we pray, we align ourselves with God's purposes and find ourselves gaining a perspective on reality that reorders our entire understanding of life. When we pray, we draw close to God in humility and dependence and begin to discover a fundamental of life stated by James: "God opposes the proud, but gives grace to the humble. Submit yourselves, then, to God. Resist the devil, and he will flee from you. Come near to God and he will come near to you" (4:6–8).

When the *Titanic* hit an iceberg in the North Atlantic at 11:40 on the evening of April 14, 1912, few of the passengers rushed to the lifeboats. Above the waterline, everything seemed normal. But below the waterline, things were very different. The iceberg had torn six relatively narrow slits across six watertight holds, and water was slowly but surely filling the hull. The crew showed no great concern. "[They] were lulled to complacency, because the ship looked so safe. Her huge bulk, her tiers of decks rising one on top of another, her 29 boilers, her luxurious fittings—all seemed to spell 'permanence.' The appearance of safety was mistaken for safety itself."[3]

We are all prone to mistake appearance for reality. But there will come a time, as we navigate life, when everything will depend on what is going on beneath the waterline. The key to what goes on in that part of our lives is directly related to our prayer lives. When we are in the storm, it is too late to develop the spiritual ballast we need. That is why wise spiritual navigators learn the habit of a rigorous prayer life.

Chapter Five

GOD'S COMPASS

In the world of country music, Alan Jackson has superstar status. Among more than sixty awards and honors, he was named Entertainer of the Year in 1995 by the Country Music Association and twice the Male Vocalist of the Year by the Academy of Country Music. In a seven-year period, an amazing twenty of his songs reached number one on the country music charts. He has sold more than twenty-five million records and amassed a fortune of more than forty million dollars. He lives in a thirty-thousand-square-foot mansion that contains most of the creature comforts known to man. Any reasonable accounting would have to consider Alan Jackson a successful man.

But appearances can be deceptive. In 1998, Alan Jackson found himself in deep personal trouble. His marriage to his high school sweetheart was on the rocks, and for the first time in his life he found himself in what he told a reporter from USA Today was "an almost suicidal depression. . . . I kept trying to let everything else make me happy. Maybe that's why I'm successful. I worked so hard to get all the stuff to make me happy. Then that didn't do it. I actually got worse."[1]

The Jacksons managed to work through their difficulties and renewed their vows as a special nineteenth-anniversary celebration. But Alan Jackson wasn't the first, and he won't be the last, to discover that in the midst of public success, he was experiencing private failure in the things that mattered most. His life required a radical course alteration if he was to get to where he wanted to go, not to where he was headed. For many of us, the danger isn't that we will fail to reach our goals but that we will have the wrong goals. The worst failure may be to succeed in things that don't really matter, to arrive at the wrong harbor.

One of the major challenges of navigating by the stars is that they are not always visible. Clouds obscure the heavens, often for days at a time. In the meantime, navigators can easily drift off course. One of the fundamental breakthroughs of the last millennium occurred when sailors began to use the compass at sea.

The origins of the compass are hidden in obscurity but are usually traced to China, centuries before the birth of Christ. But apparently it wasn't until the twelfth or thirteenth centuries after Christ that the compass went to sea. The effect was dramatic. Brave men were now equipped to venture beyond the familiar and have some way to determine where they were. The result was that new worlds suddenly were open for discovery. Sailors were free to sail familiar waters even in bad weather and emboldened to venture into the unknown with new confidence. Quickly the compass became the prime instrument of navigation.

The fundamental principle of celestial navigation is a fixed point, an unchanging North Star. The fundamental tool of navigation is a device to connect that fixed point to one's present location, such as a sextant. As we have seen, the obvious parallels are to the person of the Lord Jesus, the full and final revelation of the triune God, and to the Bible as the Word of God. Having discussed prayer as our spiritual ballast, we now return to the idea of navigational instruments and to another God-given spiritual navigational device, one too little understood and too often misused. I am speaking about the conscience, which is intended to serve as our moral compass. If we are going to arrive safely at our intended destination, we need to understand the value and limitations of our conscience.

The apostle Paul was emphatic about the need to live with a good conscience and guard against a defective conscience. He speaks with great urgency on the subject to his protégé Timothy:

> As I urged you when I went into Macedonia, stay there in Ephesus so that you may command certain men not to teach false doctrines any longer nor to devote themselves to myths and endless genealogies. These promote controversies rather than God's work—which is by faith. *The goal of this command is love, which comes from a pure heart and a good conscience and a sincere faith.* Some have wandered away from these and turned to meaningless talk. They want to be teachers of the law, but they do not know what they are talking about or what they so confidently affirm. . . . Timothy, my son, I give you this instruction in keeping with the prophecies once made about you, so that by following them you may fight the good fight, *holding on to faith and a good conscience.* Some have rejected these and so have shipwrecked their faith. Among them are Hymenaeus and Alexander, whom I have handed over to Satan to be taught not to blaspheme. (1 Timothy 1:3–7, 18–20, emphasis added)

There is an old adage about Christopher Columbus: when he left, he didn't know where he was going; when he arrived, he didn't know where he was; and when he returned, he had no idea where he'd been. The truth is that while Columbus did sail into the unknown, his voyage was a remarkable feat of seamanship. Besides, on his first voyage he wasn't an explorer so much as a discoverer. Scholars tell us that he discovered three things: land unknown to Europeans, the best westward sea passage to the Americas, and the best eastward route back. He may not have known his destination, but he did know the sea. He not only returned safely to Spain, but he also was able to retrace his voyages. This was remarkable because navigational techniques in his time were rudimentary. He did not have an instrument such as the sextant. Instead, he needed to rely upon his compass to set his direction, a simple quadrant to sight the stars, and dead reckoning to estimate how far he had traveled.

Wise people are destination-focused. They know that you do not arrive at your goal by drifting or by going with the wind but by design. That involves paying close attention to your instruments, knowing both their limitations and their effective use.

Effectively Navigating Life
Requires a Clear Destination

"It isn't the going out of port but the coming in that determines the success of a voyage," wrote the nineteenth-century preacher Henry Ward Beecher. To use more modern language: Begin with the end in view. That is why Paul is so determined to keep Timothy's attention focused on the goal as he encourages him to stay the course.

Timothy had been given an extremely difficult assignment: to take Paul's place in the city of Ephesus in a congregation infested with false teachers who loved speculations and novel interpretations. From all we can tell, Timothy was a man who was aware of his limits and inadequacies. He did not have a powerful presence. It wasn't his style to face down opponents by the sheer force of his personality. He was not a persuasive or charismatic speaker. Nor was he a fighter, a confronter who loved a good battle. From all accounts, he was a good, reliable, faithful man who loved his Lord and served Him well. But this task felt like it was too much for him. He yearned for peace and quiet, and he was tempted to go along to get along.

Wisely, Paul told Timothy to focus on the goal. He needed, as we all do, to understand why this battle was worth fighting. "The goal of this command [to reject the false teachers and their teachings] is love, which comes from a pure heart and a good conscience and a sincere faith." This is God's goal for all Christ-followers. Love is the supreme priority for God's people. Love for whom? Paul does not tell us, but it is impossible not to think of the Lord's words when He was asked which was the most important commandment. "The most important one . . . is this: 'Hear, O Israel, the Lord our God, the Lord is one. Love the Lord your God with all your heart and with all your soul and with all your mind and with all your strength.' The second is this: 'Love your neighbor as yourself.' There is no commandment greater than these" (Mark 12:29–31). Love for God and love for people are inseparable in the gospel. Christ's people are to be like Him in love, for the glory of God and the good of others.

What is remarkable here is what Paul says about the source of love. It comes "from a pure heart and a good conscience and a sincere faith." In the Bible, the heart describes the command center of a person's inner self, the core of one's being. A pure heart is one that has been set free from motives of self-absorption to those of self-sacrifice. The conscience, as we shall soon see in more detail, is the center of one's moral consciousness. A good conscience directs us in the way of life. A sincere, or unhypocritical, faith is an authentic trust in God. Paul is not trying to make scholarly distinctions between terms or trying to dissect our inner being. Rather, he is telling us that love can flow only from a pure source. That is why false teaching must be resisted. It contaminates not just our minds but also our souls.

The central thing I need to see in these words is a God-given standard by which to measure the quality of my life. Am I living well? Would those closest to me consider verse 5 an appropriate description of my life? Can they say that I have "reached the goal of love, out of a pure heart, a good conscience, and sincere faith"? That is God's declared goal for me, the destination toward which my life should be pointed.

I must confess that, compared with the goals we usually measure people's lives by, love doesn't feel compelling. Yet I am impressed with something Malcolm Muggeridge, the English agnostic journalist who became a Christian, wrote:

> When I look back on my life nowadays, which I sometimes do, what strikes me most forcibly about it is that what seemed at the time most significant and seductive, seems now most futile and absurd. For instance, success in all of its various guises; being known and being praised; ostensible pleasures, like acquiring money or seducing women, or traveling, going to and fro in the world and up and down in it like Satan, explaining and experiencing whatever Vanity Fair has to offer. In retrospect, all these exercises in self-gratification seem pure fantasy, what Pascal called, "licking the earth."[2]

The saddest failure in life is to succeed in all the wrong things. The right thing is to succeed in love, in the name of and for the glory of Christ. An essential part of that is a good conscience, as Paul makes clear. *A good conscience is not only a source of love in our lives; it is our moral compass, preventing personal spiritual shipwreck.*

The translation of 1Timothy 1:19 in the New International Version is accurate but not quite precise. A strict translation reads, "holding on to faith and a good conscience." Some have rejected "this" (a reference to "a good conscience," rather than "these,"—that is, faith and conscience) "and so have shipwrecked their faith." I'm not trying to focus on trivialities. Holding faith is hugely important. Paul, however, lays the stress on the conscience as a crucial factor in spiritual defection. He considers a healthy conscience an indispensable attribute of a Christian leader. Deacons, he writes, "must keep hold of the deep truths of the faith with a clear [or clean] conscience" (1 Timothy 3:9). And Paul describes himself as serving God "with a clear conscience" (2 Timothy 1:3). He understands the conscience as providing essential direction for our lives. It is therefore important to get a proper biblical understanding of this central navigational tool.

A Healthy Conscience Enables Us to Navigate Life Effectively

The Holy Spirit indwells every believer at the moment of conversion. But the conscience is not just another name for God's Spirit. The conscience is a component of our humanity, given to believer and unbeliever alike. It is the inner faculty that tests and judges our thoughts and actions, our inward sense of right and wrong. It is not the source of our moral standards so much as a detection device that indicates whether we are following those standards. Conscience was deeply affected by humanity's fall into sin, so it is not automatically foolproof, as we shall see. Therefore it needs to be protected and cultivated. Paul describes the way the conscience functions in Romans 2:14–15: "Indeed, when Gentiles, who do not have the law, do by nature things required by the law, they are a law for themselves, even though they do not have the law, since they show that the requirements of the law are written on their hearts, their consciences also bearing witness, and their thoughts now accusing, now even defending them." Accusing or defending is the fundamental work of the conscience, and it is intended to keep us from shipwreck.

A healthy conscience serves as a moral compass. The compass has proven to be an extremely useful illustration in helping me think through how conscience works. A compass is valuable because it is simple and clear. It gives the user the ability to determine heading and bearing by pointing to magnetic north. Seeing where the compass points is simple. Learning how to use it properly is considerably more difficult.

A compass is a valuable but limited instrument. First, it is limited by *magnetic variation.* The compass points to magnetic north, not to true or geographic north. Magnetic variation is the difference between true north and compass north, a difference that varies depending on one's physical location. A navigator, therefore, must correct his compass heading by taking into account this variation. A compass is also affected by local conditions, such as electromagnetic fields in a plane or ship, metals, or even mineral deposits. This is called *magnetic deviation* and must be taken into account by the navigator. This means that when a navigator reads his compass, he needs to recognize that he is dealing with three courses: the compass course (what the compass reads), the magnetic course (the compass course corrected for magnetic deviation), and the true course (the compass course corrected for magnetic variation). A navigator who naively follows his compass without accounting for its shortcomings will end up somewhere different than he intended!

So will the person who simply follows his conscience, because conscience is also a valuable but limited faculty. It has a built-in variation: the sinfulness of the human heart. It is not pulled to the true north of God's will but to our desires and indulgences. As Jeremiah says so powerfully: "The heart is deceitful above all things and beyond cure. Who can understand it?" (Jeremiah 17:9). A conscience is also subject to spiritual deviation, the pull of local influences. Our family training, our personal experiences, our culture, our education and training all influence our inner moral compass in profound ways. That is why the New Testament calls us to develop and protect a good conscience, a healthy conscience, a blameless conscience, and a clear conscience. Conscience in itself will never lead us properly. A person who declares, "I just follow my conscience" is like a sailor who says, "I just follow my compass." He is headed for shipwreck. The only question is, How soon? Or, to change the image: Conscience is like a sundial; it functions properly only when the right light shines on it. As Billy Graham once observed, "Most of us follow our conscience the way we follow a wheelbarrow: we push it in the direction we want it to go."

The conscience is not intended to function on its own or as the sole instrument that steers our decisions. The Word of God provides us with the moral norms and standards by which we are to steer our course. The Holy Spirit draws us into intimacy with the Father, leading us in the ways of God, convicting us of sin, and strengthening the "inner person of the heart" to love the ways of God. The community of Christ surrounds us with godly influences and examples. Prayer sensitizes our hearts to the voice of our gracious God. The Cross washes our consciences from the defiling and hardening influences of sin and guilt (Hebrews 9:14; 10:22). When all these are present, conscience is able to serve its appropriate role in our lives.

The primary function of the conscience is to serve as a course deviation monitor. It tells us when our thinking or our actions are off course. Before we take an action, a healthy conscience wrestles with our choices and tests our motives. Thus, it is crucial that our conscience is informed by God's truth and sensitive to His Spirit. During an action, conscience is usually hardest to hear, so we need to train ourselves to be sensitive to its quiet voice. After an action, conscience sits in judgment, approving or disapproving. J. I. Packer says it well:

> An educated, sensitive conscience is God's monitor. It alerts
> us to the moral quality of what we do or plan to do, forbids

lawlessness and irresponsibility, and makes us feel guilt, shame, and fear of the future retribution that it tells us we deserve, when we have allowed ourselves to defy its restraints. Satan's strategy is to corrupt, desensitize, and if possible kill our consciences. The relativism, materialism, narcissism, secularism, and hedonism of today's Western world help him mightily toward his goal. His task is made simpler by the way in which the world's moral weaknesses have been taken into the contemporary church.[3]

An Unhealthy Conscience
Endangers Our Well-Being

One of Paul's personal priorities was to guard and protect his conscience. Therefore, he says in Acts 24:16, "I strive always to keep my conscience clear before God and man." The word *strive* is important. It reminds us that this is not something automatic or constant. A clear conscience requires careful protection and continual maintenance. One way to diagnose the health of our conscience is to consider the Bible's evaluation of defective consciences. Four varieties are described.

A weak conscience lacks mature understanding. Paul describes such a conscience in 1 Corinthians 8:4–7 (emphasis added):

> So then, about eating food sacrificed to idols: We know that an idol is nothing at all in the world and that there is no God but one. For even if there are so-called gods, whether in heaven or on earth (as indeed there are many "gods" and many "lords"), yet for us there is but one God, the Father, from whom all things came and for whom we live; and there is but one Lord, Jesus Christ, through whom all things came and through whom we live.

> But not everyone knows this. Some people are still so accus-
> tomed to idols that when they eat such food they think of it
> as having been sacrificed to an idol, and *since their conscience is
> weak*, it is defiled.

As we have seen, the basic principle is that a conscience is valuable but limited. It judges only by what it knows, and if it possesses wrong information, it will make wrong judgments. In this case, the person with a weak conscience is someone who has not understood the new principles of freedom established in Christ. Such persons are uninstructed in grace and are therefore held captive by legalisms and human taboos. Their consciences are overly sensitive, making them feel unnecessary guilt. Paul was writing to believers with a Jewish or pagan heritage who had pushed a proper concern with idolatry to unwarranted lengths. Today, our areas of concern are different, but many Christians still fall prey to a legalism that elevates human taboos to a level of divine authority. I am convinced, however, that more Christians today suffer from a conscience that is weak because it is underdeveloped than from one that is overdeveloped. We live in a culture that tolerates and even encourages sin. I am amazed how many immature Christians engage in lifestyles that the Bible clearly condemns without seeming to be aware they are doing wrong. They too lack biblical knowledge, particularly about the holiness of God. This is not to excuse their ignorance. A weak conscience is not a condition to be tolerated; it is a sickness to be corrected.

A second condition is more serious. *A wounded conscience violates its integrity.* Paul describes this condition in the passage that immediately follows the one we have just considered, 1 Corinthians 8:9–13 (emphasis added):

> Be careful, however, that the exercise of your freedom does not
> become a stumbling block to the weak. For if *anyone with a weak*

conscience sees you who have this knowledge eating in an idol's temple, won't he be emboldened to eat what has been sacrificed to idols? So this weak brother, for whom Christ died, is destroyed by your knowledge. When you sin against your brothers in this way and *wound their weak conscience*, you sin against Christ. Therefore, if what I eat causes my brother to fall into sin, I will never eat meat again, so that I will not cause him to fall.

Paul addresses a simple but significant issue. Because of the example of a fellow Christian, an immature believer is encouraged to act against his convictions and his conscience. He is conforming to another's conscience. Paul's point is clear: even if his conscience is wrong, he must not act against it. (Unless, of course, following conscience means disobedience to God. But Paul is not discussing such a case.) A person who acts against conscience to please others or to conform to the crowd "wounds" another person's conscience. Paul's language is picturesque. The word *wound* means "to beat or to strike," and, as a result, this brother is "destroyed." By violating the integrity of his conscience, this person has effectively disconnected it. It will no longer serve as a reliable guide.

When we are tempted to follow the example or the reasoning of another person, no matter how much we respect that person, we may be running the red light of conscience. As Martin Luther said at a moment of critical choice in his life: "To go against conscience is neither right nor safe. Here I stand. I can do no other. God help me! Amen."

A wounded conscience may lead to the third defective conscience. *A seared conscience desensitizes the soul.* Paul describes this pattern in 1 Timothy 4:1–4 (emphasis added):

The Spirit clearly says that in later times some will abandon the faith and follow deceiving spirits and things taught by demons.

Such teachings come through hypocritical liars, *whose consciences have been seared as with a hot iron.* They forbid people to marry and order them to abstain from certain foods, which God created to be received with thanksgiving by those who believe and who know the truth. For everything God created is good, and nothing is to be rejected if it is received with thanksgiving.

A seared conscience may be one that is branded as belonging to Satan. More likely, the idea is that it has been seared or cauterized so that it feels no pain. The people he is speaking of here formerly professed allegiance to Christ. Now they are teaching ideas plainly contrary to the gospel. In this case, these people are ascetics, denying the goodness of God's creation. In other contexts, such people could be libertines, throwing off any moral restraint. Whether by indulgence or by denial, our consciences can become seared. We become desensitized when we refuse to admit the witness of conscience or to deal with its warnings.

Finally, *a defiled conscience loses all appropriate shame.* Paul uses the strongest of language to describe such people in Titus 1:15–16 (emphasis added):

To the pure, all things are pure, but to those who are corrupted and do not believe, nothing is pure. In fact, *both their minds and consciences are corrupted.* They claim to know God, but by their actions they deny him. They are detestable, disobedient and unfit for doing anything good.

"Corrupt" describes a condition of moral infection that not only makes a person sick but also infects those with whom he comes in contact. Jeremiah vividly describes such people: "'Are they ashamed of their loathsome conduct? No, they have no shame at all; they do not even know how to blush. So they will fall among the fallen; they will be brought down when I punish them,' says the LORD" (Jeremiah 6:15). Paul doesn't use the expression "corrupt conscience" in Romans 1:28–32, but there is no clearer depiction of the corrupting influence of people who have lost their sense of shame (emphasis added):

> Furthermore, since they did not think it worthwhile to retain the knowledge of God, he gave them over to a depraved mind, to do what ought not to be done. They have become filled with every kind of wickedness, evil, greed and depravity. They are full of envy, murder, strife, deceit and malice. They are gossips, slanderers, God-haters, insolent, arrogant and boastful; they invent ways of doing evil; they disobey their parents; they are senseless, faithless, heartless, ruthless. Although they know God's righteous decree that those who do such things deserve death, *they not only continue to do these very things but also approve of those who practice them.*

WE NEED TO ACTIVELY
MAINTAIN A HEALTHY CONSCIENCE

In contrast to the graphic picture Scripture gives us of an unhealthy conscience, it also tells us how to maintain the health of our moral conscience. *First, our conscience needs cleansing.* A guilty conscience will not signal true north. Neither will a dirty, sinful one that denies its true guilt. Just as a navigator must consider magnetic variation and deviation, we must take into account moral and spiritual deviation. The Lord Jesus died not only for our sins but also for our consciences. "How much more, then, will the blood of Christ, who through the eternal Spirit offered himself unblemished to God, cleanse our consciences from acts that lead to death, so that we may serve the living God!" . . . "Let us draw near to God with a sincere heart in full assurance of faith, having our hearts sprinkled to cleanse us from a guilty conscience and having our bodies washed with pure water" (Hebrews 9:14; 10:22). The initial cleansing of salvation needs to be renewed by our consistent acknowledgment of guilt and by our continual reception of the forgiveness of the Father.

Second, our conscience needs instruction. Only a biblically informed conscience is a reliable guide. Our conscience, apart from Christ, is deeply influenced by our sinfulness, our life experiences, and our sinful culture. These deviations from true north must be corrected by the eternal truths of God's Word. We need to fill our minds with Scripture. The compass of conscience is not enough.

Third, our conscience needs to be carefully protected. "Hold on to faith and a good conscience" (1 Timothy 1:19). "I strive always to keep my conscience clear before God and men" (Acts 24:16). "But in your hearts set apart Christ as Lord. Always be prepared to give an answer to everyone who asks you to give the reason for the hope that you have. But do this with gentleness and respect, keeping a clear conscience, so that those who speak maliciously against your good behavior in Christ may be ashamed of their slander" (1 Peter 3:15–16). It has been a great help to me, when I have faced a difficult situation, to remind myself to act in such a way that I will have a good conscience, whatever the other outcomes may be. A good conscience must be chosen, followed, and protected.

Life would be simpler if all we needed to do was choose our destination, set an automatic pilot, and then sit back and enjoy the ride. But it doesn't happen that way. We do choose our destination, either intentionally or by default. But life consists of millions of little choices that either keep us on course or steer us in another direction. God has given us a wonderful but limited navigational instrument—the conscience. Wise people take good care of it!

Chapter Six

LOAD LIMITS

S amuel Plimsoll was a man with a burden. Involved in the coal trade in nineteenth-century England, he became aware of the terrible dangers faced by sailors. Every year hundreds of seamen lost their lives on ships that were dangerously overloaded. Unscrupulous ship owners, pursuing ever greater profits, were more than willing to put the lives of others at risk. Ships loaded almost to the deck line left port, only to founder at sea, an event received with delight by owners, who stood to make even greater profits from insurance. In 1873, an astonishing 411 ships sank, taking hundreds of men to watery graves. To make matters even worse, if a man signed up for a voyage, he couldn't back out, no matter how unsafe he considered the ship to be. The law firmly supported the ship owners and made it a crime to jump ship, no matter how unsafe the vessel was. In the early 1870s, one of every three prisoners in southwest England was a sailor who had refused to sail on what had become known as "coffin ships."

This problem became Plimsoll's mission. His idea was simple. Every ship needed a load line, indicating when it was overloaded. With that in mind, Plimsoll ran for Parliament in 1868 and was elected. Immediately he began an intense campaign to save the lives of British sailors. He gave passionate speeches in the House of Commons and wrote a book that shocked the public by its exposure of conditions. Not surprisingly, his charges aroused the vehement opposition of many ship owners, who struck back with a campaign of character attacks and endless lawsuits. But Plimsoll persisted, attacking "the speculative scoundrels in whose hearts is neither the law of God nor the fear of man." Gradually he won over public opinion and shamed the government into taking action. The Unseaworthy Vessels Bill was passed in 1875, and the following year, a bill written by Plimsoll, which required a load line, passed. But, under pressure from vested interests, Parliament compromised. It allowed a ship's owner to put the line wherever he desired, which was a lot like putting the fox in charge of the hen house. Plimsoll saw one ship with the load line painted on the funnel, showing the captain's contempt for the new law.

Plimsoll fought on for another fourteen years until laws were passed to make sure that the line was set at a level that would ensure the safety of the ship. In time, his load line became the international standard. Today, in every port in the world you will see the results of Plimsoll's work, which led him to be called "the Sailor's Friend." On the hull of every cargo ship you will see the Plimsoll line, indicating the maximum depth to which a ship can be safely and legally loaded.

Life would be a lot easier if there were a Plimsoll mark for people. Navigating life requires more than navigational skills. We have looked at the navigational principle of the North Star and the navigational tools of Scripture, prayer, and conscience. To these we need to add navigational safeguards, and that brings us to some important biblical insights into load limits. We will not arrive safely at our destination unless we understand God's Plimsoll line.

Fast Company is a magazine that seeks to address the realities of the new economy. In a provocative issue in 1999, at the peak of the dot-com craze, it addressed, in secular terms, the issue of load limits:

> In the world of work, the hot button today is not the IPO market, which is turning Web-entrepreneurs into instant millionaires.
>
> It's not the raging war for talent, which is leading teams of workplace wizards to put themselves up for auction to the highest bidder.
>
> It's not the insatiable appetite for growth, which is converting productless startups into priceless R&D labs.
>
> It's not the desperate search for greater efficiencies and for new markets, which is resulting in ever-larger combinations of old, established corporate giants.
>
> It's not even the spiraling rewards that seem to flow to those who are brave—or brazen—enough to declare themselves brands, to assert their economic independence from the traditional workplace, and, in the process to free themselves from the constraints of salary, bureaucracy and corporate gravity.
>
> The hot button today embraces *all* of those developments of modern life—all of those developments, and more.
>
> The hot button today is a question that hangs in the air in corporate boardrooms and at cocktail parties, in IPO road shows and at the kitchen table: *How much is enough?*
>
> How much money—to compensate you for your work? How much time—to devote to your family? How much public glory—to satisfy your ego? How much opportunity for private reflection—to deepen your understanding? How much *stuff* is enough for you? And, no matter now much stuff you have, how do you find—and define—satisfaction?[1]

Those are probing questions, especially for a Christ-follower concerned about living by kingdom values. In a society that is built on chronic and compulsive consumerism, how do we set load limits? Twice we are told in the New Testament that greed, or covetousness, is idolatry (Ephesians 5:5; Colossians 3:5). The issues of contentment and covetousness are among the most pressing we confront as we seek to navigate our culture. Paul's words in 1 Timothy 6:3–16 have special relevance:

If anyone teaches false doctrines and does not agree to the sound instruction of our Lord Jesus Christ and to godly teaching, he is conceited and understands nothing. He has an unhealthy interest in controversies and quarrels about words that result in envy, strife, malicious talk, evil suspicions and constant friction between men of corrupt mind, who have been robbed of the truth and who think that godliness is a means to financial gain.

But godliness with contentment is great gain. For we brought nothing into the world, and we can take nothing out of it. But if we have food and clothing, we will be content with that. People who want to get rich fall into temptation and a trap and into many foolish and harmful desires that plunge men into ruin and destruction. For the love of money is a root of all kinds of evil. Some people, eager for money, have wandered from the faith and pierced themselves with many griefs.

But you, man of God, flee from all this, and pursue righteousness, godliness, faith, love, endurance and gentleness. Fight the good fight of the faith. Take hold of the eternal life to which you were called when you made your good confession in the presence of many witnesses. In the sight of God, who gives life to everything, and of Christ Jesus, who while testifying before Pontius Pilate made the good confession, I charge you to keep this command without spot or blame until the appearing of our Lord Jesus Christ, which God will bring about in his own time—God, the blessed and only Ruler, the King of kings and Lord of lords, who alone is immortal and who lives in unapproachable light, whom no one has seen or can see. To him be honor and might forever. Amen.

The story is told of a young girl whose father was a chronic complainer. One evening, at the dinner table, she proudly announced, "I know what everyone in our family likes!" She didn't need any coaxing to reveal her information: "Johnny likes hamburgers; Janie loves ice cream; Jimmy loves pizza; and Mommy likes chicken." Her father waited for his turn, but there was no information forthcoming. "Well, what about me!" he asked. "What does Daddy like?" With the innocence and painful insight of a child, the little one answered: "Daddy, you like everything we haven't got!"

One observer describes ours as "a society of inextinguishable discontent." We have been trained by the hidden persuaders in our society that we need to acquire, consume, upgrade, and enlarge. In such a context, the concept of "enough" is rare. No one is advertising the virtues of contentment. But the Holy Spirit uses just that word to put His finger on one of the most significant and sensitive issues in our lives.

In the Timothy passage, three ideas point us to the need for a Plimsoll line in our lives if we hope to navigate a materialistic culture successfully. Those ideas revolve around the words *covetousness, contentment,* and *character.*

WE MUST SENSITIZE OURSELVES TO THE DANGERS OF COVETOUSNESS

Pastors are often in the position of hearing people disclose the darkest secrets of their lives. Over the years, you come to believe that you have heard almost every sin confessed. So I was taken aback when I read that the great nineteenth-century preacher Charles Spurgeon had once commented that he had heard virtually every sin confessed, except the sin of covetousness. I realized that my experience more than a hundred years later was the same. I have never had anyone confess covetousness, even though there have been times when it was a pretty obvious diagnosis. I also realize, in my more honest moments, that I struggle with covetousness myself, with wanting what others possess that I do not. Money is not the only focus of covetousness, but in our culture it is a primary one.

Paul wants us to recognize that the issue is not money but the love of money. In 1 Timothy 6:9, he tells us that it is those who are eager to get rich who are in spiritual danger. Paul's precise words are "those who want to get rich"; that is, those who have set their hearts on wealth. It is tempting to see covetousness as someone else's problem, especially those who have more money than I do. But we know that "wanting to get rich" is not exclusive to the well-to-do. In fact, often those without money are consumed with a desire to acquire it. That is why we need to read Paul's words carefully. They do not apply only to those in the higher tax brackets. First Timothy 6:10 is one of those verses that people often misquote and distort. We hear it said that the Bible teaches that "money is the root of all evil." Wealth is not without its dangers, but what Paul says indicates that the problem is not money but the "love of money," an affection that can overtake rich and poor alike.

It is important to maintain the balance of Scripture. Wealthy people are to use their wealth and to enjoy it responsibly, but they are not to love it. Some of the heroes of faith in the Bible were people of great wealth, believers such as Job, Abraham, David, and Nehemiah. Others enjoyed positions of prominence and prosperity, such as Joseph and Daniel. None of these men were condemned for what they possessed, and they did not live for their possessions. Abraham was able to handle wealth; his nephew Lot was seduced by it, making foolish and evil choices. The issue is not net worth but heart values.

The issue of covetousness is a pressing one in our affluent culture. As I write, there is concern that we are sliding into recession after a decade of phenomenal expansion in the economy. Whatever direction the economy goes, the fact is that we are a people who measure success in terms of affluence and material success. The instant profits made during the heyday of the dot-com craze, the jaw-dropping contracts signed by athletes, and the drumbeat of emphasis on what the Dow or NASDAQ has done today seduce us into measuring our personal value by our bottom line. But enough is never enough. Athletes who signed headline-making contracts threaten to hold out two years later because they are underpaid and unappreciated. The ancient writer of Ecclesiastes said it thousands of years ago: "Whoever loves money never has money enough; whoever loves wealth is never satisfied with his income. . . . As goods increase, so do those who consume them" (Ecclesiastes 5:10–11).

In the edition of *Fast Company* mentioned earlier in this chapter, the editors reflected on the results of a survey they had taken among their highly successful readership:

> Sooner or later, it all comes down to money. For most respondents, money matters most. Money, the majority of them reported, is the most powerful factor in their success, in their satisfaction, and in their ability to determine the structure and substance of their lives.
>
> If money is so important, how much more of it would people need in order to stop worrying? The sums that most people named were surprising—not because they were so large but because they were so relatively small: In an age of

multibillion-dollar IPOs and multimillion-dollar lottery win-
nings, 70% of respondents said that it would take no more than
an extra $50,000 a year to free them from money worries and to
permit them to work the way they wanted to.

Enough is never enough. The ultimate question that we were
asking was How much is enough? The ultimate answer appears
to be that there is no such thing as "enough." The more people
have, the more they want.

We also asked people to designate various goods and services
as a marker of success or a sign of excess—and a similar pattern
emerged. The more money people made, the more likely they
were to view expensive cars, big houses, and dinners at fancy
restaurants as their just desserts. . . .

We want to have it all: More money and more time. More
success and a more satisfying family life. More creature comforts—and more sanity.[2]

In some ways it seems strange to read some of those words now, on
this side of the collapse of many technology companies and the decline
in stock values. Many people who seemed wealthy beyond imagining
because of the value of their stock options found themselves in quite
different financial circumstances less than eighteen months later. Paul
describes the uncertainty of wealth in 1 Timothy 6:17, but for the present
his concern is with the corrupting effects of the love of wealth. It is true,
as the editors of *Fast Company* recognize, that enough is never enough.
But what the editors fail to do is to give the disease its proper name:
covetousness. The fundamental law is that as acquisitions increase, so do
aspirations. The Greek word translated "covetousness" means "a desire
to have more." In the view of the Lord Jesus and the apostles, this is not
merely a tendency to avoid in a capitalistic, consumer society. It is, in

truth, a deadly enemy of the soul that tempts us to ignore the Plimsoll line and dangerously overload our lives.

The love of money has corrupting power in at least four ways.

1. Covetousness corrupts our view of God's truth.

Throughout 1 Timothy, Paul is engaged in conflict with false teachers. In 1 Timothy 6:3–5, he describes them for the final time in this letter. His point is straightforward: defective theology produces defective lifestyles. But behind the false message of these teachers is a false motive: they "think that godliness is a means to financial gain." This seems to mean that they pretend to be godly and spiritual so that they can deceive others to pay for their false teaching. Behind their façade of learning and spiritual insight is a corrupt desire to make money.

2. Covetousness contaminates our values.

"People who want to get rich fall into temptation and a trap and into many foolish and harmful desires" (1 Timothy 6:9). All of us encounter temptations. But Paul suggests that there are special temptations for people who have their hearts set on becoming wealthy. Here there is a fascinating play on words embedded in the original language. The Greek word for "financial gain," or profit, used in 1 Timothy 6:5 is *porismos*. The Greek word for "temptation" is *peirasmos*. Paul's opponents imagine that "godliness is a means to profit (*porismos*)." But their covetousness means that their pursuit of profit has become an encounter with temptation (*peirasmos*). It isn't hard to recognize what Paul has in mind. A desire to get a promotion or a contract pressures me to ignore my family. An opportunity too good to miss entices me to compromise my integrity. The desire to ingratiate myself with those who can further my career lures me to fudge my convictions and to imitate their lifestyle. The possibility of having a few more dollars seduces me to distort my expense account or my tax form. "An obsession with acquiring wealth is a self-feeding fire. It consumes not only time and energy, but also values. . . . Wealth leads people into circles where the rules are different, the peer pressure is tremendous, and the values are totally distorted."[3] The desire for wealth breeds other desires and things spiral downward.

3. *Covetousness capsizes our lives.*

When Paul writes of "desires which plunge men into ruin and destruction," he uses language borrowed from the world of sailing. The only other time the word *plunge* is used in the Bible is in Luke 5:7. As Peter and his helpers attempted to pull in the miraculous catch of fish, they "filled both boats so full that they began to sink [plunge]." Just as Samuel Plimsoll recognized the need for a load line on a ship to prevent it from being overloaded, we need a "covetousness line" to avoid exposing our lives to "ruin and destruction." In the most direct sense, because we cannot love or serve both God and Money (Luke 16:13), those who love money do not know Christ and are destined for utter destruction. There is also, however, an application for the Christ-follower. The word "[ruin] in biblical usage implies the loss of all that makes life worthwhile."[4] Warren Wiersbe puts it well:

> Money is the "god of this world," and it empowers millions of people to enjoy life by living on substitutes. With money they can buy entertainment, but they can't buy joy. They can go to the drugstore and buy sleep, but they can't buy peace. Their money will attract a lot of acquaintances, but very few real friends. Wealth gains them admiration and envy, but not love. It buys the best of medical services, but it can't buy health. Yes, it is good to have the things that money can buy, provided we don't lose the things that money can't buy.[5]

4. *Covetousness chokes out faith.*

"Some people, eager for money, have wandered from the faith and pierced themselves with many griefs" (1 Timothy 6:10). The Lord Jesus sees greed as a deadly enemy to the soul, and His warning is direct: "Watch out! Be on your guard against all kinds of greed; a person's life does not consist in the abundance of his possessions" (Luke 12:15). Life is not about possessions. God alone is the source of life; God alone is in control of life; God alone gives life. Trust in money cannot coexist with living faith in God.

Navigating life safely in a world of chronic and compulsive consumerism requires that we develop clear load limits. Materialism represents a hazard every bit as dangerous as the Labrador iceberg fields were to the *Titanic*. It is easy, with hindsight, to see the foolishness of the captain and the owners of that great ship, steaming at full speed through those dangerous waters. Icebergs are beautiful to admire but dangerous to encounter. They demand that we proceed with caution. So does materialism. When a culture of consumerism and a heart of covetousness converge, disaster is waiting. However, Scripture never simply calls us to avoid a negative. It challenges us to pursue a positive.

WE MUST CULTIVATE A HEART OF CONTENTMENT

The antidote to covetousness is contentment, a quality that is an indispensable part of true spirituality. Paul's words are striking: "Godliness with contentment is great gain." I doubt that Paul is suggesting that there is such a thing as genuine godliness without contentment. I suspect that he is saying that mature godliness always has contentment as an inseparable component.

"Godliness" is a favorite term of the apostle Paul in the book of 1 Timothy. He uses it eight times (four in this passage) to describe what we might call "authentic spirituality." He has taken a term much used by his contemporaries to describe their pagan concept of piety and given it a distinctively Christian meaning. The term describes an inner attitude of reverence and respect that is expressed in outward acts. Authentic godliness begins with "the fear of the Lord," reverential awe in His presence, which produces not only acts of worship but also a lifestyle that is consistent with the character and requirements of the God we love and serve. It is a God-centered life, a passion for God that translates into worship and appropriate conduct. For Paul, this quality is what it means to be a Christ-follower. As he has already written in 1 Timothy 4:7–8: "Train yourself to be godly. For . . . godliness has value for all things, holding promise for both the present life and the life to come."

True godliness always travels with "contentment." For the Greek and Roman philosophers, this was a significant word, one that described an attitude of self-sufficiency, the ability to rely on one's resources and not on others. For the Stoic philosophers, the ideal man was an independent man, in need of nothing and no one else. On Paul's lips, however, contentment takes a different meaning. As he wrote to the Philippians from a prison cell, "I have learned to be content whatever the circumstances. . . . I have learned the secret of being content in any and every situation, whether well fed or hungry, whether living in plenty or in want. I can do everything through him who gives me strength" (Philippians 4:11–13). Contentment, then, is not about self-sufficiency but Christ-sufficiency. It is not resignation but satisfaction. It is not acceptance of the status quo or surrender of ambition but submission to Christ and His purposes. Godly contentment isn't about complacency or passivity or an otherworldly detachment from life. Rather, as G. K. Chesterton says, "It is the ability to get out of a situation everything that is in it." It is a deep-seated satisfaction that is the gift of Christ.

It has been extremely helpful for me to distinguish between what someone has called "the contentment of aspiration" and "the contentment of acquisition." Aspiration is about who I am—my character, my relationships, my values. Acquisition is about what I possess. Godliness involves choosing satisfaction with acquisition and dissatisfaction with aspiration. It involves contentment with what I have but discontent with who I am. I want to become wiser, deeper, more loving, more Christlike.

The Jamaican bobsled team became the darlings of the 1988 Winter Olympics held in Calgary, where we lived at the time. It seemed amazing and amusing that athletes from a tropical nation would compete in an event like the bobsled. In the movie loosely based on that event, *Cool Runnings*, John Candy plays the coach of the team. He is a former American gold medalist, forced out of the sport by a cheating scandal. One of his athletes asks why he would cheat if he already had a gold medal. Candy's response is all about contentment: "I had to win. I learned something. If you aren't happy without a gold medal, you won't be happy with one." The contentment that wins the battle over covetousness is an inside job, which ultimately comes from the presence of the indwelling Christ.

Contentment is also the product of an eternal, kingdom perspective. That is where Paul directs our focus in 1 Timothy 6:7: "For we brought nothing into the world and we can take nothing out of it." This statement is obvious but easily forgotten. Things seem so real, and eternity seems so unreal. But faith tells us that the opposite is the truth. "So we fix our eyes, not on what is seen, but on what is unseen. For what is seen is temporary, but what is unseen is eternal" (2 Corinthians 4:18). Present things have no lasting value. They are ours to enjoy but not to keep. Life in this world is a lot like a Monopoly game. No matter how much you acquire, in the end it all goes back in the box.

John Piper invites us to imagine a visitor to an art gallery who begins to take pictures off the walls and carry them under his arm toward the exit. You watch for a while and then ask, "What are you doing?" "I'm becoming an art collector," he responds. "But they're not really yours, and they won't let you take them out of here. You can enjoy them, but you can't keep them!" "Sure, they're mine. I've got them under my arm! And I'll worry about how to get them out of here when the time comes."[6] We would have no difficulty in seeing the foolishness of that kind of behavior. Yet we often view our material possessions, which are entrusted to us by God, in the same way. We view money and things properly only when we recognize that they have no lasting value.

Paul also wants us to recognize that life's greatest values transcend money. "If we have food and clothing, we will be content with that." Those of us who live in the Western world have so much more than the basic necessities of life that it is very difficult to think only of food and clothing. Our list of "essentials" is much longer. But at various times in other countries I have met Christ-followers who had little more physically than meager supplies of food and clothing, yet I have felt humbled by their authentic joy in Christ. Food and clothing are important, but they are not the stuff of life. So the Lord tells us, "I tell you, do not worry about your life, what you will eat or drink; or about your body, what you will wear. Is not life more important than food, and the body more important than clothes?" (Matthew 6:25).

We accumulate money and possessions because they provide a feeling of security against the uncertainties of the future. But even at their best, riches are uncertain. They give no real certainty in the present world and absolutely none for the eternal world. That is why God describes as a fool the rich man who imagined that he had "plenty of good things laid up for many years," only to have God call the loan on his life. He not only doesn't control his wealth; he doesn't control his life. His money could not shelter him from the certainty of death, from his accountability to a sovereign God, or from the loss of all that he had accumulated. The Lord's verdict is, "This is how it will be with anyone who stores up things for himself but is not rich toward God" (Luke 12:21). Our greatest security comes not from the power of our wealth but from the certain promise of our God. "Your heavenly Father knows that you need [food and clothing]. But seek first his kingdom and his righteousness, and all these things will be given to you as well" (Matthew 6:32–33).

Warren Buffett no longer heads the list of America's wealthiest people, but he remains close to the top. For forty years he has had an amazing track record of success as an investor, and he has amassed a fortune measured in the billions. And he isn't ready to stop. He loves to acquire money, and he hates to spend it. He still lives in a relatively modest house in Omaha, Nebraska. He also hates to part with his money by giving it away—to his children or to charity. His friend Ann Landers said of him, "I tried my darndest to get him interested in what he could do for the world. What he does is piling and heaping and piling and heaping." Buffett is also notorious for his fear of death. One biographer pulls the pieces of his life together with this observation: "It is scarcely implausible that Buffett's fear of death has contributed to his drive to accumulate. Agnostic and hyper-rational, he has few other opiates. His passion is to accumulate."[7]

Someone shrewdly observed that we fear death in proportion to what we have to lose. If we store up treasure for ourselves on earth, we stand to lose everything. The Lord's counsel is, "Store up for yourselves treasures in heaven, where moth and rust do not destroy, and where thieves do not break in and steal. For where your treasure is, there your heart will be also" (Matthew 6:20–21). Contentment is the product of security in God, the product of trust in His character and His promises.

WE MUST FOCUS ON THE CENTRALITY OF CHARACTER

Having directed Timothy away from covetousness and toward contentment, Paul then directs him to his prime consideration. The false teachers may be absorbed with the pursuit of wealth, but Paul wants Timothy (and us) to be engaged in the pursuit of godly character. The materialists plaguing the congregation in Ephesus had a model of success, the person who single-mindedly pursued the goal of present financial wealth. "But you, man of God, flee from all this." Money is a great resource but a terribly inadequate goal. In fact, it is an extremely dangerous goal. So dangerous that we are called to flee the desire to get rich, to flee the love of money. This sounds strange in a society that has sanctified the pursuit of wealth and in a Christian community that often sounds more capitalist than Christian. The seduction of "prosperity theology" attempts to sanctify what God has called us to flee, a consumerist, materialistic philosophy of life. I find this a lot easier to preach than to practice.

We are not merely to flee, however. The call of the Christ-follower is to do just that, to follow the Lord. "Pursue righteousness, godliness, faith, love, endurance and righteousness." We will focus on the primacy of character in a later chapter. It is enough to notice here that we are to replace the pursuit of things with the pursuit of character. *Pursue* is a significant word. It reminds us that character is forged over time, not found in an instant. While there may be instant wealth, there is never instant character. The word also reminds us that while these qualities may be the product of God working in our lives, we also play a critical part. Character must be developed and pursued with vigorous energy. *Pursue* also reminds us that this is intentional activity, *pursued* in the daily experiences of life.

Phillips Brooks was a nineteenth-century pastor and preacher, now best known as the writer of "O Little Town of Bethlehem." He writes helpfully about what it means to pursue character: "Someday in years to come you'll be wrestling with the great temptation, or trembling under the great sorrow of your life. But the real struggle is here, now, in these quiet weeks. Now it is being decided whether, in the day of your supreme sorrow or temptation, you shall miserably fail or gloriously conquer. Character cannot be made except by a steady, long-continued quest."

We are not just to flee and to follow. We are also to "fight the good fight of the faith." For while the Christian life is always personal, it is never private. A Christ-follower is called to promote the cause of the kingdom of Christ and of the glory of Christ in the world. A covetous life is a selfish life. A kingdom life is a sacrificial life. In a time of warfare, we view financial resources differently. So a third phrase needs to be added to the way a Christian views money. We reject covetousness. We cultivate contentment. *And* we practice commitment in the use of our resources to further the cause of Christ in the world. Giving is the way we flee covetousness, because generosity builds our immunity against greed. Giving is the way we develop contentment, as we make a deliberate choice to employ our resources for others, not just for ourselves. And giving is the way we demonstrate and develop commitment in the fight of faith.

Our concern in this chapter has been to think about load limits, about the Plimsoll line we need to draw in our lives to prevent dangerous overloading with things. Here are four suggestions to help us to focus our thinking about personal load limits.

1. *Develop a lifestyle of limits, not luxury.* Go countercultural. Underbuy or do without. As an act of self-discipline and as a means to loosen the hold of covetousness, choose to do with less than you can afford.

2. *Cultivate generosity, not greed.* Compassion and generosity are the drain plugs for covetousness. Give more than you think you can to a cause the Lord has laid on your heart. Take a kingdom risk!

3. *Emphasize personal worth rather than net worth.* Determine to spend more time thinking and working on your future character than on your financial future. If your financial retirement plan is in place, what about your character retirement plan? You are determining your future

financial assets now. The same is true of your future character assets. What kind of an older person are you choosing to be?

4. *Invest in the eternal, not just the temporal.* Pray for a kingdom project that will capture your passion, challenge your giftedness, and inspire the investment of your treasure.

Chapter Seven

MONEY MATTERS

Although he never joined any of his men on their history-making voyages, he has gone down in history as Henry the Navigator. The fourth son of the king of Portugal, he became convinced that beyond Muslim North Africa was a land teeming with natural resources and raw materials, rich treasures for a trading nation. He was also a religious man, desiring to break the hold of Islam and to take the truth of Christianity into Africa.

Henry knew, however, that it would be difficult, if not impossible, to travel through Muslim-occupied territory. The wiser alternative was to send ships that would follow the African coast southward around enemy territory. But no such voyages had ever been made. Up until that time, Portuguese sailors had followed traditional navigational practices, using sea currents, winds, sea birds, and stars for guidance. They sailed familiar waters and almost never ventured out of sight of land. Myths and legends about the sea reinforced the problem. No experienced sailor wanted to venture into the unknown.

Henry's first expedition made its way down the African coast but was unable to get beyond Cape Bojador, a small cape south of the Canary Islands. The cape marked the end of the known world, and in that area the sea had an ominous red color, due to the amount of desert sand blown offshore. The currents were strong, the water shallow, and heavy swells made passage dangerous. For fifteen years, Henry sent expedition after expedition, promising his captains glory, honor, and wealth if they would round the cape. But year after year they turned back, afraid to venture into what they called "the Sea of Darkness." There was an obvious barrier of fear and superstition, but there was also a physical problem. If they sailed too close to land, they risked running aground; if they headed into open water, they ran the risk of being blown out to sea.

Finally, in 1433, Henry sent a sailor named Gil Eannes. Overcome by fear, he turned back, like all of his predecessors. But Henry sent him back the next year, with warnings that made Eannes more afraid of Henry than of the cape. Determined to succeed, Eannes steered a risky course westward, out of sight of land, into the Atlantic. He then turned east, back toward land. When he saw the coast again, the feared cape was behind him. He returned to Portugal, having broken the impenetrable barrier and the myth of "the Sea of Darkness." As years passed, Henry's men pushed further and further south, gaining knowledge and experience, until the Portuguese navigator Bartolomeu Dias rounded the Cape of Good Hope in 1488.

The Portuguese navigators not only needed to conquer their fear to challenge "the Sea of Darkness"; they needed to learn new skills. Out of the sight of land, the old rules and the old ways no longer applied. There was no obvious way to chart their course or to determine their position. They also needed to reengineer their ships to meet the challenges of the open ocean, with its high swells and heavy winds. Ships capable of handling sheltered waters had no chance of survival in the open Atlantic.

Traditional navigators knew how to sail in bounded waters, but no one knew how to navigate the open ocean.

That resembles life in the twenty-first century. We are sailing into a brand-new world, startlingly unlike anything we have ever encountered. We need to learn new navigational skills. If we are to chart our course, we also need to reengineer our lives so that we can survive rapidly changing conditions.

As sailors grew wiser about the ways of the sea, they increasingly turned their attention to seaworthiness. The development of the Plimsoll line greatly enhanced the safety of cargo and crew by indicating the maximum depth to which a ship could be legally loaded. Sailors also recognized the need to stabilize their ships, to counteract the tendency to pitch and roll, especially in heavy seas. The technology to do that came into existence with the gyroscope, an instrument familiar in its most simple form in a child's toy, the top.

In 1852, a French scientist named Leon Foucault discovered the principle and invented the first gyroscope. It remained a scientific toy until 1911, when an American scientist named Elmer Sperry patented the gyrocompass, an instrument that has proved to be of great importance in a variety of great navigational applications, not least of which are automatic pilots and guidance systems in ships, aircraft, missiles, and spacecraft. His company also developed massive gyrostabilizers that were used in ships to counteract the rolling motion of the ship in the ocean. In more recent technology, smaller gyroscopes have been used in connection with stabilizer fins to reduce roll and therefore increase safety and comfort.

If we are going to navigate the changing, tumultuous ocean of modern life successfully, we need a stabilizer, and I want to suggest to you that *generosity* is intended by God to serve as a personal gyroscope in the pitch and roll of modern materialism. In the verses that follow those we have been looking at in 1 Timothy 6, which warn against the danger of the love of money, Paul addresses those with money and gives them some direct instructions that provide relevant navigational safeguards for us as well.

> Command those who are rich in this present world not to be arrogant nor to put their hope in wealth, which is so uncertain, but to put their hope in God, who richly provides us with everything for our enjoyment. Command them to do good, to be rich in good deeds, and to be generous and willing to share. In this way they will lay up treasure for themselves as a firm foundation for the coming age, so that they may take hold of the life that is truly life. (1 Timothy 6:17–19)

Several years ago, the infamous shock-jock radio host, Howard Stern, announced that he was considering running for governor of New York State. However, as the deadline drew near for formalizing his candidacy, he withdrew, announcing that the financial disclosure statements he would have to file were "too personal." This from a man who made his reputation by probing and disclosing the most intimate, and often sordid, details of his and his guests' sexual lives!

It may be that the last taboo of the twenty-first century is personal finances. We become protective, even as Christians, about our money, even as we practice conspicuous consumption. It is bad taste to ask anyone too directly about his or her finances. If a pastor speaks about money matters, he will arouse more negative feeling than he will addressing almost any other subject.

I am not suggesting that this reticence is always wrong. I don't feel any need to satisfy the curiosity of nosy people about my financial status. And churches can be absorbed with money and distort biblical truth for less than holy purposes. At the same time, I am troubled by the often major disconnect between faith and money. Money matters. My check-book, my credit card statements, and my savings account reveal my deep-est beliefs, values, and priorities. That is why God's Word addresses the issue so often and why Paul returns to the subject at the end of his first letter to Timothy. In 1 Timothy 6:3–16, his concerns have been captured by the words *covetousness* ("flee it"), *contentment* ("cultivate it"), and *character* ("major on it"). Now he speaks directly to the issue of *generosity*.

MONEY IS A PARADOX AND MUST BE HANDLED WITH CARE

Paul has already warned against the passionate pursuit of money and wealth, a warning we stand in need of in our consumerist world. But money is also a tool that can be used for the glory of God. Some view wealth as intrinsically evil, something Christians must reject and avoid. This is not the biblical viewpoint. Scripture is neither ascetic, rejecting all material things, nor is it naïve about the dangers posed by money. *Money is a provision of God, to be enjoyed by those to whom he entrusts it.*

Paul's message is addressed to "those who are rich in the present world." The temptation is immediately to disqualify ourselves and imag-ine that Paul is addressing only the elite few, the upper 10 percent of our society. Obviously the words apply to them, but it is far too easy to adopt a narrow perspective and to lose sight of how enormously blessed we are. Ted Turner isn't usually a source of true wisdom, but in a com-mencement address at Emerson College on May 15, 2000, he did convey an important fact:

> It's all relative. . . . I sit down and say, I've only got $10 billion, but Bill Gates has $100 billion; I feel like I'm a complete failure in life. So billions won't make you happy if you're worried about

someone who's got more than you. . . . So don't let yourself get caught in the trap of measuring your success by how much material success you have.[1]

The issue goes beyond our definition of success. Western Christians take for granted a standard of living that is the envy of the world. A staggering 1.3 billion people earn less than one dollar a day. One hundred million children around the world are homeless, and many more live in accommodations worse than we provide for our pets and animals. Famine and disease are a deadly, daily reality to multitudes. Charles Colson's words on the subject bear repeating:

> We Americans enter the twenty-first century and the new millennium as the most economically prosperous people in the history of the world. By any historical comparative, or cross-national measure, we Americans enjoy unprecedented private affluence and enormous national wealth. Despite huge gaps in income and high concentrations of wealth, most poor Americans today are better housed and better fed and own more personal property than average Americans throughout this century.[2]

However, God's call is not for the rich to feel guilty about their wealth or to divest themselves of it. The pattern of Acts 2, where the early Christians sold "their possessions and goods, and . . . gave to anyone as he had need" (Acts 2:45), is a stirring example of Christian love but not a rigid pattern. Wealth may be a divine blessing, often given indirectly by our birth in a prosperous nation, or through our innate skills and abilities, or because of the unique opportunities a sovereign God has set before us. Only the most self-deceived or arrogant fail to recognize how much of their current blessing is due to factors beyond their control.

Wealth, however, is not an absolute right. I am not free to do with my money whatever I desire.

The laws of the Old Testament make it clear that the Lord does not sanction the uncontrolled accumulation of wealth at the expense of others. God makes a direct claim on our money through tithes and offerings, and His laws relativize the rights of private property, including the ownership and use of land, and the lending of money in exploitative ways. The prophets are full of condemnations of the rich, of a class system that manipulates and exploits, and of business practices that plunder and oppress. You cannot read Amos, Isaiah, or Joel without recognizing that many practices in our current market system fall far short of God's standards for a just and merciful society. Our economic system may be the best ever devised by selfish and sinful human beings, but it is deeply tainted by our depravity. We must not be blind to this and uncritically accept the status quo because we are comfortable.

That said, it remains true that money is to be enjoyed, because God "richly provides us with everything for our enjoyment." Earlier in his letter, Paul confronts the ascetic worldview, which rejected marriage and the enjoyment of certain foods. "Everything created by God is good," he writes, "and nothing is to be rejected if it is received with thanksgiving, because it is consecrated by the word of God and prayer" (1 Timothy 4:4–5). In the context of all that God's Word teaches, this cannot be said to sanction a self-indulgent, excessive enjoyment of our possessions. After all, 1 Timothy 5:6 tells us that the person "who lives for pleasure is dead even while she lives." But God does provide us everything "for enjoyment," a word approving pleasure in God's gracious provision. Or, as the writer of Ecclesiastes expresses it:

> Then I realized that it is good and proper for a man to eat and
> drink, and to find satisfaction in his toilsome labor under the

sun during the few days of life God has given him—for this is his lot. Moreover, when God gives any man wealth and possessions, and enables him to enjoy them, to accept his lot and be happy in his work—this is a gift of God. (Ecclesiastes 5:18–19)

The enjoyment of our material blessings without covetousness and with contentment is one side of the biblical equation. The other side is no less significant. *Money can become a substitute for God and must be kept in its place.*

"Command those who are rich not to be arrogant nor to put their hope in wealth, which is so uncertain." The danger is that we use money as a scorecard of our success in life and become proud of our achievements and arrogant and scornful toward those who have not done as well financially. All too easily we imagine that we are the authors of our success, and we give ourselves full credit. Others foster the feeling because of the way the well-to-do are treated. Money gives power, privilege, and opportunity, and we begin to feel entitled, as if we are of greater worth and value than lesser folks, who do not possess as much. A second danger is that we set our hope on what we possess. It becomes our security against an uncertain future, our shelter against the uncertain storms of life. Ironically, we put the phrase "In God we trust" on our money, but "in money I trust" is written on the secret places of our heart.

But money has its limitations. Trusting money is foolish, because at best it is uncertain. We all know the ways in which this can be true: a stock market downturn, a real estate collapse, superinflation, a dishonest manager, an unexpected job loss, a traumatic illness that wipes out savings. An article in the morning paper tells the story of people in high-tech jobs who only a year ago were giving very expensive Christmas gifts because they were rich in stock options. This year they are scrounging for company giveaways to send as gifts, and the value of their stocks has collapsed with their companies. Many are out of work. An article in the *Wall Street Journal* chronicles the changing fortunes of "centimillionaires," people who at the top of the technology boom found their companies' initial public offerings skyrocketing in value in 1999. Overnight they had net worths in the hundreds of millions of dollars, and they spent accordingly. Then, as the NASDAQ plummeted, things changed quickly. As one "ex-centimillionaire," whose stock fell 96.8 percent in a few months, said, "Going up was easy. But when it starts to go down, no one wants to talk to you. It's been the most challenging personal experience of my life."[3]

> Do not wear yourself out to get rich;
>   have the wisdom to show restraint.
> Cast but a glance at riches, and they are gone,
>   for they will surely sprout wings and
> fly off to the sky like an eagle. (Proverbs 23:4–5)

Trusting money is also faithless. The American dream has great power. It has made the United States the envy of the world, not only for the standard of living we enjoy but also for the possibilities it gives to every citizen. But there is a down side. The pursuit of more is endless. We believe that if we try harder, if we do more, we will not only achieve the dream but also fill our souls. We not only need to have it all; we need to have it now. We not only need to have more; we need to have better. And credit makes it so easy that there seems to be no reason not to have what we want when we want it. Money and things are the way to the good life.

The Word of God teaches otherwise. "Set your hope in God," Paul exhorts, recognizing that money is a tempting but terribly inadequate substitute. Job also felt the power of this:

> If I have put my trust in gold
>> or said to pure gold, "You are my security,"
> if I have rejoiced over my great wealth,
>> the fortune my hands had gained,
> if I have regarded the sun in its radiance
>> or the moon moving in splendor,
> so that my heart was secretly enticed
>> and my hand offered them a kiss of homage,
> then these also would be sins to be judged,
>> for I would have been unfaithful to God on high.
>>> (Job 31:24–28)

Because of human nature, money becomes a paradox, capable of doing great good or doing great harm. Therefore, Paul insists, we must use it with care. The first and most important step is to guard our hearts and to make sure that we are trusting God, not our money. In 1 Timothy 6:18, he stretches our thinking one step further.

Money Gives the Potential to Make a Difference, Not Just to Make a Living

Christ-followers are to imitate their Lord in developing a lifestyle of good works: "Command them to do good, to be rich in good deeds." The God who provides for us richly expects us to respond richly by practicing good works. No one insists more strongly in Scripture that we are not made right with God by good works but by God's free grace. At the same time, no one is more emphatic that God's people will demonstrate the reality of their new life by good works empowered by the Holy Spirit. The emphasis of the New Testament is consistent:

Let your light shine before men, *that they may see your good deeds* and praise your Father in heaven. (Matthew 5:16)

For we are God's workmanship, *created in Christ Jesus to do good works,* which God prepared in advance for us to do. (Ephesians 2:10)

Our great God and Savior, Jesus Christ, who gave himself for us for us to redeem us from all wickedness and to purify for himself a people that are his very own, *eager to do what is good.* (Titus 2:13–14)

I want you to stress these things, so that those who have trusted in God may be careful *to devote themselves to doing good.* (Titus 3:8)

Our people must learn to *devote themselves to doing what is good,* in order that they may provide for daily necessities and not live unproductive lives. (Titus 3:14)

Let us consider how we may spur one another on toward love and *good deeds.* (Hebrews 10:24)

Through Jesus, therefore, let us continually offer to God a sacrifice of praise—the fruit of lips that confess his name. And *do not forget to do good* and to share with others, for with such sacrifices God is pleased. (Hebrews 13:15–16)

Live such good lives among the pagans that, though they accuse you of doing wrong, *they may see your good deeds* and glorify God on the day he visits us. (1 Peter 2:12)

Paul does not specify what these good deeds are. Clearly he has in mind acts of caring and compassion, which meet the needs of people. And it is significant that he mentions good deeds before he speaks of generosity. Those with money often find it easier to give cash than time, but the Lord will not allow those with money to think they have this option. They are not only to do good works; they are to be rich in them.

Christ-followers are also to develop a lifestyle of generosity: "Command them . . . to be generous and willing to share." The two words, "generous" and "willing to share," are virtually the same and serve to reinforce the idea of financial generosity. The New Testament makes no mention of tithing as the Christian standard. It was a clear law under the Old Covenant, but the New Covenant, instead, points us to God's grace as our pattern. Generosity is the New Testament standard of giving.

> In everything I did, I showed you that by this kind of hard work we must help the weak, remembering the words the Lord Jesus himself said: "It is more blessed to give than to receive." (Acts 20:35)
>
> Remember this: Whoever sows sparingly will also reap sparingly, and whoever sows generously will also reap generously. Each man should give what he has decided in his heart to give, not reluctantly or under compulsion, for God loves a cheerful giver. And God is able to make all grace abound to you, so that in all things at all times, having all that you need, you will abound in every good work. (2 Corinthians 9:6–8)
>
> Freely you have received, freely give. (Matthew 10:8)

Generous giving is proportional giving, not merely percentage giving. While tithing may provide a useful guideline, it falls short of generosity for those who have been richly blessed by God. As Fred Smith comments, "I firmly believe that tithing for wealthy people is an escape from giving."[4] Generous giving is also joyful giving, because "God loves a cheerful giver." And generous giving is intentional giving. It is not impulsive or spasmodic but thoughtful and prayerful.

Generosity serves as a drain plug for greed in our lives. When Karl Menninger wrote a book in 1981 entitled *Whatever Became of Sin?*, he received a letter from the author of a book on money, expressing his appreciation for Menninger's chapter on avarice. Menninger responded: "I think your question, 'How do we help people shift from greed to generosity?' is one of the great moral questions of the age. I would add, 'How do we get them to shift from vengeance to magnanimity?' Greed is one of the diseases that doesn't 'get well'; it can be incurable. People with mental disease who come to our Menninger Clinic are likely to get well—even without professional skill applied—but greed is not that way."[5] That is a remarkable statement from a secular perspective. However, there is a cure for greed, and it involves the intentional cultivation of generosity.

Rich Mullins's life was tragically cut short in a car accident in 1997, but he left behind a rich legacy of music, the best known of which is the song "Our God Is an Awesome God." He also left behind a powerful example. As his music ministry began to flourish, he found himself fascinated by the life of Francis of Assisi. Mullins chose to take a vow of poverty and asked the elders of his church to serve as his board of directors. He was paid the average annual salary of a working person in America, in 1997 about twenty-four thousand dollars. Everything else was either given away or invested, as decided by the elders. Mullins had no idea what his real income was or what his royalties were. "If I knew how much it was, it would be harder to give it away," he explained. I'm not suggesting that Rich Mullins is an example we should follow. I don't believe the Lord has called me to follow that pattern. But his is an *attitude* I need to consider as I recognize the power money can have, either over my life or through my life.

Generosity is a commanded lifestyle for God's people. We are to be richly generous because God has been richly generous to us. Generosity is also a chosen lifestyle. It is the intentional decision of the Christ-follower to imitate his self-giving, generous Lord. This happens because those who are rich in this present world know that they do not live solely for this present world. That is why Paul directs our attention beyond the present age to the coming age in 1 Timothy 6:19.

Money Needs the Perspective of the Eternal

Generous people, Paul says, "will lay up treasure for themselves as a firm foundation for the coming age." *Wise stewardship accumulates eternal reward.* Giving and good works are an investment in eternity. The Bible consistently reminds us that our faithfulness here and now has eternal consequences. God rewards His people. Our generosity not only helps others here and now; it provides blessing for us throughout eternity. Giving isn't about losing wealth but about laying up heavenly treasure. The Lord Jesus is the one who taught us to think about heavenly treasure:

> "Do not store up for yourselves treasures on earth, where moth and rust destroy, and where thieves break in and steal. But store up for yourselves treasures in heaven, where moth and rust do not destroy, and where thieves do not break in and steal. For where your treasure is, there your heart will be also." (Matthew 6:19–21)

Our giving reveals whether we are motivated primarily by eternal values or by present values. D. L. Moody observed, "It doesn't take long to tell where a person's treasure is. In fifteen minutes, with most people, you can tell whether their treasures are on earth or in heaven." The Lord's counsel is not that we do not invest our money to make a profit. Rather, He wants us to be sure that we take the long view and are more concerned about eternal yields than earthly ones.

Generous people also "take hold of the life that is truly life." *Wise stewardship lays hold of life.* We hear people say, "This is the good life. This is really living!" Often that describes a time of special self-indulgence. There is such a thing as real life, and it refers to living life at its fullest here and now in a way that is consistent with God's promises for eternity. As Paul wrote earlier in this letter, "Godliness has value for all things, holding promise for both the present life and the life to come" (1 Timothy 4:8). There is a richness to life when we use the abilities and resources that God has made available to us to make a difference in the lives of other people. And there is a huge difference between living with a thirst for pleasure and living with a sense of purpose. The richest times in life come when we use our money to further God's kingdom. That is real living, and its value extends far beyond the present world into eternity.

In 1999, the death of Oseola McCarty received national attention. On one level this was surprising, because Miss McCarty had lived a life of obscurity. She had lived all her life in Hattiesburg, Mississippi, doing laundry for the well-to-do, at fifty cents a load, using an old-fashioned washboard.

Then, at the age of eighty-seven, she stunned officials at the University of Southern Mississippi by making a donation of $150,000. Where had she obtained that kind of money? She had lived frugally, saved carefully, and invested wisely. As an elderly woman, she found herself with $150,000 and decided there was something better to do with it than spend it on herself. "I had more money in the bank than I could use," she said. "I can't carry anything away from here with me, so I thought it best to give it to some child to get an education." She was embarrassed by all the attention, but when asked by reporters why she had done what she had done, she borrowed some familiar words: "It's more blessed to give than to receive—I've tried it."

Generosity is a God-given gyroscope that brings stability to our lives.

Paul draws a vivid contrast between two ways of life, only one of which is appropriate for a follower of the Lord Jesus Christ. Those who desire to get rich, who are characterized by greed, "plunge into ruin and destruction" (1 Timothy 6:9). Their ship capsizes in the seas of materialism and consumerism. But those who live with Christ-imitating generosity "lay up for themselves a good foundation for the future." They not only reach their destination safely; they flourish when they arrive. The writer of Hebrews offers the same message:

> Keep your lives free from the love of money and be content with what you have, because God has said,
> "Never will I leave you;
>   never will I forsake you."
> So we may say with confidence,
> "The Lord is my helper; I will not be afraid.
>   What can man do to me?" (Hebrews 13:5–6)

CHARACTER COUNTS

On June 17, 1913, the Canadian Arctic Expedition sailed out of Victoria, British Columbia, aboard the *Karluk* to explore Arctic waters. The expedition was the most ambitious and elaborate Arctic expedition ever mounted and was under the leadership of Vilhjamur Stefansson, a Canadian born to Icelandic parents. Stefansson was convinced that there was a vast undiscovered landmass underneath the polar ice cap, and he intended to prove it. He had already made two expeditions to the north, had become enamored with the lifestyle of the Eskimo (or Inuit) peoples, and had gained a reputation as "the prophet of the North." He would later be known as the last of the dog-sled explorers.[1]

Stefansson's expedition left for the Arctic only sixteen months before Ernest Shackleton set out for the Antarctic in the *Endurance*. (In chapter 2, we discussed Shackleton, the hero of an amazing expedition.) Both men experienced remarkably similar catastrophic circumstances, but the outcomes were dramatically different, because the two men were so different. In the difference lies a profoundly important message about navigating life.[2]

The *Karluk* set sail with a party of twenty-five, including Stefansson, sailors, scientists, an Eskimo woman with two young daughters, twenty-nine sled dogs, and a cat. The ship was a poor choice, a wooden brigantine purchased for a bargain price and inadequate for Arctic conditions. It was a sailing vessel, equipped with a steam engine for fishing. Although it had been reinforced, it was ill-suited for ice breaking. The ship was not the only problem. The crew was inexperienced and poorly trained. And although the captain, Robert Bartlett, was experienced and highly capable, he was given no voice in the selection of the ship and no time to prepare his crew adequately.

The ship experienced numerous difficulties, and Bartlett suggested turning back. Stefansson refused. Then unseasonably cold weather set in, and on August 13, the ice pack closed around the *Karluk*. For weeks the ship drifted west with the ice, and it is here that the difference between Stefansson and Shackleton becomes most apparent.

After waiting for five weeks for the ice to open, Stefansson, who craved action and hated waiting, announced that he was leaving to hunt for caribou (an interesting choice since caribou were apparently extinct in that area). He took two sledges piled with food and ammunition, and three men, and set out over the ice, promising to return in ten days. He never did. The ship drifted away, and he later claimed that his attempt to follow had proven futile. In any case, he decided to pursue his own agenda. He made no effort to provide help for the people he had recruited, but instead set off on an expedition of discovery, traveling by dog sled, adopting an Inuit lifestyle, and not reappearing for five years. It was an incredible abdication of responsibility. He left twenty-one people at the mercy of the ice and the durability of an inadequate ship.

For five months the ship drifted west with the ice flow. Then, on January 11, 1914, the inevitable happened. Ice tore a hole in the hull, Bartlett gave the order to abandon ship, and the *Karluk* quickly sank.

All twenty-one people were alive, and half the supplies were saved, but the situation was desperate. They were marooned in the middle of the Arctic Ocean, hundreds of miles from land, north of Siberia. Also, Stefansson's actions had left a leadership vacuum, and the survivors not only found themselves facing life-threatening conditions but also dealing with intense internal conflicts and rivalries. Within weeks, one party of four set out in the direction of Alaska, never to be heard from again. Bartlett led the others in a battle against the ice, snow blindness, brutal cold, darkness, and fear. They sledged for five terrible weeks and finally reached Wrangel Island. From there, Bartlett set out with an Eskimo companion to cross the 110 miles to Siberia, a journey that was difficult beyond imagining.

Bartlett's journey was epic, but he was finally able to reach civilization in Siberia (a trip of seven hundred miles across ice and barren shoreline that took thirty-seven days), cross to Alaska, and arrange for a whaling vessel to return to Wrangel Island. On September 8, 1914, nine survivors were rescued.

In the year that Steffansson had been gone, eleven people had died—some trying to reach land, two by malnutrition or disease, and one by gunshot wound, perhaps suicide or even murder. The survivors on Wrangel Island had broken into four groups, each of which pursued its own self-interest. When game was shot, the successful hunters gorged themselves rather than share. People stole from one another, and violent arguments broke out over biscuits. Some sixty-three years later, William McKinlay, the twenty-five-year-old expedition meteorologist, wrote:

> In our very mixed community we had all the seeds of future disaster. In normal circumstances we might have got by as very ordinary chaps, our frailties and idiosyncrasies unnoticed by any but our nearest and dearest. A good leader might have brought

out the best in everybody. . . . But on our own, the misery and desperation of our situation multiplied every weakness, every quirk of personality, every flaw in character, a thousandfold.[3]

The story of the *Karluk* is a story with many themes: survival, incompetent leadership, courage, and heroism. But most of all, it is a story about character. Stefansson was not only an incompetent leader, he was also selfish. Following the example he had set by his abandonment of responsibility, his crew developed into a band of self-serving individuals, willing to lie, cheat, steal, and perhaps even kill one another. In contrast, Shackleton's indomitable example in the Antarctic ice created a team who worked together and survived together.

The success of a journey is not measured by how impressively we leave port or how imposing we look in calm waters. The ultimate test is whether we arrive safely at the proper destination. In the same way, success in life is not ultimately about what I have or what I do or how I seem to others. Success is measured by who I have become—who I truly am. No question is more important than, Where do I want to go? But it is inseparable from the question, Who do I want to be?

It is often easy to see the importance of character when we have an example like the destruction caused by the character flaws of a Vilhjamur Stefansson, or the examples of significant people in our own lives. Michael Josephson offers a helpful illustration:

Suppose you saved the life of a leprechaun, and in gratitude, he said he would give the man your daughter will marry one exceptional quality of your choosing. This man could be very smart, enormously rich, remarkably good-looking, unusually strong and athletic, highly creative and artistic, or singularly competent—or he could possess extraordinary character. What would

you choose? Now, suppose you were picking a principal for your
kid's school, or a business partner, or your own boss: what would
you choose?

I would pick character every time. When we have to relate to,
work with, and depend upon someone, nothing is more important than personal ethical virtues, like honor, reliability, trustworthiness, and kindness.[4]

It is difficult to argue with Josephson. Character does not replace the
need for competence. A plumber who has good character but low competence will leave behind a mess, no matter how hard he tries. But without
character, competence—and so many other traits or abilities—are hol-
low. One legacy of the Clinton presidency is the recognition that clever-
ness, competence, and charm are not enough. Character touches all a
person does, for better or for worse. Marriage, family, work, friendships,
community involvement, ministry, personal choices—all are indelibly
marked by who I am and who I am becoming.

Navigating life successfully requires that we place the highest importance on allowing God the Holy Spirit to reproduce the character of
the Lord Jesus in our lives. What He desires to produce and how He
does that is a constant theme of Scripture, stated most memorably in
the familiar passage on the fruit of the Spirit (Galatians 5:16–26, NASB).

But I say, walk by the Spirit, and you will not carry out the desire
of the flesh. For the flesh sets its desire against the Spirit, and
the Spirit against the flesh; for these are in opposition to one
another, so that you may not do the things that you please. But
if you are led by the Spirit, you are not under the Law.

Now the deeds of the flesh are evident, which are: immorality, impurity, sensuality, idolatry, sorcery, enmities, strife,

jealousy, outbursts of anger, disputes, dissensions, factions, envying, drunkenness, carousing, and things like these, of which I forewarn you, just as I have forewarned you that those who practice such things will not inherit the kingdom of God.

But the fruit of the Spirit is love, joy, peace, patience, kindness, goodness, faithfulness, gentleness, self-control; against such things there is no law.

Now those who belong to Christ Jesus have crucified the flesh with its passions and desires. If we live by the Spirit, let us also walk by the Spirit.

Let us not become boastful, challenging one another, envying one another.[5]

Two main themes run through this passage. The first is that the Holy Spirit is the one who brings true freedom into our lives. Freedom from bondage to the flesh, the power of the old life within us, and freedom from the idea of the law as an external code imposed upon us. The other great theme is that the Holy Spirit produces the fruit of His presence in the lives of Christ-followers. We are Spirit people, indwelt and empowered by God the Spirit. He makes His presence known in the transformation of the character of His people. It is that truth we are going to focus on in this chapter, although we must not forget that the fruit of the Spirit is produced in the wider context of the freedom of the Spirit as He works in our lives. (Later we will consider the specific qualities that are described as the fruit of the Spirit.)

SOME BASIC FACTS ABOUT SPIRITUAL FRUIT

First, *the source of Spirit fruit is the Spirit.* This is obvious, but it needs to be said.

A Christian is a complex person. The "flesh" is a term that Paul uses to describe our old life—all that we were and are outside of Jesus Christ. Before we trusted Christ, we could be described as "in the flesh." As believers, we are changed at the core of our being, and we are now "in Christ" or "in the Spirit." We are no longer "in the flesh," but the flesh is still in us. That is to say, the habits of the old life and the continuing reality of our fallenness are at work in us to oppose the Spirit. The "flesh" produces its "works," the ugly list of fifteen vices described in Galatians 5:19–21. Unaided by the Spirit, that is what our life will manifest.

However, the Spirit manifests His presence within us by producing His "fruit," the natural product of His life within us. While all these qualities have a natural counterpart (unbelievers display something of love, joy, peace, etc.), these qualities are not merely the result of our early training or our inborn temperament. They are the measure of God's Spirit within us. We should also observe that believers are not passive in the process. Every aspect of the fruit of the Spirit is also commanded of believers. I am to love, to rejoice, to be at peace with all people, to be patient, and so on. I am actively to cultivate these qualities in my life. Yet at the same time, the fact that this is fruit reminds me that it is produced by a power that I do not have. I cannot *make* fruit, but the Spirit can and does.

The law of gravity is a continuing fact of life on planet Earth. However, by the application of what we can call the law of flight, the law of gravity can be overcome. The law of flight does not cancel the law of gravity, but it overpowers it. The presence of the Spirit does not eliminate the power of the flesh within us, but He does overpower it, as we walk in the Spirit. The central truth of the Christian life is not that the flesh has gone but that the Spirit has come. And when He comes, so does the fruit of His presence.

Second, *the nature of Spirit fruit is character*. The fifteen works of the flesh described in Galatians 5:19–21 are those things that produce conflict and brokenness—broken homes, broken relationships, broken hearts, broken dreams. The fruit of the Spirit is seen in a godly character that produces wholeness, and that character involves the growing reproduction of the moral character of the Lord Jesus in God's people. In fact, the supreme evidence of the presence of the Spirit in our lives is not acts of power, or remarkable gifts and abilities, or awesome experiences. The supreme evidence of His presence is a growing moral likeness to the Lord Jesus, which is here described as the fruit of the Spirit.

Third, *the production of Spirit fruit is gradual.* Fruit grows and develops; it does not suddenly appear. Neither does character. I do not become kind or faithful because of a single dramatic encounter, even with God. Such an encounter may turn my life in a different direction, but character, like fruit, is a product of time and relationship. The Lord Jesus had this in mind when He commanded: "Abide in me and let me abide in you. Just as a branch cannot bear fruit by itself, but must abide in the vine, neither can you unless you abide in me" (John 15:4, author's translation). At a certain stage, small buds and then early fruit appear on the tree or vine. If the relationship with the branch is broken by picking the fruit, there will be no mature fruit. The relationship with the branch is crucial, as is time to ripen. The same is true of Spirit fruit. Only a relationship with the Spirit over a period of time will produce the likeness of Jesus.

Fourth, *the development of Spirit fruit is holistic.* Paul does not talk about the fruits of the Spirit but the fruit of the Spirit. While it is possible that "fruit" is used as a collective noun, it seems more likely that Paul is emphasizing that the fruit of the Spirit has a unity and a harmony. The Spirit does not produce isolated characteristics, such as love, joy, and peace, but an integrated character of all these qualities that increasingly resembles the Lord Jesus. As has been observed, Paul is not describing nine jewels but a single jewel with nine distinct facets. This is not a complete description of all that could be considered the fruit of the Spirit (in Galatians 5:23, Paul speaks of "such things"), but it is a representative description of the character of the mature believer.

This has some important implications. The Lord's purpose in my life is not realized when only some of these qualities are present. While it is true that some qualities are more highly developed in some believers than in others, the Spirit's purpose is to produce a complete and balanced character in every believer. It does not honor God if I am high in joy but low in faithfulness or high in self-control but low in love. It is mixing the metaphor, but it has been helpful to me to think of the fruit of the Spirit in terms of an old-fashioned rain barrel made up of nine wooden staves held together by iron bands. If the staves are of uneven length, water will pour out at the level of the lowest stave. In the same way, the level of our lowest character quality will determine the level to which we can experience God's fullness. It is also at this level that effectiveness and influence will be lost from our lives.

Fifth, *the purpose of Spirit fruit is ministry*. Fruit is not on a tree for display but for the benefit and nourishment of others and to enable the tree to reproduce. Personal blessings do accompany the presence of the fruit of the Spirit in our lives, but Spirit fruit is also visible evidence to others of the presence of God within us, so that they may receive a blessing from what God is doing in our lives.

THE DESCRIPTION OF SPIRITUAL FRUIT

The nine qualities Paul describes can be conveniently divided into three categories. The first three (love, joy, and peace) tell us that the Holy Spirit reshapes our fundamental attitudes to life; the second three (patience, kindness, and goodness), that He produces essential qualities for ministry to others; and the final three (faithfulness, gentleness, and self-control), that He builds within us the attributes essential for personal integrity.

First, the Spirit produces the fruit of godly attitudes. It is no surprise that Paul begins as he does: the fruit of the Spirit is *love*. In fact, some have suggested that love *is* the fruit of the Spirit and the other eight qualities are merely a further description. That seems unlikely, but love does belong first. It is the defining characteristic of God, because God is love. It is the opposite of the flesh, which is self-centered, self-indulging, and self-aggrandizing. It is to be the distinguishing mark of a Christ-follower, the predominant characteristic by which "all [people] will know that you are my disciples" (John 13:35). John Stott says it well, "Love is the principal, the paramount, the preeminent, the distinguishing characteristic of the people of God. Nothing can dislodge or replace it. Love is supreme."[6]

The love that God gives is the love that God shows. It is more than warm feelings of affection, more than romantic attraction. Spirit love is a self-giving concern for others that produces sacrificial action. The emphasis in these attributes is on our relationships with other people. Thus, the love that is described is love for people. It imitates the God of love by seeking the best for others, whatever the personal cost. This is the first and prime evidence of the presence of the Spirit in our lives. Not power or knowledge or ministry, but love.

The second attitude produced by the Spirit is *joy*. This is a word that is notoriously difficult to define, because Spirit joy is different than happiness or even enjoyment, both of which are dependent on external circumstances. Joy is the inner sense of well-being that comes from satisfaction in God, which produces a delight in life. The picture that comes to my mind is a spring, relentlessly forcing its way through the mud to reach the surface. You can throw dirt in a pond or a well and foul the water. But a spring will bubble its way through whatever is in its way.

The wonder of Spirit joy is that it can coexist with sorrow. Thus, Paul, who knew firsthand about life at its most difficult, can describe himself as "sorrowful, yet always rejoicing" (2 Corinthians 6:10). He reminds the Thessalonians that "in spite of severe suffering, [they] welcomed the message with the joy given by the Holy Spirit" (1 Thessalonians 1:6). I have seen this paradox at work in the lives of believers in times of intense personal suffering or catastrophic events. I have felt it in my own life, at the graveside of my parents, in the experience of my wife's cancer, in the midst of a serious medical situation. The pain is real and intense, but the joy of God's grace is almost tangible.

The joy of the Spirit is the joy of the Lord Jesus, the joy with which He lived life and enriched everyone around Him. No one has described this better than William Morrice, in a delightful book entitled *Joy in the New Testament*:

> There was in the life and teaching of Jesus an abounding joy that surpassed and transformed all the sufferings and sorrows he had to bear. If he can justly be characterized as 'a man of sorrows and acquainted with grief,' he can with equal truth be described as 'the man of joy.' Shining right through his life—even at its darkest moments—there was a note of radiance and triumphant joy. Optimism and joyful trust in his heavenly Father were the keynotes of his life and ministry. Joy was thus an ever-present reality in the life and work of Jesus. Everywhere he went in Galilee, he left some mark of cheerfulness and hope in the lives of the common people. An atmosphere of sheer exuberance surrounded his public ministry.[7]

It is something of that exuberance in God and in life that the Holy Spirit produces in our lives. In the vivid language of John Wesley, "Sour godliness is the devil's religion."

The third attitude produced by the Spirit is *peace*. When people in Paul's day used the word *peace*, they tended to think in negatives. Peace was the absence of conflict or the absence of troubles in mind or body. The Hebrews, however, thought of peace in terms of the word *shalom*, a word that expresses the idea of wholeness and harmony. For me, the most helpful description is that peace is the deep inner sense of well-being that comes from the possession of adequate resources. Think of the anxiety you feel when tax time comes or when a sudden, unexpected expense arises when you are already overdrawn at the bank. Contrast that to your response to the same situation when you have sufficient savings to handle the expense. One of my most vivid memories is of driving with my family late at night on a deserted piece of highway. Suddenly I realized that I might have miscalculated how much fuel I had left and how far I had to go. Because I wasn't sure when or if I would find an open service station, and the thought of stranding my family in the middle of nowhere was upsetting, I began to get very anxious. (I was, however, not prepared to awaken my sleeping wife and tell her what was going on!) But then I rounded a bend, and there it was! When I pulled out of that station, with my gas tank full, I knew what peace was—the possession of adequate resources.

The Spirit assures us that we have adequate resources spiritually. He brings the certainty of peace with God, because we have been declared righteous through faith in our Lord Jesus Christ (Romans 5:1). He also gives the blessing of personal peace, the peace of God that guards our hearts and minds in Christ Jesus (Philippians 4:7). And finally, we have the blessing of relational peace, the presence of wholeness in our relations with others, "the unity of the Spirit through the bond of peace" (Ephesians 4:3).

Lilias Trotter was an aristocratic woman born to the luxuries of life in Victorian England. She had before her a comfortable life as a socialite and a successful life as an artist. John Ruskin, the noted English art critic, said that she had challenged his prejudices that a woman could not draw or paint, and he was convinced that she had the potential to become one of the great artists of her day. But at the age of thirty-four, Lily Trotter left behind a world of comfort and potential fame to invest her life in reaching the Muslim peoples of Algeria. For forty years she poured out her life in an often difficult ministry, starting a mission agency that still continues. No higher compliment was paid her than the description of her by an Algerian: "She is still and created stillness. She is beautiful to feel near. I love the quiet of her." This is not the description of a recluse, hiding from life. Lily Trotter was a risk-taking, strong-minded woman. She needed to be to survive forty years in an often-hostile environment. But she was a woman who made visible that part of the fruit of the Spirit called peace.[8]

Second, the Spirit produces the fruit of healthy responses to others. Paul's mention of peace leads to three qualities essential for harmony in relationships. The first of these is *patience.* The Greek language has two words for patience, one of which primarily describes patience with circumstances, the other, patience with people. It is the second that is used here, an important reminder that the fruit of the Spirit operates in a world in which people disappoint us or hurt us or betray us. The fruit of the Spirit is not for living on Fantasy Island, a place inhabited only by perfected saints. It is for living with people who are sinners, like we are.

The Greek word for patience has the literal meaning of "a long temper." We are familiar with someone who has a short temper, but our culture does little to produce people with a long temper, people who take a long time to get hot. We drive with special care because we know that road rage is not just a clever phrase but a far too prevalent reality. "Going postal" describes an outpouring of violent rage that hits the news far too often. In contrast, the Spirit builds in us the capacity to keep on keeping on with people who wrong us or irritate us. Patience is the opposite of anger, a refusal to give up on people or to get even. It is the ability to count down before you blast off.

Far too often I am characterized by impatience rather than patience. I can identify only too well with the four-year-old who just knew that a trip was taking far too long. "Mommy, are we there yet?" "Daddy, when will we get there?" "I'm bored." Finally, his mother had had enough. "Timmy, that's enough. I don't want to hear another word. We won't be there for a long time, time for two Barneys. So you just sit still, and I'll tell you when we're getting near." There was silence for a few minutes. Then a little voice was heard from the back seat: "Mommy, when we get there, will I still be four years old?" Timmy and I have something in common, and I need the Spirit to work patience within me.

The second quality of the Spirit directed toward our relationship to others is *kindness*. Kindness describes a sensitivity to others that leads us to do what is useful. It is the opposite of harshness or severity. Patience causes us to hold back anger; kindness compels us to reach out, so that others feel valued and valuable. It is not merely a feeling or a disposition. It moves us to action.

I will never forget a sermon I heard when I was a college student. The speaker was an internationally known Christian leader whom I deeply respected. In the course of one message, he declared, "I pray every single day, 'Lord, keep me from becoming a cranky old Christian.'" I don't know why that impressed me so deeply. Perhaps it was the suggestion that this was a course he had seen many older Christians follow. Years later, I discovered that this was a prayer that the great man of faith George Muller had prayed regularly as well. Aging Christians can become cranky as they deal with the changes in their bodies and in their world. But maturing Christians become kind, under the softening influence of God the Holy Spirit.

A third relational quality produced by the Spirit is *goodness*. In absolute terms, goodness is a quality that belongs to God alone, for as the Lord Jesus said, "No one is good—except God alone" (Mark 10:18). Goodness is closely aligned to kindness, and it also involves actions. As Gordon Fee rightly comments, "When put into practice it takes the form of 'doing good.' Indeed, goodness does not exist apart from its active, concrete expression."[9] In Paul's mind, a distinction can be drawn between a good person and a righteous person. "Very rarely will anyone die for a righteous man, though for a good man someone might possibly dare to die" (Romans 5:7).

Justice gives people what they deserve. It does what is required. Goodness goes one step further, doing what is needed. Goodness is expressed as generosity, a giving attitude to others that goes far beyond what is required. The Holy Spirit cannot coexist with an ungenerous heart. When the Spirit truly fills our lives, He flows out to others with His grace.

Third, the Spirit produces the fruit of personal integrity within us. As Paul shifts to the qualities that concern our inner resilience, he begins with *faithfulness*. In another context, the word describes the faith in God that brings us eternal life and is the basis of a Christ-follower's relationship with God. But true faith produces faithfulness and reliability. That is what the Spirit produces in the lives of people of faith. Faithfulness is a loyalty to commitments and convictions, even when one is experiencing downside costs. It is a loyalty to people whom others are abandoning. It is a dependability that means that I can be counted on to do what I said I would do.

We live in a serve-yourself society where we see even professing Christians walking away from marriages and families and obligations. "Many a man claims to have unfailing love, but a faithful man who can find?" (Proverbs 20:6). Spirit people are trustworthy.

A second quality is *gentleness*. The older translations render this as "meekness," a word that has a bad connotation: "meekness is weakness." It is hard to find a good translation because "gentleness" conveys only a portion of the idea, as does "humility." The Greek word conveys the idea of strength under control. It describes a horse broken to the bridle or an ox submitted to a yoke. For Aristotle, it was the golden mean between excessive anger and the inability to be angry. A gentle person is someone who is angry with the right person for the right reason on the right occasion in the right manner for the right length of time. He or she has a submissive, teachable spirit before God, which produces gentleness with people. It is the opposite of an arrogant, self-righteous attitude.

The epitome of gentleness in the Old Testament is Moses. Obviously he was a strong, dynamic leader, able to confront Pharaoh and to lead millions of people out of Egypt and through the wilderness. Yet he is described in Numbers 12:3 as "a very humble [or gentle] man, more humble than anyone else on the face of the earth." The supreme example is, of course, the Lord Jesus, who describes himself as "gentle and humble in heart" (Matthew 11:29).

The final quality of the fruit of the Spirit is *self-control*. This is the mastery of self, with strong emotions and impulses under control. It is the ability to live with strong desires and drives but to keep them under the control of one's convictions and choices. It describes the self-discipline of an athlete in 1 Corinthians 9:25 and sexual self-control in 1 Corinthians 7:9.

Self-control is the foundation of all moral living. "Like a city whose walls are broken down is a man who lacks self-control" (Proverbs 25:28). Daniel Goleman, who is famous as the popularizer of the concept of emotional intelligence, observes, "The bedrock of character is self-discipline; the virtuous life, as philosophers since Aristotle have observed, is based on self-control."[10]

The Father's purpose in giving us His Spirit is at least in part to reproduce the character of His Son in His people. But how do these qualities begin to appear in our lives?

THE PRODUCTION OF SPIRITUAL FRUIT

On the one hand, we are to "walk in the Spirit" (Galatians 5:16) and "to keep in step with the Spirit" (Galatians 5:25). Both expressions convey the idea of living in obedience to the Spirit as He sets the direction. "Walking" and "keeping in step" with the Spirit mean that the Spirit sets the pace, sets the direction, and establishes the path we are to follow. The fruit of the Spirit does not grow in our lives when we are quietly passive. We are required to live with discipline and in obedience to the will of the Spirit.

At the same time, Christians are to be "led by the Spirit" (Galatians 5:18). Here, the Spirit is the active one, whom we are to follow. We must yield to the work of the Spirit within us. His presence is certain, and His purpose is to produce His fruit in our lives. But we also have a role to play. We must be actively obedient and passively dependent on His work within us.

A writer named Tom Anderson describes part of the process of the development of the fruit of the Spirit in his life.

> I made a vow to myself on the drive down to the vacation beach cottage. For two weeks I would try to be a loving husband and father. Totally loving. No ifs, ands, or buts. The idea had come to me as I listened to a commentator on my car's tape player. He was quoting a biblical passage about husbands being thoughtful of their wives. Then he went on to say, "Love is an act of the will. A person can choose to love." To myself, I had to admit that I

had been a selfish husband—that our love had been dulled by my own insensitivity. In petty ways, really: chiding Evelyn for her tardiness; insisting on the TV channel I wanted to watch; throwing out day-old newspapers before Evelyn had a chance to read them. Well, for two weeks all that would change.

And it did. Right from the moment I kissed Evelyn at the door and said, "That new yellow sweater looks great on you." "Oh, Tom, you noticed," she said, surprised and pleased. And maybe a little shocked.

After the long drive, I wanted to sit and read. Evelyn suggested a walk on the beach. I started to refuse, but then I thought, Evelyn's been alone here with the kids all week and now she wants to be alone with me. We walked on the beach while the children flew their kites.

So it went. Two weeks of not calling the Wall Street investment firm where I am a director; a visit to the shell museum, though I usually hate museums; holding my tongue while Evelyn's getting ready made us late for a dinner date. Relaxed and happy, that's how the whole vacation passed. I made a new vow to keep on remembering to choose love.

There was one thing that went wrong with my experiment, however. On the last night at our cottage, preparing for bed, Evelyn stared at me with the saddest expression.

"What's the matter?" I asked her.

"Tom," she said, in a voice filled with distress, "do you know something I don't?"

"What do you mean?"

"Well . . . that checkup I had several weeks ago . . . our doctor . . . did he tell you something about me? Tom, you've been so good to me . . . am I dying?"

It took a moment for it all to sink in. Then I burst out laughing. "No, honey," I said, wrapping her in my arms, "you're not dying; I'm just starting to live!"[11]

If you began to show the fruit of the Spirit, would your family think someone was dying?

Chapter Nine

STAYING POWER

A s far back as the French and Indian War of the eighteenth century, special troops have tried to protect the American people. Led by Major Robert Rogers, and following his advice to "move fast and hit hard," Rogers' Rangers moved through the forests of the New World to carry out unexpected and devastating attacks on the enemy. It was, however, two centuries later, in the Cold War years after World War II and during the Vietnam War that special operations forces came into their own, and the Green Berets, Delta Force, the Army Rangers, the Navy SEALs captured the public imagination for their daring and courage.

Special forces operate in the shadowland between diplomacy and overt military action, often in remote areas and hostile environments, carrying out dangerous, complex, and usually covert operations. They operate as small, self-contained units, with a minimum of external direction and support. They have military skills, trained to the highest level of proficiency, but they must also be resourceful, resilient, and reliable.

The Cold War years fostered the image of the special forces soldier as Rambo, a highly efficient and ruthless killing machine. That is obviously a stereotype. But in the days before the fall of the Soviet Union, the mission of the special forces was challenging but clear, as was their composition. They were rough-and-ready individuals prepared to defy death, celebrated for their ability to face danger and their willingness to do whatever it took to bring the bad guys down.

But then the Berlin Wall fell, the Soviet Union collapsed, and the old Cold War ended. Suddenly the rules changed. General Peter Schoomaker served as the commander in chief of the United States Special Operations Command in the closing years of the twentieth century and had to lead the forces in a time of significant change. As he describes the new situation: "We know that we're going to have fewer 'wars' but a lot more 'conflicts.' There's a real blurring between the definitions of 'war' and 'peace,' 'domestic' and 'nondomestic,' 'economic' and 'military.' All of this means that we need to be able to thrive in uncertainty."[1] And this was before September 11!

The challenge is obvious. People attracted to the special forces do not tend to thrive on uncertainty and ambiguity. They are far more comfortable in a black-and-white world, where the enemy is clear and the situation military. But this new world requires a different mindset. Special Forces might find themselves helping to distribute humanitarian aid, training the forces of other nations, calming ethnic hostilities, engaging in counter-drug operations, or responding to crisis situations. Terrorist groups have adopted new tactics, striking at America's vulnerabilities in unorthodox ways rather than confronting America's strengths directly. Sometimes these actions are sponsored by private individuals rather than by rogue nations. Religious groups, rather than those promoting secular ideologies, may be the instigators of violence. Drug lords and organized crime systems have more power in some countries than the official government. All these factors mean that the special operations forces are as relevant to the new context as they were to the Cold War. For example, in 1998 these forces were sent into 152 countries, nearly always into fast-moving, fast-changing situations.

But the rules have changed, and the self-image of these special forces has had to change with the changing climate. Without in any way compromising the quality of their military training, they have come to regard themselves as "warrior diplomats" and "quiet professionals," able to operate in fluid, ambiguous situations. Schoomaker describes the new requirements this places on his troops:

> We need people who can operate in an increasingly complicated, subtle and sophisticated world. You can't put out a checklist that tells you, "If this happens, you do that, and if that happens, you do this." In our business, you encounter situations in which you have to rely on internalized skills. For that reason, we focus on teaching our people not just what to think, but how to think.[2]

What Schoomaker is describing as a requirement for his troops is a specific example of what is required to navigate a new world. Their mission to defend the interest of the United States has not changed, but the context in which they carry out that mission, and the enemy they face, keep changing. Because of this, they can not operate by the rulebook of the 1980s.

The same is true for the Christ-follower. We live in a fast-changing, fast-moving world, where maps and checklists quickly become outdated. The rules that many Christians use to guide them in the modern world seem curiously out-of-date in a postmodern culture. It is not that God or His standards have changed. He and they are eternal. But the enemy's attack comes in new and distinct forms. To be unprepared is to be unprotected.

A Christ-follower, therefore, needs to learn how to navigate highly fluid situations with proven principles. As a Christ-follower grows, he increasingly learns more about those things that he needs to know as he establishes fundamental beliefs and convictions. He also increasingly does what he needs to do as he develops the habits and skills of a mature disciple. Most important of all, a follower of Christ who wants to thrive in challenging situations increasingly becomes what he needs to become, developing the character and virtues that God desires in our lives. As Christ-followers, we need to live as people with internalized convictions, skills, and character.

Navigating life means living by faith. So at this point, we are going to focus our attention on one of the great chapters of the Bible, Hebrews 11. It has been called "the Hall of Faith," because it sets before us the lives of people who navigated by faith in the living God for hundreds of years. The details of their lives differ dramatically from one another, and from us, but we can distill from their stories the essence of the life of faith.

The author of Hebrews writes with great passion to a group of believers who find themselves living as an embattled minority, tempted to turn back from their allegiance to Christ. We do not know the identity of the writer of Hebrews, but he spends the first ten chapters of his letter giving some sturdy theological support for clinging to allegiance to Christ, and we are left with no doubt as to His excellence as the Son of God and as God's perfect and final solution to our deepest needs. If we grasp what the writer is telling us about the supremacy of the Lord Jesus as our great High Priest, we will be anchored in the truth, no matter how stormy life gets. The basis of this spiritual stability is a firm grasp on the person and work of the Lord Jesus Christ.

While our *supreme* encourager is the Lord Jesus, we sometimes need human examples to be of encouragement to us. So in Hebrews 11, the writer wraps his message in flesh and blood as he sets out brief case histories of men and women who lived by faith in times of great difficulty. Their lives are powerful reminders of the ways God enables His people to live with integrity and endurance, even in the most difficult of circumstances. And we have an advantage they never had: these people could not look back upon the great facts of faith and history that we celebrate in the gospel.

It is important to remember that Hebrews 11 was not written in a vacuum. The author had a specific message to communicate to his original readers, as well as to us. That message stands out more clearly when we read it in its original context. The final eight verses of Hebrews 10 appeal directly to these struggling Christians and call them to stay the course. It is a challenge that lays the foundation for Hebrews 11 and helps us to understand the main message of that chapter.

AUTHENTIC FAITH IS AN INNER CONVICTION THAT PRODUCES STAYING POWER

Remember those earlier days after you had received the light, when you stood your ground in a great contest in the face of suffering. Sometimes you were publicly exposed to insult and persecution; at other times you stood side by side with those who were so treated. You sympathized with those in prison and joyfully accepted the confiscation of your property, because you knew that you yourselves had better and lasting possessions. So do not throw away your confidence; it will be richly rewarded. You need to persevere so that when you have done the will of God, you will receive what he has promised. For in just a very little while,

"He who is coming will come and will not delay.
But my righteous one will live by faith.
And if he shrinks back,
I will not be pleased with him."
But we are not of those who shrink back and are destroyed,
but of those who believe and are saved. (Hebrews 10:32–39)

In 1990, I had the great privilege of visiting Romania only six weeks after the overthrow and execution of the dictator, Nicolae Ceausescu. Christians had experienced intense persecution during his regime, and when the visit was planned, it was intended that I would teach at an underground Bible school. By the time I arrived, the people were celebrating their newfound freedom, although the situation was very fluid. Romanian flags flew proudly, with holes in them where the hammer and sickle, the hated symbol of the old oppression, had been cut out. I was there to preach and teach, but I was the one who was learning. As I shared with my brothers and sisters, often through an interpreter, visited in their very plain homes, and worshiped in their physically small but overcrowded and spiritually energized churches, I felt humbled. These were people who knew what it was to suffer greatly for their faith. They had developed a depth and maturity in their walk with Christ that challenged me deeply. My greatest concern was that their contact with the Western church would lead them away from their "sincere and pure devotion to Christ" (2 Corinthians 11:3).

The people to whom the book of Hebrews is addressed knew what it was to live under pressure. These Hebrew Christians lived in a climate that was growing increasingly hostile to their faith in Christ, and part of the opposition was coming from their own Hebrew roots. They had broken with the temple and the synagogue because they had found fulfillment in Christ. But families, friendships, and cultural background exert a strong hold, and some of them were beginning to struggle with the cost of loyalty to Christ. Opposition was also coming from the wider pagan culture, which had little sympathy with either Judaism or Christianity. Thus, these believers felt they were continually swimming upstream, against the current, and some of them were beginning to feel exhausted. Worn down by opposition, they were losing their endurance. Their great need was staying power.

Our life setting is very different from theirs, but our problem is the same. It is never easy to live as a Christ-follower, and our culture is increasingly contrary to the purposes of God. For some, the battle is primarily with internal temptations and desires that the culture promotes. It seems so much easier to just give up and give in. For others, there are significant personal costs to following Christ. It means misunderstanding and alienation from some we deeply love. So we, too, know what it is to be under intense pressure and to feel worn down by it, and we need to see staying power in operation.

Genuine faith produces endurance, and that is the great theme of Hebrews 11. But before the writer describes faith in action, he passionately pleads for the Christ-followers to keep on keeping on. The God who sustained them in the past is fully able to sustain them in the future. That is why the writer first turns his attention to the past and reminds the believers how a faithful God has enabled them to be faithful.

Staying power is not mere wishful thinking. These Christians had experienced it, and they could be an example to themselves. When they were new Christians, babies in the faith, they had encountered intense pressures. The writer doesn't want them to forget: "Remember those earlier days after you had received the light." We can only guess what happened, but it was something he describes as "a great contest." Although this Greek word is the term from which we get our word *athletics* and was used to describe the intensity of an athlete's efforts, here it has the sense of "combat." Greek and Roman sports were often brutally physical. These believers had found themselves fighting for their very lives, an experience many of our brothers and sisters in Christ are experiencing even as you read these words. These people had experienced opposition to their newfound faith that had been severe and prolonged. We cannot be sure of the details of that persecution—perhaps it was related to events connected with the expulsion of Jews and Jewish Christians from Rome in A.D. 49. Regardless, they were not unique. The Lord Jesus had told His followers, "In this world you will have trouble" (John 16:33). They were not the first to fight the good fight of faith, and they would not be the last.

The good news was that they had held firm. "You stood your ground in the face of suffering." They had endured. They may have been shaken, but they had not been moved. They had not fled the field of battle. I'm sure that, in the deepest parts of their being, these people knew that their resistance had been more about God than about them. He had been faithful to keep their feet firmly planted.

What *had* they endured? The writer reminds them and informs us. Some had undergone public humiliation: "you were publicly exposed to insult." The word behind the translation "publicly exposed" is *theatrizo*. Some of them had been used for public entertainment, exposed in public, subjected to physical mistreatment and emotional abuse for the amusement of the masses. "Insult and persecution" describe verbal attacks and physical violence carried out before a jeering, cheering mob. The Roman authorities relished such opportunities. It gave them favor with the public, who loved such spectacles, and offered a vivid reminder of the penalty for displeasing Rome.

Disgrace and humiliation are powerful weapons. I remember an elderly Chinese believer telling the story of enduring such a trial in China, when family, friends, and even some fellow church members had publicly accused him of crimes against the state during the infamous Red Guard period.

It is tempting, when some are experiencing public abuse, for others to distance themselves, hoping they will escape the attention of the authorities. That had been Paul's experience. Facing his second appearance before the bloody emperor Nero, the apostle makes the sad observation that "at my first defense, no one came to my support, but everyone deserted me" (2 Timothy 4:16). These Christians being addressed by the writer of Hebrews had done nothing of the sort: "You stood side by side with those who were so treated." They had courageously identified with their suffering brothers and sisters and identified themselves as followers of King Jesus.

Another way they had shown their faith was by demonstrating their fellowship with those who had been imprisoned for their faith. Imprisonment was and is a regular part of religious persecution. "You sympathized with those in prison" does not merely mean that they felt sorry for them. At that time, prisoners were not supplied with food, clothing, and medicine by the state. If they did not have resources of their own, they were dependent on the kindness of others. So when we read that these people "sympathized with those in prison," it means that they had visited them and shown compassion by ministering to their needs. In such dangerous circumstances, that was an act of great love and bravery, and it is this the writer has in mind when he exhorts in Hebrews 13:3, "Remember those in prison as if you were their fellow prisoners, and those who are mistreated as if you yourselves were suffering."

That was not all. Many of them had had their possessions confiscated. We can't be sure whether this involved judicial action, mob attack, or perhaps looting after imprisonment. Whatever occurred, it was a devastating blow—to lose not only one's freedom but also one's material possessions. Seemingly there was no indignity to which they had not been subject.

Remarkably, these believers had not only endured such things; they had accepted them "with joy." There is a play on words here that the New International Version does not quite capture: "You joyfully accepted the seizing of your property, because you knew that you had better and enduring property." They had property not subject to confiscation, property located in the same city the heroes of faith lived for: "a better country—a heavenly one" (Hebrews 11:16). That is the essence of faith. It is an entirely different perspective on reality. Faith tells us that the eternity promised in Christ is something far more valuable, far more secure, and far more enduring than anything that can be taken away by police, judges, or mobs. Their hope was not based on what people could take by force but on what God had given by grace. They were identified with the Lord Jesus Christ, and "they had been counted worthy of suffering disgrace for the Name" (Acts 5:41).

True joy is the inner spring of well-being that comes from having resources that circumstances cannot touch. Faith sees what our physical eyes cannot see. This is the paradox of God's joy. It can coexist with suffering and persecution.

The experience of these Christ-followers had been difficult. Yet, by God's enablement, they had stood firm. More than that, they had stayed together. Suffering had drawn them closer, not split them apart. Why? Because they had stayed focused. With the eyes of faith they had seen the future with God, and they had refused to turn back. This is an essential truth about faith, and one that built staying power into these Hebrew Christians and will build it into us. *Faith focuses on what is before us by grace, not on what is around us.* It is a profound conviction that what God has promised is true, no matter how the present circumstances may seem to contradict them.

At times, we need to look back in our life, not for the sake of nostalgia but for the sake of encouragement. God's grace experienced in the past is not just a memory to be cherished. It is a foundation on which to build. Past victories over difficulty build confidence to face what lies ahead.

But life is lived in the present, not the past. The fact is that continued pressure grinds us down. Hard times can dull the edge of faith, especially when there seems to be no end. Just after my twenty-first birthday, I found myself in hospital with a retinal detachment in my right eye. The state of medical technology then was very different than it is now, and it was by no means certain that my vision could be saved. I had surgery, then spent three weeks motionless on my back with both eyes bandaged. It was, on one hand, a difficult time. On the other hand, God was so real to me in His grace and presence that it remains one of the most significant experiences of my life. However, six weeks after I got out of hospital and returned to university, the retina detached again. Despite all the blessing of that first experience, this time I found it much harder. The medical procedure was much easier the second time. In that brief period, new technology became available, making the surgery easier and more successful. But the inner battle was much harder. Sustained pressure grinds us down.

But if hard times can grind us down, good times can soften us up. We can lose the sharp edge of faith under prosperity perhaps even more readily than under adversity. I suspect for most who are reading this book the absence of staying power will be more the product of good times and prosperity than of adversity.

Having reminded them of their strength and endurance in the past, the writer of Hebrews next voices concern that things have changed. Before, they had stood firm; now, they seem to be growing fearful. Before, they had stayed together; now, some are in danger of drifting away. Before, they had remained spiritually focused; now, the present is clouding the eternal. They are losing their confidence in the certainty and supremacy of God's promise. They are loosing their hold on the great certainties of

Christ. So, building on his account of their past experience, the writer shouts his appeal: "Don't abandon! Don't throw away your confidence in Christ, in His work and His promise, that has given you endurance in the past." The picture is of an army in full flight, panic-stricken, abandoning whatever they think will hinder their retreat. Such an army is defeated already. When a Christ-follower abandons confidence in Christ, he has already lost.

Despite all that the Hebrews had experienced and achieved by God's strengthening power on that earlier occasion, this time they are finding it much harder. All of us face situations that make us want to pack it in, to take the easy way, to go with the flow of our culture. When others around us seem to flourish, despite their indifference or even hostility to spiritual things, we wonder whether godliness has any real value. When others challenge us because of our allegiance to the Lord Jesus and His standards, conforming to the prevailing life-style can look attractive. When the temptations of the culture become powerfully attractive, we are tempted to seize the highly enticing and available opportunities. At that time we need to hear the voice of the Spirit: "Don't throw away your confidence in God; it will be richly rewarded."

Confidence is linked to endurance. "You need to persevere; you need to develop endurance." *Endurance* is a word that always challenges me. It describes the attitude that stays under the hard circumstances of life, rather than seeking the easy way out—that keeps on pressing toward the goal. But endurance isn't an end in itself. It isn't about just surviving but about doing the will of God. Earlier in this chapter of Hebrews, the writer has reminded us that this was the motivating principle of the Lord Jesus Christ. In fact, he goes so far as to say that as the Lord Jesus left heaven to enter the world, He took the words of Psalm 40:6–8 as His motto:

Therefore, when Christ came into the world, He said:

"Sacrifice and offering you did not desire,
 but a body you prepared for me;
with burnt offerings and sin offerings
 you were not pleased.
Then I said, 'Here I am—it is written about me in the scroll—
I have come to do your will, O God.'" (Hebrews 10:5–7)

Doing the will of God is the lifestyle of the Lord and all who claim to be His followers. But just as He "endured the cross" (Hebrews 12:2) to do the will of God, so must we endure to do His will. When we do that, we "will receive what he has promised" (Hebrews 10:36).

This is a second great truth about faith. *Faith is not the absence of fear but the facing of it with confidence in God.* The mark of the reality of faith is staying power, endurance, produced by the indwelling Spirit of the living God.

Having looked at their past record of staying power under great conflict and having challenged them to present endurance through confidence in God's promise and God's reward, the writer summarizes his preparation for the great roster of faith by anchoring his appeal in the eternal principle found primarily in Habakkuk 2:3–4:

"He who is coming will come and will not delay.
 But my righteous one will live by faith.
And if he shrinks back,
 I will not be pleased with him."

"He is coming" is the Lord Jesus. The Coming One is the Messiah and Redeemer. The entire book of Hebrews is an eloquent exposition of the

truth that the Lord Jesus is the full and final fulfillment of that promise.
In the same way, "the Coming One will come" has now become the promise to people of faith who look forward to the return of Christ in power
and great glory. He will not delay. He will come in precise fulfillment of
God's timetable. That may not be the timetable we desire, but our confidence is grounded in the promise of our God. "We have this hope as an
anchor for the soul, firm and secure" (Hebrews 6:19).

In the light of this promise, God says, "my righteous one shall live by
faith." The reason we don't cast away our confidence is because "the just
shall live by faith." It isn't on the basis of our works, our achievements,
or our merits that we stand accepted by a holy God. We are declared
righteous on the basis of what the Lord Jesus has done on our behalf,
through faith and trust in Him. Our confidence is Christ-confidence,
not self-confidence. We come to life in Christ by faith, because "without
faith it is impossible to please God" (Hebrews 11:6).

The righteous—that is, sinners declared righteous through faith—
not only come to life by faith but also continue to live by faith. They
don't start and then shrink back. They don't begin and then withdraw.
The faith that saves continues, and it produces faithfulness, because it
is ultimately the product of the Holy Spirit at work within us. That is
why the writer of Hebrews says with such confidence, "We are not of
those who shrink back and are destroyed, but of those who believe and
are saved." People of faith desire to please God, and they please Him by
trusting Him. And they trust Him because they believe not only that He
is the One who has come, but also that He is the Coming One.

This becomes the central exhortation that leads us to the great roster
of faith in Hebrews 11. People of faith keep on keeping on. The essence
of the Christian life is that those who are God's people live by faith in
the Coming One. Faith isn't just an event but a living heart-relation with
God. Faith isn't simply a decision made at a moment. It is a reliance

upon God that sustains and keeps. Faith is not merely intellectual assent to spiritual truth, or a passing decision, or a momentary experience. Genuine faith is a living thing.

Because faith is intimately related to the work of the Holy Spirit within us, "those who believe and are saved" press on. They do not shrink back in unbelief. *Faith is a lifestyle, not an event.* We have spiritual staying power because of the Spirit's enablement. Authentic faith is an inner conviction about the Lord Jesus, His person, His performance, and His promise that produces staying power within His people. At the same time, we are not passive in the process. We need a commitment of heart and the inspiration of others who have walked the way of faith before us, which is why the writer of Hebrews leads us to consider the example of those who have modeled the staying power of faith down through the ages.

FAITH IS A COMPELLING VISION OF GOD AND HIS PROMISE THAT BUILDS STAYING POWER

The opening verses of Hebrews 11 build on the exhortation of Hebrews 10:32–39. We have need of endurance and we need faith to endure.

Now faith is being sure of what we hope for and certain of what we do not see. This is what the ancients were commended for.

By faith we understand that the universe was formed at God's command, so that what is seen was not made out of what was visible. (Hebrews 11:1–3)

These verses tell us three things about faith. First, *faith is a commitment to God that relies on His promise.* Verse 1 is not a formal definition of faith so much as a description of it. There is something dry and cold about a dictionary definition; it dissects what is alive. Whereas we are shown in Hebrews 11 that faith is living and active, and part of its essential nature is that it is forward-looking. It reaches for the coming blessings promised to us in the Lord Jesus Christ.

Yet while faith focuses on the future, it is grounded in the past. Faith is our personal response to what God has done for us in His Son. That is why the first ten chapters of Hebrews have been devoted to the finished work of Christ, showing that He is the fulfillment of God's promises by His coming, His death, His resurrection, and His present position at the right hand of the Father. True faith stands on a firm foundation of objective fact. It is not a vague trust in God or a subjective response to personal experiences. It is reliance on God's actions on our behalf.

This is important because faith is only as good as its object. When we lived in Calgary, where the winters get very cold, people would too often venture out on the ice of the local reservoir. It looked solid and secure, but what they did not realize was that the city had often drawn down the water supply, and the ice was unsupported. More than one person lost his life trusting something that looked safe and secure but wasn't. In a similar sense, faith in the wrong thing will bring danger and even disaster. There is no virtue in faith per se. That is why authentic and saving faith rests on the firm foundation of the person and work of the Lord Jesus.

But faith not only looks back; it looks forward to what God has promised. In fact, this is the major emphasis of Hebrews 11. Faith reaches for the future, for the blessings that God has promised. Faith takes God at His word, and, on that basis, acts in the present. We see this in the lives of each of the heroes of faith. Because they had a profound trust in God and His promises, they took actions that often appeared to the unbelieving to be risky and even foolhardy. They acted with courage and vision, supported by their certainty that God will do what He has promised.

"Faith is being sure of what we hope for." The word translated "being sure" was used for a title deed, which legally guaranteed the possessor future possession of a property. Faith gives certainty to our hopes. Faith is not the projection of our wishes and desires into the future, a kind of spiritual wishful thinking; rather, faith is the title deed to what we hope for. It gives solid confidence—a compelling certainty that what God has said, He will do. This is no wish or dream. It is a certainty planted in the heart by God's Spirit, based on God's Word. Adoniram Judson, the pioneer American missionary who endured years of suffering and imprisonment in Burma and yet kept on, caught the mood of faith in his declaration, "The future is as bright as the promises of God."

Faith also makes us "certain of what we do not see." This certainty is spiritual, not tangible. The term *certain* comes from the legal system. It means "proof" or "evidence," the kind of proof that brings conviction. Legal certainty or proof is not the same as scientific proof. Scientific proof is reproducible. Others can repeat the experiment you have done under the same circumstances and receive the same results. Legal proof is the compelling preponderance of evidence, a recognition that the facts can be credibly explained in no other way.

In the physical realm, my eyes see the world around me, and through them I reach conviction and certainty. In the spiritual realm, the eyes of faith see the invisible, eternal world and reach an even deeper conviction and certainty. I cannot see my forgiveness by God, my adoption into His family, the indwelling of His Spirit, and the home prepared for me in heaven. Yet His Word tells me the truth of these things, and His Spirit bears witness to their reality. Faith is a robust confidence in God's person and God's promise. Faith grasps the unseen future because it relies on the certainty of God's promise.

The second affirmation is that *faith is a confidence in God that receives His approval*: "This is what the ancients were commended for." Here, "the ancients" refers to the heroes of faith we are about to meet in the verses that follow. These were obviously people of special character, men and women who lived exceptional lives. Yet they were also ordinary, deeply flawed human beings. Abraham, Jacob, Moses, Rahab, Samson, David, and the others were all people who knew what it was to fall into sin. The point is not that they were exceptional or special in and of themselves. They were commended by God not for their exceptional qualities but for their faith.

The way God dealt with these men and women because of their faith is a pattern for how He deals with people of faith in all ages. When the writer tells us that they were commended for their faith, he means that they were commended by God, they were testified to by God, they gained God's approval. This will be reiterated in Hebrews 11:6: "Without faith it is impossible to please God, because anyone who comes to him must believe that he is and that he rewards those who earnestly seek him." Trust in God and in His grace wins His approval. In fact, faith is, and always has been, the only way a sinful human being can experience God's salvation and blessing. As Martin Luther said, "To be without faith is like someone who has to cross the sea, but is so frightened he does not trust the ship. And so he stays where he is, and is never saved because he will not get on board and cross over."

The final affirmation about faith is that *faith is a confidence about God that recognizes His power*. "By faith, we understand that the universe was formed at God's command, so that what is seen was not made out of what was visible." This is the first of eighteen uses of the phrase "by faith" in this chapter. In the other cases, it will describe the specific acts of faith of the heroes of faith. In this case, it describes the understanding of life shared by all who follow Christ. The truth of the creation of the universe recorded in Genesis 1 does more than introduce the Bible. It teaches us that "the God who is there" is all-powerful and all-wise. The immensity of the created universe is one side of the equation. Only a God of infinite might and ability could account for such a massive reality. Faith knows a God who is more than adequate for any demand that life places upon us.

The other side of the equation is the complexity, intricacy, beauty, and design of creation. Although a huge segment of our society insists on missing the evidence, claiming that this is all a product of unguided time and chance, faith knows better. The irreducible complexity of creation bears witness to the knowledge, wisdom, and sovereign control of God. Faith is not belief without proof. God's creation gives evidence of His power and wisdom, and on that evidence we trust without reservation.

This gives faith confidence to trust that God knows best, that to follow His direction is to walk in the path of wisdom, even when our initial intuition is that there is a better way. Faith listens to and lives by the familiar words of Proverbs 3:5–6:

> Trust in the Lord with all your heart,
> and lean not on your own understanding:
> in all your ways acknowledge him,
> and he will make your paths straight.

God's agent in bringing about creation was His command, His spoken word. That word has power and wisdom. The writer's point is clear: We can and must respond to God's command as well. Because of God's word, something came out of nothing, the visible from the invisible. God, and only God, is ultimate. Faith relies on His promise, receives His approval, and recognizes His power—and that inspires staying power in our own lives.

Dawson Trotman, the founder of the Navigators, wrote a little booklet entitled *The Need of the Hour*. In it he asked, "What is the need of the hour?" and then answered his own question:

For a beggar on the streets it is a piece of bread. For the Christian community it is not more money or better literature or better programs or better facilities. It is for people of faith—people who believe that God is God and he can fulfill every promise he ever made.[3]

That was true five decades ago when Trotman wrote those words. It was true two thousand years ago when the writer of Hebrews penned his appeal to a group of embattled Christians in need of endurance. And it is true today as we navigate the changing world of a new millennium.

Chapter Ten

By Faith Alone

The news story seemed bizarre. Two Air Force F-15 jets were shadowing a Learjet as it flew steadily north across the heart of the United States. Flight controllers had been unable to make contact with the plane, and the pilots of the military jets reported that the windows of the plane were frosted over and there was no sign of life. Six people, including the two pilots and the reigning champion of the U.S. Open golf championship, Payne Stewart, were known to be aboard. The saga played out over four hours. Finally, the ghost flight came to a tragic end when the plane ran out of gas over South Dakota and spiraled into the ground at a speed estimated at more than six hundred miles an hour, blowing a huge crater in the ground. There were no survivors.

Payne Stewart had left home that Monday morning, October 25, 1999, intending to fly to Dallas for some golf course design business discussions. The jet, flown by an Air Force veteran, took off at 9:19 A.M. with a flight plan designed to take it northwest to Ocala, Florida, and then west toward Dallas. But the plane never made the turn west. It kept flying northwest, and air-traffic controllers reported that they had lost contact fourteen minutes into the flight. The plane kept going higher and higher, reaching an altitude of more than fifty thousand feet. When all attempts to reach the pilots were unsuccessful, military jets scrambled to follow the plane and perhaps even to tip the wings of the Learjet to see if they could rouse the pilots. One of the military pilots later said: "It's a very helpless feeling to pull up alongside another aircraft and realize the people inside that aircraft are potentially unconscious or in some other way incapacitated. And there's nothing I can do physically from my aircraft, even though I'm fifty to one hundred feet away."[1]

When there was no response, experts quickly diagnosed a decompression problem. A sudden loss of pressure during the plane's climb after take-off had caused all six people to pass out. Long before the plane had crashed, everyone was unconscious, and probably dead, from lack of oxygen. For four hours, an expensive, high-performance jet was assisted by the most advanced help from air-traffic controllers and military pilots. The plane had state-of-the-art guidance systems and access to the finest navigational direction. Everything necessary to safely reach the intended destination was present, except oxygen. But as the results show, nothing else matters if oxygen is missing.

There is a spiritual counterpart to this. *The life of faith is the only life that pleases God, and nothing else matters if faith is missing.* No matter how many navigational devices may be present in our lives, if we lack faith, we lack the indispensable. The good news is that Payne Stewart was a man who had come to faith in the Lord Jesus Christ, and his memorial service became a powerful testimony to the country about the difference the Lord Jesus can make, as he had in Stewart's life. As fellow golfer and Christ-follower Paul Azinger said during the service, "During the past year, everyone who knew Payne Stewart saw this dramatic change in his life. They saw in Payne what the Bible calls a 'peace which passes understanding.' Only God can do that because only God can change a heart."[2]

Hebrews 11 reminds us over and over about the priority of faith in the living God. There is no virtue in faith in and of itself. Faith has value because it is placed in the triune God, who has made himself known in Scripture, in history, and, supremely, in the person of the Son. Hebrews 11 begins with an account of three who lived millennia ago, but whose lives still have a fresh message for followers of the same Lord.

> By faith Abel offered God a better sacrifice than Cain did. By faith he was commended as a righteous man, when God spoke well of his offerings. And by faith he still speaks, even though he is dead.
>
> By faith Enoch was taken from this life, so that he did not experience death; he could not be found, because God had taken him away. For before he was taken, he was commended as one who pleased God.
>
> And without faith it is impossible to please God, because anyone who comes to him must believe that he exists and that he rewards those who earnestly seek him.
>
> By faith Noah, when warned about things not yet seen, in holy fear built an ark to save his family. By his faith he condemned the world and became heir of the righteousness that comes by faith. (Hebrews 11:4–7)

The description of faith given in the first verses is now wrapped in flesh and blood, as the writer begins his account of the heroes of faith. He expects us to be familiar with the stories to which he refers, and so he compresses his accounts to get to the main point. He begins by taking us to the dawn of human history to demonstrate that the way of faith has been the consistent, indeed the only, path to right standing with God. The life of faith is, and always has been, the only life that pleases God.

FAITH ALONE BRINGS APPROVAL FROM GOD

As far as the biblical account is concerned, Cain and Abel are the first two human beings born on planet Earth (Genesis 4). The two sons of the first human couple lived in a world that was fresh with the creative genius of God. But because of the sinful choice of their parents, humanity's first children were fallen people living in a fallen world. They knew drives and desires within them that not only pulled them away from the presence of God but also put them into competition with one another. As brothers, they had much in common. They had the same parents, experienced the same environment, and shared the same gene pool. But like most siblings, they were gifted in different ways. Abel was a man drawn to living things, a herdsman, a person who found delight in raising and working with animals. He was the first to domesticate sheep and goats and to develop a herd. Cain was a man of the fields, an agriculturalist who loved to feel the dirt on his hands and to see crops grow.

These two brothers also shared something else. They were religious men. Where they learned to bring an offering to God, we are not told. Almost certainly God had revealed it to them or to their parents. But there was a set time when they came into the presence of God and made an offering to him, a *minhah*. The word itself is a general word for an offering to God, a gift presented to Him. It is used often in the Old Testament to describe offerings made to God, and often refers specifically to a grain (rather than an animal) offering. Both men brought offerings that represented their sphere of life. Cain, the farmer, brought a gift of produce. Abel, the herdsman, brought part of an animal.

All of this seems normal. But as they presented their offerings, religious men doing what God had commanded, somehow it became evident that God's response to the two sacrifices was not the same. He accepted Abel's offering but rejected Cain's. As Genesis 4:5 tersely says, "The

LORD looked with favor on Abel and his offering, but on Cain and his offering he did not look with favor."

Questions jump out at us here. How did God show this to them? Did He speak audibly? Did He send fire from heaven and consume Abel's offering but not Cain's? Did He give some other supernatural signal? There is no way for us to know. But the brothers knew.

The other question is much more important. Why? What made Abel's offering acceptable and Cain's unacceptable? People have suggested a multitude of answers. Some have suggested that Abel offered a blood sacrifice, while Cain self-righteously offered the work of his hands. This makes great preaching, but it assumes an awful lot of later theology, and also assumes that this was intended to be a forgiveness sacrifice. God later required many grain or produce offerings. Others have suggested that God had no reason, that His preference was arbitrary, a view that squares neither with the character of God nor the statement of Hebrews that Abel's was "a better sacrifice." Others point out that Abel offered "*fat portions* [a valued part] from some of the *firstborn* of the flock," while Cain offered "some of the fruits of the soil." They suggest that Abel offered what was special and costly, while Cain offered what was ordinary and not especially valuable. But such suggestions are mere speculations. The text does not tell us *why*.

Whatever the reason and whatever the method, Cain knew that God had not accepted his offering, and his response was neither repentance nor regret. He was angry—an anger mixed with depression. He was angry with God and with his brother.

God was not silent. He intervened, challenging Cain's response and calling him to repentance: "If you do what is right, will you not be accepted?" But Cain refused to hear. Stomping out of God's presence, he went in pursuit of his brother. Abel was a convenient scapegoat for Cain's rage, and Cain met him with a heart full of anger, self-pity, jealousy, hatred, and all those other passions that haunt our souls when we turn our back on God. "And while they were in the field, Cain attacked his brother Abel and killed him." Abel's blood soaking into the ground offered a sad preview of human history, marked as it is by the bloody trail of Cain.

Dramatic and instructive as this story is, the writer of Hebrews wants to fix our eyes on the major issue. What distinguished Cain and Abel was not so much their offerings as their faith, or lack of it. "*By faith* Abel offered a better sacrifice than Cain." Abel, the man of faith, came to God in trust and belief. Cain mechanically did the "rite thing," but his response to God's rebuke showed that he was a man of unbelief. Cain wasn't rejected because he had followed the wrong ritual or because he had offered the wrong offering. He was rejected because he had come to God with a wrong heart. It was not the offering but the offerer. (Note the order: God rejected Cain and then his offering.) It was who Cain was that was wrong, not what he brought. And he is an eloquent reminder that God puts no value on acts of religion as such. Cain possessed religion, but he lacked faith.

"By faith [Abel] was commended as a righteous man, when God spoke well of his offerings." Faith is not devoid of works. Abel's outward offering was the product of his inward faith. The offerings were accepted because of the heart of the offerer.

Genuine faith causes us to do what pleases God. But works can be devoid of faith, as Cain's were. This is a message our pluralistic world needs to hear. All around us we hear the claim that there are many ways to reach God. But at the beginning of God's Word, at the first offering in the Bible, we learn that God puts no value on works of religion per se. It is by faith, and by faith alone, that we are made right with God. "By faith, Abel still speaks, even though he is dead."

Abel also had to provide his own sacrifice. Anyone who has read the book of Hebrews knows that *we* don't need to bring a sacrifice. God has provided the perfect sacrifice. He has sent His Son. "He has appeared once for all at the end of the ages to do away with sin by the sacrifice of himself. . . . Christ was sacrificed once to take away the sins of many people. . . . And where these [sins] have been forgiven, there is no longer any sacrifice for sin" (Hebrews 9:26, 28; 10:18). When Christ died on the cross, that was the end of sacrifices. God allowed the temple to be destroyed not long after the crucifixion of the Savior, because its usefulness had passed. The Lord Jesus met 100 percent of the righteous requirement of God and ended the era of sacrifices. But the value of the death of Christ has no personal effect for us apart from faith in the Lord Jesus.

The content of our faith is much richer and more profound than Abel's. But for him and for us, the truth is the same: faith alone in Christ alone brings the gracious approval of our God.

Faith Alone Enables Us to Please God

Abel's story is brief, but it contains a huge principle. The same is true of Enoch, the second man we meet in Hebrews 11. We know even less about him than we do about Abel, all that we know being found in a few verses in Genesis:

> When Enoch had lived 65 years, he became the father of Methuselah. And after he became the father of Methuselah, Enoch walked with God 300 years and had other sons and daughters. Altogether, Enoch lived 365 years. Enoch walked with God; then he was no more, because God took him away. (Genesis 5:21–24)

The Septuagint, the Greek translation that the writer of Hebrews knew and used, renders the beginning of the last sentence, "Enoch pleased God; then he was no more." There is not much material there, but out of it emerges one of the primary principles of God's dealings with human beings.

The account of Enoch occurs in the middle of a chapter that at first glance is one of those notorious lists of names that tempts us to abandon our plans to read through the Bible. Yet hidden in such places, we often find great truths. In this case, there is a phrase that is repeated eight times in Genesis 5, tolling like a bell announcing funeral after funeral: "and then he died . . . and then he died . . . and then he died." It is a solemn reminder from God that His warning in Genesis 2:17 was not an empty threat: "When you eat of [the tree of good and evil] you will surely die." The wages of sin really is death.

There is one remarkable exception, however. In the midst of this trail of death, we come to Enoch and read, "Enoch was no more, because God took him away." The phrase is cryptic, but the writer of Hebrews leaves no doubt as to the meaning: "By faith Enoch was taken from this life, so that he did not experience death." God took Enoch into His presence without requiring him to pass through the gates of death. The only other human being to share such an experience was the prophet Elijah, whose ascent to heaven in a chariot of fire is described in 2 Kings 2:11–12. Enoch's exit from life was remarkable; he was caught up to God without experiencing death. That alone makes him interesting and worthy of examination.

Enoch lived in a time of increasing wickedness and immorality. Society around him was on the downhill moral toboggan ride that led God to bring the flood upon humanity. We know nothing of the first sixty-five years of Enoch's life, but apparently the birth of his son Methuselah was a defining moment. "After he became the father of Methuselah, Enoch walked with God 300 years." When Enoch realized he was responsible for the physical and spiritual well-being of a child, he apparently began to look at life and God in a different way. He wasn't the last father to straighten up spiritually when he realized that he was responsible for a little one. But the striking thing is that Methuselah never knew a time when his father wasn't walking with God. What a special legacy! The text says it simply but powerfully: Enoch walked with God. God didn't walk with Enoch. No, God set the pace, and Enoch walked with God. This becomes one of the most common New Testament descriptions of the Christian's life: a walk with God. When the Greek translators came to this phrase, they chose not so much to translate it as to interpret it: Enoch pleased God. The writer of Hebrews picks up that idea when he observes, "Before he was taken, he was commended as one who pleased God."

What was it about Enoch that pleased God? The answer is given in the form of one of the Bible's golden verses, a statement that captures the essence of so much biblical teaching: "And without faith it is impossible to please God, because anyone who comes to him must believe that he exists and that he rewards those who earnestly seek him." Enoch did not please God because of his religious performance or his personal attributes. He pleased God by faith. The life of faith is the only life that pleases God. Nothing counts if faith is missing.

But what do we mean by faith? In an op-ed article in the *Los Angeles Times*, an engineering professor ridicules the whole idea of faith: "Faith is belief without evidence or despite evidence to the contrary. Faith occurs when a person believes that something is true even though he suspects it is false. . . . Religious faith is beliefs without such [testable] logic or facts."[3] I hope this professor is more rigorous with his scientific definitions than he is with this one, because this is a classic straw man definition.

Faith is not believing that for which there is no evidence or accepting what you suspect is false. Quite the contrary. True faith rests on solid and substantial reasons. We believe in the Lord Jesus Christ on the basis of solid historical and compelling rational evidence, as well as profound personal experiences. Granted, there is a difference between scientific proof and the kind of proof faith rests upon. I cannot test the truth of the Incarnation in a test tube. But I cannot prove my wife's love in that way, either. I cannot even prove that the car coming toward me will stop at the stop sign. I may have a high degree of confidence that it will, but that is in the realm of faith, not scientific proof. In fact, a moment's thought will leave us amazed at how many acts of faith we practice in a given day. Faith takes us beyond proof, but it does not take us away from it. It is a confidence built on deep experience. That is especially true of faith in God, and we have profound and powerful reasons to trust Him.

The essence of faith is trust. To trust someone is to respect who that person is, to rely upon that fact, and to act on that basis. You don't trust someone until you find yourself dependent on him. Faith is faith in God, the God who has chosen to reveal himself in Scripture, in history, and, supremely, in His Son. We could read the statement "Anyone who comes to God must believe that He exists" in the most superficial way, saying that faith involves belief in God's existence. That is self-evident, but I doubt that is what the passage means. The question in biblical times was never the existence of God—or gods. (The world is full of gods, all of them the result of the sinful and distorted imaginations of human beings.) The real question is the character of God—whether God is who He says He is, whether the God who is there is the God of Scripture. Faith believes that the God of Scripture, the God of Israel, the God and Father of our Lord Jesus Christ *is*. Faith rests and relies on the God of revelation—the majestic, infinite, holy God who alone is worthy of worship and service. Faith believes that God *is*, that the God who *is* is awesome beyond imagining, and that the God who *is* is utterly consistent and reliable.

Faith believes not only that God is real but also that He is worth knowing. "He rewards those who earnestly seek him." The greatest privilege in life is knowing God; the greatest reward in life is intimacy with God; the greatest purpose for life is the service of God. He is good, gracious, and forgiving. He is holy, generous, and loving. Faith believes that God is worth seeking, that He is worth pursuing. Faith places the highest possible value on God himself.

At this point, the modern secular worldview collides with the biblical worldview. Modern man considers God optional at best, but essentially irrelevant to a meaningful life. Everyone is entitled to his or her own understanding of God, but it is bad taste to take Him too seriously or to insist that there is any ultimate truth behind anyone's viewpoint. And if my idea is as good as yours, why take any of this too seriously? Life can be lived well without bringing God into daily life!

But the fact is that people who are indifferent to God are insulting Him. I remember vividly a man who didn't like my leadership in a church context. When I sought him out for a conversation, he told me, "You know, sometimes I hear you talk about baseball or something else, and I think you might even be worth getting to know. But then you do something else, and I decide that you aren't." I have been insulted before, but that insult was easily the most painful. To dismiss someone as not worth getting to know shows immense contempt for that person.

That is what we display toward God when we refuse to seek Him or trust Him. "I've lived a good life. I've tried to behave. Sure, I haven't been very interested in you or paid you much attention throughout my life. But still, why shouldn't I get into heaven?" Yet you've lived your life on the basis that God isn't worth knowing, that He isn't worth worshiping or serving, that He has no meaningful place in your schedule or in your values! "Without faith, it is impossible to please God."

Therefore, the most basic question in life becomes, Do you believe God? Have you trusted in His Son as your Lord and Savior? The picture of Payne Stewart's jet reminds us of this truth: No matter how well the plane is equipped, nothing else matters if there is no oxygen. And the life of Enoch sends this message: No matter how well your life is equipped, it doesn't matter if you don't trust in the God of Scripture.

FAITH ACTIVELY RESPONDS TO GOD'S WORD

The third of our heroes of faith is Noah, and he is by far the best known of these first three. His action in building the ark and saving a remnant of humanity from the flood of God's judgment is one of the great events in biblical history. Noah is the first person in the Bible whom we see acting in direct response to God's command. His life teaches us that the kind of faith the Bible celebrates is not passive faith but active, obedient faith.

> By faith Noah, when warned about things not yet seen, in holy fear built an ark to save his family. By his faith he condemned the world and became heir of the righteousness that comes by faith. (Hebrews 11:7)

Noah lived in tumultuous times, when "the LORD saw how great man's wickedness on the earth had become, and that every inclination of the thoughts of his heart was only evil all the time" (Genesis 6:5). Yet Noah "was a righteous man, blameless among the people of his time, and he walked with God" (Genesis 6:9). But nothing in Noah's experience could have prepared him for God's direct command to him. God warned Noah that there was going to be a flood of catastrophic proportions, unlike anything he had ever seen. There was no physical reason to believe such a thing would happen, no meteorological evidence, and no ominous warning signs. All he had to go on was the word of God. Faith means actively responding to God's Word.

And the task Noah was asked to undertake was no small task. It involved a massive infusion of physical energy, technological skill, and personal resources. It wasn't a project of a few weeks or even years, but an undertaking so immense he knew that it would take decades to complete. It also would inevitably attract scorn and ridicule from Noah's neighbors, who already had little sympathy for his faith and his lifestyle, both of which put him out of step with the surrounding culture.

The writer of Hebrews summarizes Noah's response to God's astonishing command: "By faith Noah, when warned about things not yet seen, in holy fear built an ark to save his family." Noah heard God's word of warning, and he paid attention. The word translated "holy fear" does not refer to a response of dread but to an attitude of respect. He took God's word seriously, and therefore he paid close attention to the instructions he received. The bottom line is that he acted on God's word. He built the ark.

When did Noah believe God? Noah's faith became visible when he picked up his axe for the first time, walked over to the first tree, and made the first cut. There would be countless more cuts before the task was finished, but that first cut set the course of Noah's life.

Over the next 120 years, Noah relentlessly worked on the massive floating barge God had instructed him to build. Every day was a new venture of faith. Not once in that entire period was there any external reason to believe that this project made sense. But he kept on, despite the protests of his aging body and the taunts of his neighbors. Then came the time to gather the animals, to gather his family, and to enter the boat, even as the derision of his society reached fever pitch. When he tried to explain, things only got worse. But God's commands were more real to Noah than the faces of his enemies, and God's approval more precious than their approval, and so he completed God's assignment.

Two results of Noah's actions are described. The first is that "by faith he condemned the world." Noah's life was a condemnation of those around him. When the culture was rushing away from God, Noah modeled a life of righteousness and holiness. Noah was also "a preacher of righteousness," as Peter calls him (2 Peter 2:5). Undoubtedly, as people came to see this strange monstrosity that Noah was constructing, he took the opportunity to explain the project and to proclaim God's warning. Now they had exactly the same information Noah had. The people had heard God's word, but they chose to ignore it. Perhaps they rejected it out of hand. Perhaps they persuaded themselves that they could wait until the first drops of rain started to fall. Whatever the reason, none of them entered the ark. Noah and his family alone were saved. But by his faith in God and his life of righteousness, Noah condemned the world. He stood in dramatic contrast to an unbelieving, guilty generation.

We are also told that "by faith Noah . . . became heir of the righteousness that comes by faith." This is great biblical language that takes us to one of the great truths of Scripture—that is, justification by faith. Righteousness before a holy God is not a human achievement; it is the gift of a gracious God because of the finished work of Christ. Even though Noah lived and died millennia before the Lord Jesus died on the cross, it was on the basis of Christ's finished work on the cross that Noah was declared righteous. The same is true for us. When we trust in the Lord Jesus Christ, the holy God declares us righteous on the basis of the finished work of Christ.

Faith means building the boat before you see the rain. It means taking God at His word when He speaks about the future. It means stepping out and acting on the basis of God's word. The only faith the Bible knows is faith in action.

Two fascinating passages in the Gospels describe the Lord's response to people's faith or lack of faith. In Mark 6, we read that the Lord Jesus returned to Nazareth, where He taught in the synagogue, performed a few miracles, and "many were amazed" (Mark 6:2). But amazement quickly turned to offense at the Lord's claims. The account ends with Mark's comment: "And he was amazed at their lack of faith" (Mark 6:6). The second fascinating passage is found in Luke 7. There we read that the Lord was in Capernaum, and a Roman centurion came to Him in great confidence that if Jesus would only speak the words, his deathly ill servant would be healed. Luke then comments: "When Jesus heard this, he was amazed at him, and turning to the crowd following him, he said, 'I tell you, I have not found such great faith even in Israel'" (Luke 7:9).

In one case, Jesus was amazed by unbelief. It is an amazing thing that human beings cannot trust the God who created and redeemed them. In another case, Jesus was amazed by faith, the faith of a Gentile. Genuine faith is such a rare commodity that when it appears, it stands out like a precious jewel. The question is, What would the Lord be amazed at in my life—my belief or my unbelief?

Faith is not merely a nice quality; it is an absolute necessity. "Without faith, it is impossible to please God." Like oxygen, without it, nothing else matters.

Chapter Eleven

TRAVEL GUIDES

Robert Ballard has spent most of his life exploring a part of our world about which most of us know very little. He calls himself an "undersea exploration scientist," and he gained fame primarily as the locater of the *Titanic*. On September 1, 1985, he took the submersible *Alvin* to a depth of 12,400 feet to view and to film the most famous wreck of the twentieth century.

Over the years, Ballard has led or taken part in more than one hundred expeditions under the world's oceans and seas. In the process, he has mapped underwater mountains, discovered hydrothermals and underwater volcanoes, and located ships ranging from Roman times to famous twentieth-century vessels such as the *Lusitania* (sunk by the Germans in an act that helped draw the United States into World War I), the *Bismarck* (a ship sunk by the Allies in a major World War II sea battle), and the *Titanic*.

Ballard's passion is exploring uncharted territory, and the bottoms of the great oceans represent the last major frontier for such exploration on planet Earth. He sees his exploration as a metaphor for life:

We're all explorers. We're all in pursuit of fundamental truths. That's what exploration is all about. To be an explorer is to have a dream. Your dream gives your life direction and helps you navigate day-to-day decisions. Let your dream inform your life: Look at opportunities through the dream's filter and ask yourself whether any given situation will move you closer to final realization.[1]

Christ-followers are not so much explorers as navigators. Explorers venture into the unknown. They don't know where they are going or what they will encounter along the way. Navigators are people who are headed for a destination. They know where they want to go. The Lord Jesus has opened the frontier for us. We know where we are headed, although we do not know all that we will encounter on the journey. And we have something much more tangible than a dream. A dream is often nothing more than a projection of our inner desires on the future. Instead, Christ-followers possess a God-given promise and calling.

The certainty of our destination enables us to navigate day-to-day decisions. Our calling not only informs our decisions but also shapes our lives. We could debate what shapes us more, our vision of the future or our experiences in the past. Both are powerful, but there can be no denying that what we believe about the future directly determines our present. We see this in many areas of life. An athlete determinedly keeps training because his eye is on the coming competition. A student prepares and studies because she has her eye not only on the coming examinations but also on an ultimate career goal. An entrepreneur takes time, money, and energy that could be used in a multitude of ways to bring immediate enjoyment and invests them with the intent of building a profitable business for the years that lie ahead. An explorer navigates past the known and the familiar because he is headed for a destination that takes him off the maps. But people with no compelling vision of the future drift aimlessly in the present. If a person has nowhere to go, he will tend to go nowhere.

In this book we have used the metaphor of navigation to emphasize that in a world in which all the maps are out of date, a Christian needs to learn how to navigate. We have been given navigational principles—fundamental guiding truths. We also need navigational skills—habits that are internalized so they become second nature. But if these principles and skills are to be of value, we must also have navigational seaworthiness—a character that is able to handle rapidly changing conditions.

The whole purpose of navigating is to reach an intended goal. That is a central message of Hebrews 11. *Faith is a hope-filled view of life, grounded in confidence in God and directed toward the promise of God.* People of faith are not driven by fear or by duty; they are inspired and sustained by a future painted and promised by God. That quality of faith is seen most clearly in the life of Abraham, the man who is the premier graduate of the Bible's school of faith. The writer of Hebrews devotes more space to his story than to that of any other Old Testament figure, and he begins with the story of God's call and Abraham's response.

By faith Abraham, when called to go to a place he would later receive as his inheritance, obeyed and went, even though he did not know where he was going. By faith he made his home in the promised land like a stranger in a foreign country; he lived in tents, as did Isaac and Jacob, who were heirs with him of the same promise. For he was looking forward to the city with foundations, whose architect and builder is God.

By faith Abraham, even though he was past age—and Sarah herself was barren—was enabled to become a father because he considered him faithful who had made the promise. And so from this one man, and he as good as dead, came descendants as numerous as the stars in the sky and as countless as the sand on the seashore. (Hebrews 11:8–12)

Valuable as navigational skills are, we also stand in need of travel guides. Wise people listen carefully to those who have ventured out on the ocean of life and safely reached the other side. We want as much information as possible about where we are headed and what we will encounter on the way. That is, in a sense, what Hebrews 11 is all about. It is the story of those who, because of their journeys of faith, have become travel guides to those of us who follow behind. Of all who can serve us in that way, none is more significant than Abraham. He is "the father of the believing," who lived his life journeying through uncharted territory in obedience to his God.

In Hebrews 11:6 we encountered the fundamental principle of spiritual life, that "without faith it is impossible to please God." Faith is how we begin the Christian life, and faith is how we continue on. If that is so, then it stands to reason that one of God's great purposes is to strengthen and deepen our trust in Him. Many things in our lives make sense when we realize that God is pursuing His agenda of building faith deep within us, an agenda we see at work in the life of Abraham.

There is much we do not know about Abraham. His earliest years are hidden in obscurity. We are told that his father was an idolater and a worshiper of false gods in his Mesopotamian homeland (Joshua 24:2). But we are not told about the earlier stages in Abraham's spiritual journey. All we know—all we really need to know—is that the defining moment for him came when his life was intersected by the sovereign and mysterious call of God. That moment became for Abraham, as it does for us, life's decisive moment.

FAITH RESPONDS OBEDIENTLY TO THE CALL OF GOD

God's call came to Abraham in the city that was apparently the most advanced of the time. Located in what is today southern Iraq, Ur was beginning a time of flowering in what is now known as its third dynasty. It was culturally advanced, offering the finest of the ancient world's advantages. It was technologically advanced for its time and economically prosperous. But Ur also was thoroughly pagan, a city given over to polytheism and idolatry. Abraham's father, Terah, carried the name of the moon god, the preeminent deity of the culture. From all we know, Abraham was not a seeker who stumbled upon the truth or a religious genius who broke through with new insight. He was a sinner whose life was suddenly and graciously intersected by the grace of God.

When that occurred, Abraham was a man in middle life. He was also a man of considerable wealth, and undoubtedly he was comfortably settled in Ur. He was married to a strikingly beautiful woman, Sarah, a woman other men desired. Abraham and Sarah shared the sadness of not having been blessed with children, but that did not diminish the strength of their commitment to one another. There is no indication that he was restless, seeking new spheres to explore or new worlds to conquer. Abraham was at ease in Ur, quietly satisfied in his comfort zone.

One of the realities of faith is that it is like a muscle. It grows stronger only when it is used. And it is rarely used in our comfort zone. So God sovereignly, powerfully, and directly nudged Abraham out of that zone. "The God of glory appeared to our father Abraham while he was still in Mesopotamia" (Acts 7:2). The details are hidden from us, but the central message is not:

> The LORD had said to Abram, "Leave your country, your people and your father's household and go to the land I will show you.

> I will make you into a great nation and I will bless you; I will make your name great, and you will be a blessing. I will bless those who bless you, and whoever curses you I will curse; and all peoples on earth will be blessed through you." (Genesis 12:1–3)

Those words not only mark a new chapter in Abraham's life; they mark a new stage of human history. This is the Abrahamic covenant, one of the crowning moments in the unfolding drama of salvation, which leads to the saving work of the Lord Jesus Christ and will lead on to the coming kingdom of Christ on earth. God offers a promise of *a people*, who will become the nation of Israel; the implied promise of *a place*, which will be the land of Palestine; and the promise of *a program* that will bring blessing not only to Abraham and to his descendants but also to the nations, a promise fulfilled in the Lord Jesus Christ.

From that moment, nothing is the same. This vision of the glory of God transforms Abraham. He will never again bow before an idol, imagining that it represents a divine being. He will never again see the sun, moon, or stars and be drawn to worship them. He has met the living God, and life is forever changed.

On a personal level, God's call is a summons to a radical break with the past. "Leave your country, your people and your father's household and go to the land I will show you." Abraham was to leave behind all that was known, familiar, and comfortable and to live in radical trust in God. It was also a call to a radical trust in God's future. Abraham could undoubtedly predict what the future would be like if he remained in Ur. But this was a call to head for an unknown, unnamed place, "the land I will show you." Abraham ended in Canaan, but when he left Ur, he had no idea that was his destination. "When called to a place he would later receive as his inheritance, he obeyed and went, even though he did not know where he was going." I have often wondered how Abraham explained this to Sarah. "Honey, it's time to pack. We're moving. No, I don't know where. No, I don't know what the weather's like. No, I don't know anybody there. I'm just doing what God told me to do."

Faith is at once simple and profound. It is simple in concept: Faith means taking God at His word and acting on what He says. It is profound in its requirement. It is staking everything on the goodness, truthfulness, and faithfulness of God. *Faith is following God's clear leading.* It is *not* doing what is dramatic or unusual or immense. While it may involve some of those things, in essence, faith is following God's clear leading. That is what Abraham did: "By faith Abraham, when he was called to go . . . obeyed and went."

Abraham teaches us that faith is confidence *about* God and confidence *in* God. There is so much that Abraham did not know. He couldn't see the nation that would descend from him. He couldn't even see one child who was his. He couldn't define the blessing that God had promised through him. And he couldn't describe the place to which he was going. But he did know God. Abraham believed that God was who He claimed to be and that God would do what He said He would do. Abraham had so little to go on, compared with us. No written Scriptures. No travel guides to point the way. No community of faith to support, encourage, and pray for him. All he had was an encounter with God's person and God's word, and that was enough. Faith meant trusting a God he could not see for blessings he had not received in a place he did not know.

In Romans 4:11, Paul tells us that Abraham is "the father of all who believe." The Lord has given us a much richer and fuller revelation of himself, but faith is still about trusting who God is and believing what He has said. God calls us to trust Him, to believe something that is beyond anything in our experience. We are to believe that what Someone did for us on a cross two thousand years ago can make an eternal difference for us now. Can we prove it or see it? No. But a Christian is staking everything on the fact that Jesus is who He said He is and that He will do what He promised. Faith is not blind; it rests on good and reliable evidence. Faith is taking God at His word.

Faith is also active, not passive. Inward faith produces outward obedience. Faith does not simply accept what God has said; it acts upon it. Furthermore, Abraham acted immediately. Genesis 12:4 simply says, "So Abram left, as the LORD had told him." The writer of Hebrews says, "When he was called, he obeyed and went." He left Ur with God's voice ringing in his ears. Immediate obedience is not easy obedience. I cannot help but believe that there were tears and fears as Abraham set out. But, by faith, set out he did.

The journey starts in faith, but the need for faith doesn't end when Abraham and his family leave Ur—or even when they finally arrive in the Promised Land.

FAITH TENACIOUSLY AWAITS THE TIMING OF GOD

I do not know what Abraham expected when he finally reached his God-intended destination, but I doubt that it was what he found. The writer of Hebrews simply says, "By faith he made his home in the promised land like a stranger in a foreign country; he lived in tents." When Abraham did reach the land, God not only repeated His promise (Genesis 12:7); He also confirmed it in a solemn ceremony (Genesis 15:7–20) and established the covenant sign of circumcision (Genesis 17:1–27). But still, Abraham lived in tents. He had no permanent status. He was a resident alien, a sojourner. He had no permanent home. He lived semi-nomadically, moving from place to place. When Sarah died, after sixty-two years in the land, Abraham owned no land where he could bury her. He had to make special arrangements to buy a cave in which he could place her body. He was wealthy and influential, but he was an outsider.

There is a remarkable story in Genesis 14 that tells of a group of petty kings who formed an alliance and made war against the tribal chiefs in Palestine. In the process, Abraham's nephew Lot was taken as a prisoner of war. Abraham raised an army of 318 trained men who were born in his household and marched off to rescue Lot. Abraham drove his enemies all the way beyond Damascus in Syria, then returned to his tents near Hebron. The point is significant. Abraham had all the resources to take as much of the land as he desired at any time he wanted. But he didn't. Faith involves trusting God's timing as well as God's promise. He would receive the land as a gift of God, not as something he acquired on his own.

I do not find this easy. I can identify with the story of Phillips Brooks, the nineteenth-century Boston pastor who wrote "O Little Town of Bethlehem." A friend once discovered Brooks fretting and fussing. Asked what the problem was, Brooks responded, "I'm in a hurry, and God isn't!" I can identify with that. I want guidance and direction now. I want to see the results of my efforts now. I want relief from my problems, release from my sufferings, answers to my prayers, change in my spouse or children *now*.

Being patient isn't something twenty-first century people do very well. But faith means trusting not only God's guidance but also His timing. This is one of life's most difficult lessons. Richard Halverson challenges my demands on God with some penetrating words:

> To say "Now!" to God is as presumptuous as saying "No!" And it can be just as rebellious.
>
> Someone has defined sin as a shortcut: robbery is a shortcut to work. Lust is a shortcut to love. One can sin simply by refusing to wait. Wanting a good thing is virtuous. Demanding a good thing now is sin.

God has a time for everything, a perfect schedule. He is never too soon, never too late. The when of His will is as important as the what and the how.

Prayer is waiting on God . . . not being in a hurry for God to do something. We wait, because out of God's mercy He often makes us wait. We wait, because out of God's mercy He does not always give what we ask for. We are often like little children asking for machine guns or time bombs. We're unequipped to use what we request.

Submission to God's will includes submission to His schedule.

Impatience indicates a lack of trust in God's perfect will and way.

"Let patience have her perfect way, that ye may be perfect and entire, wanting nothing" (James 1:4 KJV)

"They that wait upon the Lord shall renew their strength" (Isaiah 40:31 KJV).

"He that believeth shall not make haste" (Isaiah 28:16 KJV).[2]

Waiting is not easy. Yet God often uses times of waiting as some of His most significant ways to deepen His work within us.

Abraham was forced to wait. "He made his home in the promised land like a stranger in a foreign country." He waited, trusting God's timing. How did he do that? Hebrews 11:10 gives the answer. He was able to stay and wait and trust the timing of God because he saw the ultimate outcome of God. "For he was looking forward to the city with foundations, whose architect and builder is God." By faith, Abraham looked beyond the temporal and the visible to the eternal and the invisible. His spiritual eyes saw what his physical eyes could not see. He looked beyond his tents, beyond the cities that dotted the plains, to the city that God alone could build and that God alone could give. Abraham chose to live for what was timeless, not for what was temporary.

We live in a generation that does not do very well with the ideas of heaven and eternity. The world pushes in with its noise and attractions and calls us to feed on the opportunities all around us. Talk about heaven sounds suspiciously like escapism. But at the center of faith lies the deep conviction that the ultimate fulfillment of God's promises lies beyond this life. We are going to return to this theme in the next chapter, but we must not miss the truth before us here. As my much-loved teacher and friend Howard Hendricks loved to tell us as students, "We are not in the land of the living on the way to the land of the dying. We are in the land of the dying on the way to the land of the living." Faith is not closing our eyes to reality; it is opening our hearts to hope.

Faith holds a vision of the eternal. It sees "the city with foundations, whose architect and builder is God." Faith is shaped by what the eyes do not see, by what the hands cannot touch. It is focused on the timeless, not just the timely; on the eternal, not merely the present. But that is so hard for us!

Still, the ultimate fulfillment of God's promise lies beyond this life. The call to faith is a call to live as kingdom citizens who live here as kingdom agents but who recognize that our kingdom is not of this world. That means we are pilgrims. Abraham was not a nomad, wandering aimlessly from place to place. He was not a fugitive, running away from circumstances he did not enjoy. He was not a migrant, seeking a better life. He was not a tourist, seeking exotic and interesting experiences. He was a pilgrim, heading for a new homeland. And because he knew that his ultimate destination was God's eternal city, even when he reached the Promised Land, he was a sojourner, not a settler. His values were not determined by the surrounding culture. They were determined by the city to which God had called him.

This is one of the greatest challenges to the life of faith in the twenty-first century. It is tempting to live as a spiritual tourist rather than as a spiritual pilgrim. I enjoy being a tourist. I love seeing new places and having new experiences. But only for a brief time. Then I safely settle back into the comforts of home. After a while, tourism becomes tiresome. The danger is that I will live my spiritual life that way, collecting experiences but living rooted in the present world. The other danger is that I will be a settler and not a sojourner, that my deepest loyalties will not be to God's kingdom but my own. We are in danger of destination confusion, forgetting that we are called to live as travelers and not as settlers. Christ-followers are to be defined by our ultimate destination, not our present location. So we live "as aliens and strangers in the world" (1 Peter 2:11), surrounded by an alien culture, with its alien values and alien loyalties. Our calling is to live in such a way that our relation to our God determines our relationships and our responsibility to those around us.

Faith Resolutely Holds on to God's Promise

As the writer of Hebrews says: "By faith Abraham, even though he was past age—and Sarah herself was barren—was enabled to become a father because he considered him faithful who had made the promise." If God's call of Abraham pushed him out of his comfort zone and God's dealings with Abraham put him in the waiting room, now, as it were, Abraham found himself in the doctor's office. God had promised a son, indeed a people. But, as the years went by, Sarah and Abraham were still childless. There were no fertility clinics in the ancient world to inform them that their suspicions were correct, that Sarah was incapable of bearing children. We are told this the first time Sarah is introduced in the Bible: "Sarai was barren; she had no children" (Genesis 11:30). But time had made their suspicions certain. Both of them were well past the age of having children. As Paul bluntly describes their medical condition: "Abraham faced the fact that his body was as good as dead—since he was a hundred years old—and that Sarah's womb was also dead" (Romans 4:19). Their biological clocks had run out. The problem was that their undeniable reality collided head-on with God's undeniable promise, stated most directly in Genesis 17:19: "Your wife Sarah will bear you a son, and you will call him Isaac."

Faith is not wishful thinking. Neither is it a stubborn refusal to face the facts. Faith is following God's clear leading and acting upon God's clear promise. I love Paul's description in Romans 4:18–21:

> Against all hope, Abraham in hope believed and so became the father of many nations, just as it had been said to him, "So shall your offspring be."
>
> Without weakening in his faith, he faced the fact that his body was as good as dead—since he was about a hundred years old—and that Sarah's womb was also dead. Yet he did not waver through unbelief regarding the promise of God, but was strengthened in his faith and gave glory to God, being fully persuaded that God had power to do what he had promised.

The writer of Hebrews puts it like this: "He considered him faithful who had made the promise." We are not told much about the psychology of faith. The Old Testament makes it clear that trusting God for a son was a struggle for Abraham and Sarah, and they made unwise and foolish choices along the way. But God graciously overlooks the struggles of faith to focus on the end result. Abraham chose to believe God and was strengthened in his faith, and the reason must be that he chose to concentrate his attention not on his faith but on God and His faithfulness. He trusted God's promises, made in His spoken word, and he nurtured his soul on the trail of God's gracious interventions in his life. As a result, God honored their faith: "And so from this one man, and he as good as dead, came descendants as numerous as the stars in the sky and as countless as the sand on the seashore." It has been said that faith is seeing the invisible, believing the incredible, and receiving the impossible. To the extent that that description is helpful, no one illustrates it more completely than Abraham.

As we have said, faith is a muscle. We strengthen it only as we test it by stepping out in what feels like risk-filled acts, as we follow God. *The essence of faith is not engaging in risk but in following God's clear leading and acting on His sure promise.* We strengthen faith not by focusing subjectively on our faith but by filling our hearts and minds with thoughts of God that are worthy of Him.

Hebrews 11 is a wonderful account of the biblical heroes of faith. But down through the centuries, millions more have followed that path. That is why I love to read the accounts of men and women who have shown what it means to trust God in their time and place. One of those people is the great missionary leader of the nineteenth century, Hudson Taylor. The Lord used him to begin missionary work in unreached areas of China, pioneering efforts that are bearing remarkable fruit long after Taylor entered "the city whose architect and builder is God." He was a man who knew how to be strengthened in his faith, but it came out of a struggle to grow in faith:

> Want of trust is at the root of almost all our sins and all our weaknesses; and how shall we escape from it, but by looking to Him, and observing His faithfulness? As the light which shines from the dark waters of the lake is the reflection of the sun's rays, so man's faith is the impress and reflection of God's faithfulness.
>
> The man who holds God's faithfulness will not be reckless

or foolhardy, but he will be ready for every emergency. The man who holds God's faithfulness will dare to obey Him, however impolitic it may appear.

All God's giants have been weak men, who did great things for God because they reckoned on God being with them. Oh! beloved friends, if there is a living God, faithful and true, let us hold His faithfulness. Holding His faithfulness, we may go into every province of China. Holding His faithfulness, we may face, with calm and sober but confident assurance of victory, every difficulty and danger. Let us not give Him a partial trust, but daily, hourly, serve Him, holding God's faithfulness.[3]

Faith is the God-centered conviction that a good and gracious God will not lead us astray and that He will keep His promises. God kindly looks beyond the weaknesses of Abraham—his failures, fears, and false starts—to honor him as a man of faith.

Faith nearly always begins for us where it began for Abraham, with a call to leave our comfort zone, following God's clear leading. "Leave," says the Lord. "Put me to the test and trust me." And faith sometimes lands us in the waiting room, struggling to accept not only God's will but also God's timing. But faith endures. It refuses to take shortcuts, knowing that our real destination is eternal, not temporal. And then it may land us in the doctor's office, confronting us with the fact that there seems to be no earthly way to receive what God has promised. At such times, the living God calls us to believe that what men pronounce dead, He can make alive. In all of these things, our travel guide Abraham would tell us that we can have confidence in a faithful God.

And the bottom line is this: What you believe and know about God will determine how much you trust Him.

Chapter Twelve

HOMEWARD BOUND

t is amazing how quickly we become used to events that were once viewed as extraordinary. *Apollo 13* was only the third manned mission to the moon, but the media was paying it little attention. The first two missions had gone off flawlessly, and this one was viewed as rather routine. That all changed in an instant. At 10:07, eastern standard time, on the evening of Monday, April 13, 1970, fifty-six hours into the mission, astronaut Jack Swigert's voice suddenly brought all other activity at Mission Control in Houston to an abrupt halt. "OK Houston, we've had a problem here." The controllers radioed back, "This is Houston. Say again, please." This time it was the voice of Jim Lovell, "Houston, we've had a problem."

Did they ever! An oxygen tank had exploded, setting in motion a catastrophic chain of events. The astronauts were in deep trouble. The supplies of water, oxygen, and power were quickly reaching critical levels, and the astronauts were now in a disabled spacecraft, 203,980 miles from earth. The mission had suddenly changed. A safe lunar landing was out of the question. The only goal now was survival, bringing the three astronauts home alive. Even that seemed impossible. Engineers calculated that there was not enough power to complete the journey.

The scramble to save *Apollo 13* demanded the focused skills, inventiveness, and energies of America's finest space scientists, as well as the skills, inventiveness, and determination of the astronauts themselves. Two moments were especially critical, and both involved navigation. The first required a five-minute rocket burn (263 seconds precisely) to change their trajectory back to Earth. By doing so, they would take hours off the return trip, and by now minutes were precious. The problem was that when they attempted to align themselves to acquire the proper navigational heading from the stars, they could not, because sunlight was sparkling off the debris being vented from the spacecraft, making it impossible to see the stars. Scientists at Mission Control quickly did calculations. The commander, Jim Lovell, was instructed to align his optical telescope so that the sun would be in a corner of his field of vision, allowing him to acquire approximately the correct angle. The rockets were fired with great anxiety, but the maneuver was successful.

Twenty-six hours later came an even more perilous moment. Houston control calculated that the command module needed to make another rocket burn, this time for fourteen-seconds. This was a critical moment because it would determine the angle of reentry. If they erred and had too shallow an angle, the module would skip off the atmosphere and be lost in space. If the angle was too severe, the spacecraft might burn up with the heat of reentry, and there was already concern about the condition of the capsule's protective shields. But the accident had rendered the required navigational devices inoperable. The only hope was what Houston admitted was "a last-ditch procedure." Lovell needed to center the earth in his window, with the cross hairs of his optical sight pointed at the terminator line—the twilight line where day gives way to night. Lovell remembers aligning everything carefully, then turning to Swigert and saying, "I hope the guys in the backroom who thought this up know what they're doing," and then pushing the button. Later, Lovell tried to read notes he had made at the time and discovered he couldn't decipher a single word. It was a time of tremendous stress.[1]

The movie *Apollo 13* captures this dramatic moment, as the earth fills the window of the tiny space module. Watching it, we feel something of Lovell's anxiety as he prepares to fire the rockets in a life-and-death act. The burn was a success, and *Apollo 13* splashed safely into the Pacific, with each of the astronauts alive and grateful.

To get safely home, the crew of *Apollo 13* needed to keep their destination in the cross hairs of their vision. The same truth applies to Christ-followers. As people of faith, we need to keep our spiritual eyes focused on our destination. While that may involve some earthly destination points, faith causes us to lift our eyes to our eternal destination, the city of God. In the last chapter, we talked about destination confusion, the danger of living as though our present location is our intended destination. When we do that, we cease to live as pilgrims and start to become settlers.

This is an issue of great importance to the writer of Hebrews. The people to whom he was writing had come under intense persecution. If their present location was also their final destination, it made no sense to endure persecution. The same is true for us. If this world is all there is, why put up with suffering and hardship? But if this is not our final destination, if there is a city whose architect and builder is God, then endurance is not only possible but also wise.

Questions about heaven are not theoretical and impractical. What we believe about heaven determines the way we live today. What is our true destination? If that isn't clear, we will not only waste time; we may well waste our lives.

That is why the writer of Hebrews interrupts his account of the lives of the faithful to engage in some destination thinking. The heroes of faith knew where they were going, and it wasn't a physical location on earth. A vision of the eternal city filled their navigational sights, and they steered their lives toward it. So in Hebrews 11:13–16, the writer directs our attention to the heavenly country and urges us to join Abraham and the others as pilgrims headed for the city of God, and not to be merely tourists enjoying the sights here on earth. Some might say that earlier generations of Christians were so heavenly minded that they were no earthly good, but I doubt that was ever really so. C. S. Lewis is far closer to the truth when he writes:

> If you read history you will find that the Christians who did most for the present world were just those who thought most of the next. The Apostles themselves, who set on foot the conversion of the Roman Empire, the great men who built up the Middle Ages, the English Evangelicals who abolished the slave trade, all left their mark on Earth, precisely because their minds were occupied with Heaven. It is since Christians have largely ceased to think of the other world that they have become so ineffective in this. Aim at heaven and you will get earth "thrown in": aim at earth and you will get neither.[2]

That is precisely the problem of modern Western Christians. We think about heaven far too little. We desperately need to hear the message of the heroes of faith: that the most successful way to live life is to have clearly and continually in mind what lies beyond life.

> All these people were still living by faith when they died. They did not receive the things promised; they only saw them and welcomed them from a distance. And they admitted that they

were aliens and strangers on earth. People who say such things show that they are looking for a country of their own. If they had been thinking of the country they had left, they would have had opportunity to return. Instead, they were longing for a better country—a heavenly one. Therefore God is not ashamed to be called their God, for he has prepared a city for them. (Hebrews 11:13–16)

Several years ago, our friend Miriam Bundy found herself fighting a battle against a particularly virulent form of cancer. She was a wife and mother who loved life, loved her husband, and loved her children, who were entering their adult years. She had no desire to leave them. At the same time, she was a woman of faith who was determined to honor God through all that she encountered. She committed herself, as she put it, "to be sure that the big C" in her life was not cancer but Christ. The road was not an easy one, and she has written about it in *Restoring the Soul*.[3]

I remember being with Stuart and the children, waiting for news, during one of the surgical procedures she endured. I remember the insensitivity with which the surgeon blurted out the news: "The surgery was successful—but you know she's going to die of this." He was right, but the way he delivered the news was harsh and unfeeling. As Stuart wrestled with the impending loss of his wife, a friend told him, "Imagine death as a lion. We hear him roaring through the forests of life, and sometimes in the death of a friend we see his shadow. Then, one day the leaves part, and the lion of death steps out of the forest and we see his face for the first time. Life is never the same after that encounter."[4]

Death is the final, and ultimate, test of faith. Yet it is one we rarely speak about. On her seventy-ninth birthday, two years before her death in 1989, the actress Bette Davis appeared on the *Today* show. "I'm really curious about how I will go and what will happen," she said.

"But my friends don't like it when I talk about it. 'Don't talk about it,' they say. 'We don't want to hear about it.'" But, like it or not, death is inevitable. Wise people don't spend much time thinking about how they will go. That is usually beyond our knowledge or control. They do, however, spend a lot of time thinking about where they will go, and the knowledge of their final destination determines many of their present choices.

The people to whom the book of Hebrews was first written were paying a high price for following Christ. It was true that none of them had paid the highest price: "You have not yet resisted to the point of shedding your blood" (Hebrews 12:4). But it was very possible that such a day would come, as it did for many Christ-followers in the first century, as it does for many of our brothers and sisters in the twenty-first century. Probably few who read these pages will face the possibility of martyrdom, but all of us need to recognize that our view of death determines our view of life. If we see death in terms of loss, we will flee from it and fear it. If we see death in terms of ultimate gain, we will not seek it, but neither will we dread it. Death is an enemy, and Christians grieve the loss of those they love. But it is a conquered enemy, and the risen Lord Jesus has made it different.

FAITH ENABLES US TO FACE THE FACT OF DEATH

The statement of Hebrews 11:13 is direct and unvarnished: "All these people were still living by faith when they died. They did not receive the things promised." The original Greek text is even more terse: "In accordance with faith, these all died, not having received the promises." This reflects the disappointment that Abraham must have felt. He had received a portion of the promise. He had held the promised son Isaac in his arms and watched him grow. But so many of God's promises remained visible only to the eyes of faith. There was no land that belonged to him, no nation that sprang from him, as death drew near.

Faith does not exempt us from death. Faith does not mean that we do not experience the effects of living in fallen bodies in a fallen world. People of faith die of old age; they also die of cancer and car accidents and senseless acts of violence. Faith does not exempt us from the fact of death, the pain of dying, fears about death, or the loss and grief of those left behind. "In faith, these all died."

The Bible tells us that, because of sin, death is the universal experience of human beings. This does not mean that there is a direct connection between our individual sins and death—that we die because of this specific sin or that particular act. God graciously postpones His judgment on our sins. But it remains true that "the wages of sin is death" (Romans 6:23). Sin has unleashed death in the world, and no one, rich or poor, famous or obscure, can escape it. Death is God's limit on creatures who believed the deceiver's lie and defiantly said, "We will be like God" (Genesis 3:5). Every time a person dies, we should be reminded that we are not like God, that we stand in need of what He alone can give us. So death remains the lion, the enemy, attacking us and cutting short our hopes and dreams. The Bible is intensely realistic about death. It refuses to indulge in sentiment and romantic speculation. There is no cure for death. At best, modern medicine with its amazing achievements can bring about postponement. But there is no avoidance: "these all died."

Faith may not change the certainty of death, but it does transform the experience of death. We are told of Abraham, "Abraham breathed his last and died at a good old age, an old man and full of years" (Genesis 25:8). The New American Standard Bible renders it, "an old man and satisfied with life." What a wonderful epitaph, "old and satisfied." As John Wesley once said, "Our people die well."

The greatest description of the way in which faith transforms death for the believer is found in the words of Paul in Philippians 1:21–24: "For to me, to live is Christ and to die is gain. If I am to go on living in the body, this will mean fruitful labor for me. Yet what shall I choose? I do not know! I am torn between the two: I desire to depart and be with Christ, which is better by far; but it is more necessary for you that I remain in the body." As he wrote, Paul was under house arrest in Rome, about to face the increasingly insane and evil emperor Nero, who eventually sentenced him and many other Christ-followers to brutal death. Paul's cause was just, and his legal treatment had been a travesty of justice. But his words are utterly lacking in self-pity, bitterness, escapism, fear, or denial. He tells us three things about death that are true for every Christ-follower.

First, death is a departure: "I have a desire to depart." "Depart" is elsewhere used to describe a ship weighing anchor as it begins its journey home or an army striking camp to begin its homeward march. Death, through the eyes of faith, is not a destination but a departure. It is not a termination but a terminal through which we pass on our journey. The early Christians used three symbols, which they scratched on the walls of the catacombs of ancient Rome. The most common was the fish, which spoke of Christ. Another was the dove, which symbolized the Holy Spirit. The third was an anchor representing our hope of heaven. Hebrews 6:19 describes our hope in Christ as "an anchor for the soul." Ancient ships were often pulled into harbor on their anchors. In the same way, Christ has entered into heaven, and He pulls us into His presence.

Second, death is fellowship with Christ. The believer's hope is that he or she will "depart and be with Christ." Death means not only spiritual presence with Christ but also personal fellowship with Him. There is no absorption into the cosmos in an impersonal existence or entrance into a state of unconsciousness or soul-sleep. To be away from the body is to be "at home with the Lord" (2 Corinthians 5:8).

Third, for the believer death is gain. The Spirit graciously draws a veil over the details of heaven, recognizing that such knowledge is beyond our comprehension.

In 1988, when I lived in Calgary, the Winter Olympics were held there. However, during part of the games, I was in Africa, in Liberia and Ghana. Some Africans asked me to explain things like skiing and skating, which they had briefly seen on television. How do you explain snow to someone who has never seen snow or ice, to someone who lives just north of the equator? Even if they understood my words, they had no way to share my experience of shoveling my driveway when it was 25 degrees below zero. (I can't even explain that to friends who grew up in California.) If it is impossible to explain a Canadian winter to an African, how much more difficult to describe God's city to people who have experienced only earth? How could we possibly understand the blessings that God has for us? But imagine it as you will, it is "better by far." "Blessed are the dead who die in the Lord!" (Revelation 14:13). As George MacDonald once said, "If we knew as much about heaven as God does, we would clap every time a Christian died!"

Faith Causes Us to Live in This World With a Homesickness for God's City

I do not remember being homesick very often in my life. The only two times that immediately come to mind involve being separated from my wife, Elizabeth: once when I was falling in love with her, and the other when I left to study at seminary a few days after becoming engaged to her. I had a longing in my heart and a feeling of incompleteness that no words could express. It wasn't a place I missed but a person. My body was one place, but my heart was another. The writer tells us that faith is a kind of homesickness for heaven, a place we have never seen and never been.

Faith sees the promise of heaven. "They did not receive the things promised; they only saw them and welcomed them from a distance." The city of God was not a mirage. These faithful were so certain that God would keep His promise that they saw the city and welcomed it in their hearts. The word *only* isn't in the original language. It reads, "They saw them." Through the eyes of faith, God's promises were as real to them as anything that was on their horizon. There are things we will not see or receive this side of heaven, but, by faith, we see what God has given us.

Faith seeks the values of heaven. "And they admitted that they were aliens and strangers on earth. People who say such things show that they are looking for a country of their own." Two things need to be observed about the translation here. First, the statement that "they admitted they were aliens" is misleading. It sounds apologetic. A better translation is, "they confessed they were aliens." They were making a bold declaration about their God-given status. Second, to say that "they were looking for a country" is also weaker than the original suggests. In fact, they were "seeking for a country," an indication that their attitude was one of determination and dedication. They were eagerly desiring and moving toward God's city. In Hebrews 11:16, the idea is reinforced: "They were longing for a better country," which describes an intense inner desire to lay hold of what only God can give. In the heart of faith, there is a kind of homing instinct for the eternal city.

In Genesis 23:4 we learn that Abraham approached a local tribe that owned land in the area: "I am an alien and a stranger among you," he said. "Sell me some property for a burial site here so I can bury my dead." The people responded that Abraham was a mighty prince and could use any burial site he desired. Abraham, however, insisted on purchasing land. There is more here than legal and civic niceties. Abraham was convinced that the land was his by God's promise and would be received from God's hand in God's way at God's time. But he was not a citizen of

Canaan. He was "an alien and a stranger." This is a part of the text that I can identify with. Elizabeth and I are in the process of taking American citizenship. For a number of years we have lived in the United States as resident aliens. We have rights and privileges in our country and also in the United States, but when I cross the border, or at election time, I am reminded that I do not have the rights, privileges, and responsibilities of a citizen. It is also possible that under certain circumstances, my loyalties and values would differ. Since we are not yet citizens, we are foreigners, living away from our "home and native land."

The differences between Canadians and Americans are minor (I've probably offended both sides of the border with that comment). If you didn't know my nationality, you might detect it only when I say certain words in a different (and correct!) way, or when I talk about places I have lived in my homeland. But people of faith are spiritual aliens and strangers, and the differences between us and the world around us are immense. We swear loyalty to another King; we owe allegiance to another kingdom; we have a commitment to other values. We have a country of our own and a city whose architect and builder is God. As citizens of heaven, we must resist absorption and assimilation into the culture of the world that surrounds us. We take our values from our homeland. Malcolm Muggeridge has some wise words on the subject: "The only ultimate disaster that can befall us, I have come to realize, is to feel ourselves to be at home here on earth. As long as we are aliens, we cannot forget our true homeland."[5]

Faith receives the approval of God. "Therefore God is not ashamed to be called their God, for he has prepared a city for them." It is an amazing thing that the God of the universe chooses to identify himself by His connection with sinful but believing human beings. "I am the God of Abraham, Isaac and Jacob."

My wife serves as national director of Women's Ministries for the

Evangelical Free Church. This means that she travels around the country and is well known to many people whom I have never met. I find myself known as Elizabeth Inrig's husband. Believe me, my wife is a woman of such wonderful attributes and gifts that it is a privilege to be known as her husband. People always think more highly of me when they meet her! Obviously I would feel differently about being known as Elizabeth's husband if her name brought instant recognition of some notorious behavior.

Often someone will introduce themselves to us with the comment, "I'm a friend of person X." Whether you want to or not, you will make a judgment about that individual on the basis of person X. There is reputation by association. That is what makes it so remarkable that the God of glory so often chooses to identify himself with people whose lives are full of obvious flaws. When He describes himself as "the God of Abraham," He is not merely saying, "I am God over Abraham." That is obviously true. Rather, He is saying something like this: "Do you know Abraham? Well, I'm His God!" "You know Jacob? Well, I'm His God." And even today He identifies with His people. "Do you know Gary Inrig? He trusts in my Son. I'm His God, and He's my child." He is not ashamed to be called our God, because His heart goes out in gracious love to men and women of faith. Furthermore, the statement "he is not ashamed to be called their God" is a kind of understatement. He is saying that He is delighted to be called their God, such is His gracious identification with His people. There may also be a challenge to us here—not to be ashamed of Him!

God is not only not ashamed of people of faith but He also "has prepared a city for them." This is the last of a series of descriptions of heaven. It is "a city with foundations, whose architect and builder is God"; "a country of their own"; "a better country, a heavenly one"; "a city for them." It is worth taking time to reflect on that home.

FAITH WILL BRING US HOME AT LAST

Heaven is the place where God fully reveals His character and blessing. Often in Scripture, heaven is described as a city. In Hebrews 12:22, we read of "Mount Zion, the heavenly Jerusalem, the city of the living God." In Revelation 21:2, it is "the Holy City, the new Jerusalem." In the ancient world, to live in the city where the king resided was an immense privilege. The king's presence gave a city special glory. John goes one step further, writing that this city is "prepared as a bride beautifully dressed for her husband" (Revelation 21:2). I have been the father of the bride twice. I know how much cost and care and love go into that moment when the groom sees his bride in all her wedding-day finery. That is the picture the Lord chooses to describe His preparation of His place for His people.

We are given other pictures of God's home. In the familiar words of John 14, heaven is the Father's house, a family mansion resplendent with places prepared for each member of the family. We will live in the King's palace, as close as possible to the Lord. There have been scandals associated with the price some people are willing to pay to sleep for one night in the White House. God's children are given free eternal residence in the palace of the King of kings. We are also told that heaven is Paradise, a word borrowed from the Persians to describe a royal garden or park, a place of extravagant beauty. These images and others combine to tell us that although heaven is ultimately beyond our comprehension, it is delightful beyond imagining. It is the place where God reveals himself in His goodness, without restraint. It isn't merely a state. It is the place where God rules in His majestic glory. I love the description of Psalm 16:11: "In Your presence there is fullness of joy; in Your right hand there are pleasures forevermore" (NASB).

Heaven is the place where the God of glory fully reveals himself in blessing. He is present in all creation, the all-present God, but heaven is His dwelling place, where He pours forth His glory in unrestrained measure. And we will be there in answer to our Savior's prayer: "Father, I want those you have given me to be with me where I am, and to see my glory" (John 17:24).

Heaven is the place where God makes us completely new. At the heart of John's description of the heavenly city is the divine declaration: "I am making everything new!" We will be made physically new at the rapture, when we receive our resurrection bodies, perfectly suited for life in God's city (1 Corinthians 15:50–57). We will be made morally new when we see the Lord Jesus as He is and are made like Him (1 John 3:2). We will no longer struggle with sin and temptation and failure. We will be perfected in holiness. We will also be made spiritually new when, in His presence, the words of Revelation 21:3–4 come to pass: "Now the dwelling of God is with men, and he will live with them. They will be his people, and God himself will be with them and be their God. He will wipe every tear from their eyes. There will be no more death or mourning or crying or pain, for the old order of things has passed away." We will be made personally new when all the limitations of our fallenness are removed: "Therefore, they are before the throne of God and serve him day and night in his temple; and he who sits on the throne will spread his tent over them. Never again will they hunger; never again will they thirst. The sun will not beat upon them, nor any scorching heat. For the Lamb at the center of the throne will be their shepherd; he will lead them to springs of living water. And God will wipe away every tear from their eyes" (Revelation 7:15–17).

Heaven is the place where we realize our destiny as God's people. We are told little about all that we will do in heaven, but we can be sure of some things. Above all else, we will worship in the presence of God. Every glimpse we have of heaven reveals the creatures of God of every kind pouring out their praise and adoration in unhindered ways in His presence, as they respond in awe to His glory and majesty. At the heart of all true worship is delight in God. In heaven, purged of the things that hinder our capacity to delight in God, our worship will be unrestrained. The goal of worship is the greater glorification of God by His creatures, and God is most truly glorified when He is most deeply enjoyed. In heaven, our capacity for enjoyment will be unrestrained. As A. W. Tozer properly observed, "I believe that the reverential fear of God, mixed with love and fascination and astonishment and adoration and devotion is the most enjoyable state and the most purifying emotion the human heart can know."[6] John Calvin was also correct when he stated that "The proper adoration of God is the prime purpose of Christianity."

People of faith are worshipers. As Abraham moves through the land, everywhere he builds altars. In heaven, our worship will reach new depths of conviction and new heights of praise. But heaven merely increases our capacity to do what we are called to do here and now. "I can safely say, on the authority of all that is revealed in the Word of God," said Tozer, "that every man or woman on this earth who is bored and put off by worship is not ready for heaven."[7]

Heaven is also a place of fellowship with God and one another. The essence of our experience in heaven is our relation to our triune God: "Now the dwelling of God is with men, and he will live with them. They will be his people, and God himself will be with them and be their God" (Revelation 21:3). When the perfect time comes, I will "see face to face" and "know fully, even as I am known" (1 Corinthians 13:12). I will always be a creature before an infinite God. Yet the Bible indicates that I will have a deeply enhanced capacity to experience God, up close and personal. "The Lamb at the center of the throne will be their shepherd; he will lead them to springs of living water" (Revelation 7:17). "They will see his face, and his name shall be on their foreheads" (Revelation 22:4). At the same time, we will be capable of relationships with one another free of all the effects of sin. We will know ourselves and feel no need to hide. We will know others and find no reason to condemn.

Heaven is a place of service. The picture of people sitting on clouds endlessly plucking on harps mocks the wonder of God's intention for His people. So does the idea that heaven is a place of unending rest and relaxation. We were made with a need for meaningful activity. Heaven will provide abundant opportunities to fulfill that need. "They are before the throne of God, and serve him day and night in his temple" (Revelation 7:15). "The throne of God and the Lamb will be in the city, and his servants shall serve him" (Revelation 22:3). There is little value in speculating about exactly what we will do to serve our God. We can be certain, however, that it will be significant, fulfilling, and meaningful. As least some of our service involves reigning under the authority of King Jesus. "You have made them to be a kingdom and priests to serve our God, and they will reign on the earth" (Revelation 5:10). "And they will reign for ever and ever" (Revelation 22:5).

Leighton Ford's son Sandy died suddenly as a young man. He was a committed Christ-follower whose life was making a difference for many others. On hearing the news, a missionary friend wrote the Fords to say, "I thought, 'What a waste!' But then I thought—we're so earthbound. Sandy's highest service has just begun." Somehow that will be true for every believer.

Heaven is a place of rest and reward. Revelation 14:13 lifts a veil on eternity with these words: "Then I heard a voice from heaven say, 'Write: Blessed are the dead who die in the Lord from now on.' 'Yes,' says the Spirit, 'they will rest from their labor, for their deeds will follow them.'" I think heavenly rest isn't so much about stopping activity as reaching our intended goal, the kind of rest God knew when He completed His work of creation. Whatever our service in heaven, it will not be experienced as toilsome labor but as rest and blessing. Heaven will be a time when our gracious Lord receives us into His presence and rewards us for our earthly service to Him (1 Corinthians 3:12–15).

Heaven will also be a place of glorification. That is to say, we will become all that we were created to be. "He will transform our lowly bodies so that they will be like his glorious body" (Philippians 3:21). "When Christ, who is your life, appears, then you also will appear with him in glory" (Colossians 3:4).

In 1967, the former president of Wheaton College, V. Raymond Edman, was speaking in chapel at the college. He was a much-loved and respected leader, becoming weaker with age, and the chapel was full to hear his message. He began to speak about coming into the presence of God and the need for a sense of reverence and worship. To illustrate his point, he described a time when he was invited to meet Haile Selassie, the man who was then the emperor of Ethiopia. Edman described how he carefully prepared for the occasion and the excitement he felt as he walked into the palace to meet the emperor. He told of the moment when he entered the royal presence and the respect he felt as he bowed before Emperor Selassie. At that point in his sermon, Edman paused, did a slow half-turn, and then collapsed, dead.

Dr. Edman was talking about being in the presence of an earthly king, and suddenly he was in the presence of his eternal King. What a way to go!

Our departure from this world will not likely be as dramatic, but our entrance into heaven will be every bit as glorious. For we are headed for the city whose architect and builder is God, and for an audience with the triune God.

It is important enough for us to think deeply about the nature of our hope and the certainty of our home that the writer of Hebrews has interrupted his account of the life of Abraham to direct our attention away from this world to the heavenly city. The men and women of faith were gripped by the hope of eternity, and that hope enabled them to exert a profound influence on our world.

When Ronald Reagan was president, George Schultz served as his Secretary of State. One of Schultz's duties was to appoint ambassadors to foreign nations. When the new ambassadors had an interview with him, he would test them by pointing out a large globe in the corner of his office. "Show me your country," he would say. They would go over, spin the globe, and put their finger on the country to which they were being sent.

When Mike Mansfield, a long-time senator, was appointed ambassador to Japan, even he was given Schultz's test. He, however, spun the globe and put his finger on the United States. "That's my country," he said.

From that time on, Schultz did the same test with a different ending. After the new ambassador pointed out his country, Schultz would tell the story of Mike Mansfield. Then he would tell the new appointee, "Don't forget that you may be in that country, but your country is the United States. You are there to represent us. Take care of our interests and never forget which country is your country."

The great secret of the great heroes of faith was that they never forgot their true country. They lived for God's country, and so must we.

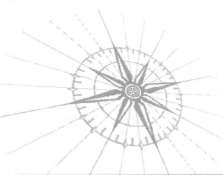

Chapter Thirteen

STRESS TEST

The America's Cup is the most coveted trophy in sailing. Every few years, syndicates from around the world spend huge amounts of money to win the right to be called the world champion. In November 1999, fifteen boats from ten countries were competing in the challenge round near Auckland, New Zealand, for the right to be the official challenger to the defending champion, New Zealand.

One of the American candidates was the entrant of the New York Yacht Club, the group that for most of the twentieth century dominated the America's Cup. They had spent more than forty million dollars to regain the trophy they felt was rightly theirs. Their boat, *Young America*, was competing against a Japanese boat in very difficult conditions. Racing through twenty-knot winds and heavy seas, the boat launched itself off a six-foot wave and slammed directly into a second one of the same size. Although the boat was designed by the most respected of naval architects and cost more than four million dollars, the hull cracked, and the boat began to take on water. The sheer force of the collision caused the deck to crumple, and the sailors had to scramble overboard for their

217

own safety. Skipper Ed Baird observed, "The boat wasn't strong enough for the conditions we had. We hit a steep set of waves at the wrong time."[1]

Some years earlier, on March 5, 1995, a state-of-the-art boat from Australia, *oneAustralia*, had met a similar fate in another America's Cup trial. That boat had folded in the middle and sunk almost instantly.

Two boats, designed by the most gifted of designers, containing the most advanced technology, and sailed by the most expert of sailors, had failed under racing conditions. It wasn't for lack of money or testing. There is such a fine line between speed and strength in these competitions that designers work with very close margins. They test with computer models, with simulations, and with test races, but none of those are the same as real-life conditions. One designer commented on this:

> It is relatively straightforward to design a structure to withstand a known set of loads. We test under realistic sailing conditions, but there are unforeseen conditions. The safety margin is as small as considered prudent. On the other hand, it is not possible or desirable to test to destruction, so generally the finished product is not tested beyond expected design conditions. There is a fine line between squeezing maximum performance out of the design and spectacular failure.[2]

Young America and *oneAustralia* managed to cross the line in spectacular fashion!

Real-life conditions are never quite the same as even the most sophisticated and expert predictions. No matter how advanced the theoretical models or how careful the preparations and practice runs, real life is different. The waves come from an unexpected angle; the winds gust in unprecedented ways; the elements converge in novel fashion. Reality has a way of catching us by surprise.

Sailing school is valuable. It first teaches us to sail in carefully controlled conditions or in a protected harbor and then prepares us for more difficult challenges. But racing day is entirely different. When your competitor is trying to take your line and to steal your wind, in the midst of rough water, steep waves, and strong winds, nothing is quite the same. When decisions have to be made in split seconds and there is no opportunity to reflect or consult, the pressures and stresses mount. That's when you discover whether or not you've got the stuff that makes a champion.

Life is like that. A Christ-follower doesn't face a stress test sitting in a service on Sunday morning, surrounded by like-minded people, affirming great and certain truths. Nor is a stress test usually found within insight-filled classrooms or in the fellowship of a small group. But Christ-followers are called to a real-world faith lived out in the open ocean of daily life, facing difficult choices, intense pressures, deep suffering, unfair treatment, and enticing temptations. It is then that we encounter the ultimate stress test, when we sail determinedly on or break and sink under the strain.

Hebrews 11:17–22 engages us with its account of a man under the most intense of tests, one engineered by God. The best of coaches will put the best of his athletes through the toughest conditioning and training program. He will stretch their limits to the extreme to help them reach beyond the norm to the extraordinary. Abraham is the great champion of faith, but God tested him in a way He tested no one else, to give a lasting vision of faith at its highest.

The story of Abraham and Isaac is full of mystery, but it also forces us to ask some hard questions about ourselves.

> By faith Abraham, when God tested him, offered Isaac as a sacrifice. He who had received the promises was about to sacrifice his one and only son, even though God had said to him, "It is

through Isaac that your offspring will be reckoned." Abraham
reasoned that God could raise the dead, and figuratively speaking, he did receive Isaac back from death.

By faith Isaac blessed Jacob and Esau in regard to their future.

By faith Jacob, when he was dying, blessed each of Joseph's
sons, and worshiped as he leaned on the top of his staff.

By faith Joseph, when his end was near, spoke about the exodus of the Israelites from Egypt and gave instructions about his
bones.

In reading this chapter, we continually need to return to the key verse,
Hebrew 11:6: "Without faith, it is impossible to please God." That means
that one of the Lord's highest priorities is to strengthen and to deepen
our faith. Abraham's whole life was an adventure in faith-building. The
call of God began his spiritual experience, a call that pulled him out of
his comfort zone and led him to spend his life awaiting the fulfillment
of God's promises. He fixed his eyes on God's city, a vision of life that
enabled him first to endure the delay of God's promise and then to face
its impossibility because of age and infertility.

But God is faithful, and there came a time when the
one-hundred-year-old Abraham held his newborn son, Isaac, in his arms.
At that moment, Abraham had no way of knowing that his toughest
challenge was still ahead. In fact, his biggest test came toward the end
of his life.

When I was younger, I convinced myself that I was fighting my toughest battles—issues of life direction, moral convictions, and a life partner.
Those *were* life-shaping issues. My mistake was to imagine that when
these were behind me, I could coast home. Since then, I have seen too
many who have not finished well. You encounter midlife, and you face
the test of values and morals; you lose your partner, and you face the

battle of loneliness; you lose your health, and you confront the test of sickness; you end your career, and you face the test of retirement; you cash in your investments, and you fight the battle of affluence. Abraham was to learn that his later years would not involve a downhill walk but a climb up the hardest mountain he would ever encounter.

Abraham's test came without warning. We are told nothing of the specific events that immediately preceded the moment that Abraham heard the most astonishing words he would ever hear from his God. "Abraham!" "Here I am." "Take your son, your only son, Isaac, whom you love, and go to the region of Moriah. Sacrifice him there as a burnt offering on one of the mountains that I will tell you about" (Genesis 22:1–2). With those words, Abraham's world collapsed and he found himself on the most incredible journey of his life. He was learning in the most extreme of ways a fundamental truth.

FAITH IS REFINED IN THE CRUCIBLE OF TESTING

Every phrase of God's instructions must have felt like a dagger in the heart of Abraham. "Take your son . . . your only son . . . Isaac . . . whom you love." There could be no doubt about God's intention. His instructions were not open to interpretation. They were not the product of Abraham's imagination. God was asking him to do the unthinkable: not only to offer a human sacrifice, not only to execute his only son, but also to kill the promise. Hebrews tells us that God was testing Abraham, and what a test it was!

God's command must have seemed unthinkable. On the most basic level, it contradicted Abraham's natural instincts as a father. Only a person who is fundamentally evil or someone who is deeply disturbed would think of taking the life of a beloved son. Abraham was neither. On a deeper level, God's command violated all of Abraham's spiritual instincts. This wasn't the God he had come to know. Abraham lived in a world where pagan gods demanded such evil acts. But the God who had called him from Ur was unlike any such beings. He was a God of grace and goodness who abhorred human sacrifices. The God Abraham knew was the God who would not destroy Sodom and Gomorrah if there were even ten righteous people. This command seemed out of character with all that he knew of God.

Furthermore, God's order contradicted the promise He had made to Abraham. God had promised that from Abraham would come a great nation and that Isaac was the one through whom this promise would be realized. Yahweh could not have been more explicit: "It is through Isaac that your offspring will be reckoned" (Genesis 21:12). If God is faithful and true, how could He be calling Abraham to take a knife to the throat of His promise? This wasn't just about Isaac; it was about God. This command seemed to make a mockery of Abraham's life. Everything he had done, he had done because he had believed in and acted upon the promise of God. Now his God was asking him to destroy that promise. However you looked at it, this seemed to be wrong. How could he obey such a command?

Abraham's test is unique. God never again asked a human being to do such a thing. We realize, from our perspective, that God never had any intention of letting Abraham go through with it. But there are times in our lives that the Lord puts His finger on something that is infinitely precious to us and asks us to put it on an altar. There are times when God's Word is clear, and it goes against our natural instincts. "Let go of that relationship and face a lonely future as a single person?" "Encourage my child to go as a missionary and miss the opportunity to enjoy my grandchildren as they grow up?" "Use this money for that project when I had intended it for this good purpose?" The call comes in a variety of ways, but the Lord summons us to trust Him more than we trust our instincts.

Faith sometimes calls us to place our future on the altar and to surrender the most precious and valuable things we possess. When Abraham was in Ur, the Lord called him to break with his past: "Leave Ur." Now He calls him to break with his future: "Sacrifice Isaac!" Which do you think is harder? Probably whatever the Lord is asking you to do at the time! The writer of Hebrews does not give any attention to Abraham's inner struggles. He simply tells us that "by faith, Abraham offered Isaac as a sacrifice." Moses tells us that "Early the next morning Abraham got up and saddled his donkey. He took with him two of his servants and his son Isaac" (Genesis 22:3).

Abraham's immediate response is amazing. I would have found every reason imaginable to delay, even if the outcome was inevitable. But Abraham obeys without delay. I feel sure that the three-day journey to Moriah was the longest three days of his life. Then immediate obedience was followed by ultimate obedience. At the top of the mountain, Abraham took Isaac and bound him and placed him on the altar. One often-overlooked detail is that Abraham was an old man, perhaps 120 years of age. Isaac was in the prime of life as a young man. It is hard to imagine that Abraham could have overpowered his son, so Isaac must have cooperated with his father. That much is speculative. What isn't is that Abraham raised his knife with every intention of plunging it into the body of his son. For him, disobedience to God, even at such a cost, was not an option. His allegiance to God transcended every other loyalty.

The writer of Hebrews makes Abraham's intention clear in an interesting way. A literal rendering reads, "By faith Abraham offered [past tense] Isaac, when he was tested, and the one who had received the promises was offering his one and only son." In Abraham's heart, the deed was as good as done, even though this was the son whom God had promised to him. Compliance to God's Word was his supreme responsibility.

How could Abraham do what he did? The answer of the writer of

Hebrews is simply that "Abraham reasoned." His was not a blind faith but a thinking faith, and what he was thinking about was the character of his God. His reasoning made him certain that the God who had made himself known to him was good, faithful, and true. He could be trusted to do what He said He would do. He would—He must—keep His promise. He also was a God who had the power to do the impossible. After all, hadn't God breathed life into Abraham's impotent body and Sarah's infertile body and enabled them to have Isaac?

Thus, Abraham drew an amazing conclusion: "Abraham reasoned that God could raise the dead." He knew that God must keep His pledge that Isaac would be the channel of the promise, so if Isaac was to be put to death, the only solution was that Isaac would be resurrected. It was an amazing leap of faith. A resurrection of a dead person had never taken place. But Abraham knew that no barrier, even the barrier of death, could stop God. No wonder he could act with poise even in the face of this incredible command of God. The promise of God trumps the problems of life. "I am so certain of God's person and of God's promise that I will do what God commands and leave the results to Him."

We don't know at what point Abraham reached this conclusion. Was it before he left for Moriah? Or along the way? Or when he raised the knife? When Abraham started up the mountain, he left behind his servants with the instructions, "Stay here with the donkey, while I and the boy go over there. *We* will worship and then *we* will come back to you." Is the "we" an indication of faith? We cannot be sure, but it seems likely.

Even with that kind of faith, the journey up that hill must have seemed like the longest trip of Abraham's life. And then his son asked, in confusion or concern, the unanswerable question, "The fire and the wood are here, but where is the lamb for the burnt offering?" How could Abraham explain all of this to his son? "God himself will provide the lamb for the burnt offering, my son," he said (Genesis 22:8). Abraham was speaking much more wisely than he realized, for he could not have imagined how remarkably God would do that. Then the rest of the drama was played out. The altar was erected; the fire was laid out; Isaac was bound. How terrifying this all must have been for him!

I imagine that, despite his certainty that his son would be raised to life, Abraham's hands trembled as he lifted the knife and "was about to sacrifice his one and only son." Then, once again, Abraham's life was interrupted by a heavenly voice: "Abraham! Abraham!" "Here I am." "Don't lay a hand on the boy. Don't do anything to him" (Genesis 22:11–12). He not only experienced God's intervention but also saw God's provision. He lifted up his head to discover a ram entangled in a thicket, the sacrifice God had provided. Hurriedly he untied his son and sacrificed the substitute as he heard Yahweh confirm His promise once again, the promise that had so recently seemed in such great peril:

> The angel of the LORD called to Abraham from heaven a second time and said, "I swear by myself, declares the LORD, that because you have done this and have not withheld your son, your only son, I will surely bless you and make your descendants as numerous as the stars in the sky and as the sand on the seashore. Your descendants will take possession of the cities of their enemies, and through your offspring all nations on earth will be blessed, because you have obeyed me." (Genesis 22:15–18)

Abraham was full of wonder at God's just-in-time provision. So much so that he named the place Yahweh-yireh (or, more commonly, Jehovah-jireh), a name that means "Yahweh [the Lord] will provide." Earlier he had come to know God as El Elyon, God most high, and El Shaddai, almighty God. Now he met God as the God who meets us in our need, the God who provides a substitute, the God who takes our

place. Centuries later, on the other side of the Cross, the apostle Paul
reflected on this story of Abraham and Isaac and penned some of the
most moving and powerful words ever written: "If God is for us, who
can be against us? He who did not spare his own Son [a clear allusion to
Abraham and Isaac], but gave him up for us all—how will he not also,
along with him, graciously give us all things?" (Romans 8:31–32). I can
never read these words without being deeply moved that the same God
who would not permit Abraham to sacrifice his son allowed *His* Son to
become the sacrifice for my sin. The eternal God provided for me at a
cost that is unimaginable and incalculable! Abraham knew the truth that
God is Yahweh Yireh, and so do I!

The God of grace often intervenes in our lives in just-in-time ways. I
can find no greater evidence of that than this: On the same piece of real
estate where Abraham offered up a ram as a substitute for his son, the
Lord Jesus died on the cross as God's substitute for my sin. That gives
me the confidence that He who paid such a great price will continue to
be the God of provision in my life.

As Abraham walked down that mountain with his son Isaac by his
side, the knowledge that he could trust his God with the most valuable
and precious things in his life had been burned on his heart. He could
trust the provision of God for the deepest needs of his life. So can we.
There are times I think that I am sacrificing my Isaac, and then I discover that God has a provision far more amazing than anything I could
have devised. There are times when I have felt that God's promises and
God's commands were in hopeless conflict. But I don't have to solve
the conflict. Faith follows God's clear leading and trusts the results to
Him.

Abraham's faith was refined in the crucible. As the angel said on the
mountain, "Now I know that you fear God, because you have not withheld from me your son, your only son" (Genesis 22:12). And his life of

faith would impact the next three generations in a significant way. None of them rose to the heights of Abraham's faith. In fact, some of the examples of faith in Hebrews seem even mundane. Yet each of them shows us one thing.

REFINED FAITH LEAVES A LEGACY OF FAITH

Abraham's faith profoundly touched the lives of those who came after him. I have been the beneficiary of that kind of powerful legacy in my life. My grandparents and my parents showed what it was to live a life of faith, and now with my own grandchildren beginning their young lives, I want to show them in some way what it means to walk in the steps of faith. One of the prime responsibilities of a navigator is to leave behind a trail or a record so that others will not need to wander in a maze of dead ends and false starts as they head toward the same destination.

Isaac, like his father, became a man of faith. I'm sure he never forgot those agonizing moments on the altar. However, he does not appear to have been traumatized by the experience. Instead, he was impressed by the faith of his father. He had seen the value his father placed on faith and was deeply affected by that. I can identify in a small way. When I was a teenager, my father was offered a promotion to vice president of a national pharmaceutical company. It would have been a great career move as well as a major economic advance. It also would have meant moving his family to a part of the country that he did not think would be good for their spiritual well-being. I watched my father put his career on the altar and put a knife in it. I mean that almost literally. There were significant negative repercussions from that decision. But he didn't lose his son! Seeing my father trust his God to that extent taught me about the reality of faith. Whatever has been accomplished in my life for God in the years since is in large measure the fruit of that decision. Isaac was not the man his father was. He was made of different stuff. But he did know what it was to trust God, and he had learned that from his father. Significantly, the writer of Hebrews chooses an episode from Isaac's life that shows Isaac at both his best and his worst.

Faith doesn't eliminate human frailty and weakness. Though Abraham and Isaac were believers, they had no strong community of faith to support them and no lineage of faith to instruct them. They were only years removed from paganism, and their families represented tiny islands of faith in an ocean of unbelief. They also battled with the realities of their fallen natures. Nevertheless, we read that "by faith, Isaac blessed Jacob and Esau in regard to their future." When he did this, Isaac was an old man, blind and failing. Much about his life was out of alignment with his trust in God. He was self-indulgent and selfish. But he recognized that his most precious possession was the promise he had received through his father, "the blessing given to Abraham" (Genesis 28:4). It was that which he wanted to pass on to his children. His son Esau was a secular man. Whatever else was true about him, he lacked any sensitivity to spiritual things and placed no value on the blessing of Abraham. Isaac's younger son, Jacob, was a deceitful schemer who had learned from his mother to do whatever it took to get what he wanted. But in this case, he wanted the right thing. God would have to perform intense therapy on his character, but Jacob valued the promise of God.

The focus of Hebrews 11 is not on the shortcomings of Isaac but on his faith. He knew the promise; he believed the promise; he valued the promise; and he transmitted the promise. What he wanted to pass on to his sons wasn't simply a view of the future but a view of the future discernible only to the eyes of faith. Faith values the promises of God and seeks to deposit them in others who will value them as well. So we hear Isaac transmitting the promise to his son: "May God Almighty bless you and make you fruitful and increase your numbers until you become a community of peoples. May he give you and your descendants the blessing given to Abraham, so that you may take possession of the land where you now live as an alien, the land God gave to Abraham" (Genesis 28:3–4). Those are the words of a person of faith.

The years went by. Jacob was a man who learned things the hard way, and many times he found himself in the crucible under the hand of God. But God was refining his faith, and as the dross was burned away, a genuine man of faith began to emerge. Jacob had been born in the Promised Land, but he had been forced to flee from it because of his mistreatment of his brother, Esau. He lived outside the land and then returned, only to be forced to seek refuge in Egypt because of famine. His final years found him once again outside the land, old, growing blind and sick. And it was on his sickbed when the moment emerged that the writer of Hebrews chooses to illustrate Jacob's faith: "By faith Jacob, when he was dying, blessed each of Joseph's sons, and worshiped as he leaned on the top of his staff."

Joseph had come to visit his ailing father and had brought with him his two sons, Ephraim and Manasseh. It was a moment filled with emotion and tenderness as Jacob reflected on the strange trail of God's grace in his own life and gave specific direction about the disposition of his affairs. Then Jacob asked his son to bring his two grandsons forward so that he could pronounce a blessing upon them. This was a solemn, significant moment. In effect, Jacob was appointing Joseph as his firstborn (his chronological firstborn, Reuben, had disqualified himself by his sin of incest) and giving him the firstborn's double portion. He surprised Joseph by crossing his hands and putting his right hand on the head of the younger son, Ephraim, and his left hand on the head of Manasseh, the firstborn. Then he pronounced the words of blessing:

"May the God before whom my fathers
   Abraham and Isaac walked,
the God who has been my shepherd all my life to this day,
the Angel who has delivered me from all harm
   —may he bless these boys.
May they be called by my name and the names of my fathers
   Abraham and Isaac,
and may they increase greatly upon the earth."

(Genesis 48:15–16)

Faith and gratitude poured out of every word. Here was a man at the end of a long and often difficult life looking back in gratitude and looking forward in hope. Nothing in his actions made sense if the children of Israel were to remain in Egypt. But he was convinced that God would keep His promise and return his descendants to the Promised Land.

Although Jacob was dying in a foreign land, he was convinced that God would be faithful to His promises. At death, Jacob was not self-absorbed. His act of reversing his hands was not the careless act of a senile old man, as Joseph first imagined. It was a deliberate act of prophecy, as he acted in sensitivity to the leading of his God.

Faith doesn't always follow the natural order of things. Jacob had learned the hard way that faith is about submission to the ways of God. As he died, he wanted not only Joseph but also his young grandsons, Ephraim and Manasseh, to grasp the certainty and the power of God's promises. He died, not looking back in nostalgia, as so many older people are prone to do, but worshiping his God with a staff in his hands, a symbol that he was ready to start walking back to the Promised Land if God would give Him strength. Jacob showed his descendants that they must be a pilgrim people, not settling down but always moving toward the city God had promised. Jacob looked forward in hope to a future seen only by the eyes of faith, and passed on a torch of faith to the generations that followed.

Our third vignette is drawn from another deathbed scene, speaking of a man whose life stands out as one of the most remarkable in the Scriptures. Joseph had lived almost all of his life in Egypt, where he had become successful and prosperous despite horrible suffering. The Promised Land held no glorious memories for Joseph. He had grown up in a dysfunctional family, full of jealousy, strife, and immorality. He had been abused by his brothers in a terrible way. But he was a man of faith, who knew his God. His declaration to his treacherous brothers stands out as one of the great affirmations in Scripture: "You meant evil against me, but God meant it for good" (Genesis 50:20, NASB). Many examples of faith can be found in Joseph's life, but I want to highlight one that occurred during his final moments on earth: "By faith, Joseph, when his end was near, spoke about the exodus of the Israelites from Egypt and gave instructions about his bones." The specific details are found in Genesis 50:24–25. These are the final instructions of a man who was one of the greatest men of his generation in Egypt. But he was not interested in a tomb, a pyramid, a memorial, or a presidential library. He wanted a coffin—but a coffin that would be taken back to the Promised Land. He wanted his descendants to keep it where they could see it, so that they would never forget that they were a people with a promise. While life in Egypt had been good to him, Egypt was not the Promised Land.

The book of Genesis ends with these words:

> Then Joseph said to his brothers, "I am about to die. But God will surely come to your aid and take you up out of this land to the land he promised on oath to Abraham, Isaac and Jacob."
> And Joseph made the sons of Israel swear an oath and said,

"God will surely come to your aid, and then you must carry my
bones up from this place."
   So Joseph died at the age of a hundred and ten. And after
they embalmed him, he was placed in a coffin in Egypt. (Genesis
50:24–26)

Joseph's faith was about confidence in God's promise. "Keep my coffin where you can see it and remember the promise." Joseph's coffin
wasn't a symbol of death; it became a symbol of living hope. "Egypt isn't
home; Canaan is. We don't live for here; we live for there." So, four hundred years later, when Israel hastily left Egypt during the exodus, they
made sure that they took Joseph's bones (Exodus 13:19), and when they
reached the land, they buried his bones in Shechem (Joshua 24:32). For
more than four hundred years, Joseph's dying request would keep Israel
focused on the promise of God.

   Abraham's faith, forged in the crucible, left a great legacy of faith to his
descendants. God allowed stress, sometimes almost unbearable stress, to
burn into their hearts the certainty that He is who He says He is and will
do what He has promised He will do. Abraham, Isaac, Jacob, Joseph—
the lives of these men show that God is concerned to build faith within
each one of us. And when He does, we need to cling hard to His promises, to obey quickly His commands, and to rely constantly on His power.

   Today we may be in a quiet harbor. But one day we will surely find
ourselves in wild waters that refuse to be controlled. The question then
will be whether the speed of life has caused us to sacrifice the strength
we need. People who design America's Cup boats may feel compelled to
make the safety margin as thin as possible. But when you do that, there
is a high price to be paid if something goes wrong. A designer of *Young
America* made the observation, "I think the boat was well designed—just
much too close to the edge."[3]

The issues of life are far more serious than a boat race, but some analogies may help us see the truth. When you hit those six-foot waves, it's too late to build in the strength you need. Whether we crack and buckle, like *Young America*, or whether we sail safely through will depend on whether or not we have built with faith beneath the waterline. Cutting corners may look good on a computer model, but it doesn't look so good on stormy seas. Sailing close to the edge sounds daring and dramatic, but in a storm, it becomes foolish. The choices we make in the harbor determine the success we will experience in heavy weather.

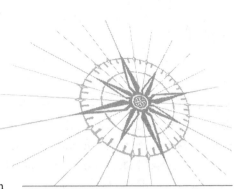

Chapter Fourteen

CHOICES

To celebrate the new millennium the *New York Times Magazine* published a series of six millennium issues, probing the past thousand years so as to predict some aspects of the future. The third in the series, which was entitled "Into the Unknown," dealt with exploration and discovery in the second millennium. The editors began with these words:

> The story of the last 1000 years can be told as a series of great adventures: Marco Polo to China, Columbus to the New World, Darwin to the Galapagos. Adventure is as old as Homer, but plunging into the unknown in quest of knowledge is the legacy of this millennium—one that began with Leif Erickson and ends with a robot on Mars. Where must the explorer go now to find terra incognito?[1]

The record of physical discovery in the past thousand years is remarkable. People of daring and imagination pushed back the barriers of ignorance, sailed uncharted waters, and opened up a world we now take for granted.

The same magazine introduced me to a person I had never heard of before, a Chinese admiral named Zheng He.[2] Almost a hundred years before Columbus, he commanded a huge navy of twenty-eight thousand sailors and three hundred ships, a navy larger than any the Western world was going to know until World War II. He led his fleet throughout the waters of southeast Asia, starting a wave of Chinese emigration. There is evidence that elements of his navy reached all the way to East Africa, which is amazing given the technology of the time.

Zheng He's expeditions were amazing, but the author who describes his accomplishments points out that they had no lasting impact. Political issues in China were such that his achievements were not followed up. Europe, not China, was to dominate exploration in the centuries that followed. As the author indicates:

> In the end, an explorer makes history but does not necessarily change it, for his impact depends less on the trail he blazes than on the willingness of others to follow. The daring of a great expedition is hostage to the national will of those who remain.[3]

He goes on to describe this as "one of history's biggest lost opportunities," due to "a culture of complacency . . . a tendency to look inward, a devotion to past ideals and methods, a respect for authority and a suspicion of new ideas."[4]

The writer is thinking of the affairs of nations. But one of his statements applies with equal force to spiritual matters: Explorers make history but do not necessarily change it, because everything depends on whether others will follow in their footsteps. Hebrews 11 is a record of a remarkable group of spiritual trailblazers, none more important than Abraham and

Moses, the two greatest figures of the Old Testament. But we are told their stories not for our fascination but for our imitation. Everything depends on our willingness to follow where they have led. The writer of Hebrews was concerned that the people to whom he first wrote were in danger of throwing away their confidence in Christ and going their own way. His concern for us is the same. He is not writing to inform us or to impress us but to inspire us to join these trailblazers in walking the way of faith.

One of the most striking things about Hebrews 11 is that it is not populated by people whose lives were error-free. The heroes of faith were not perfect people. They were failing people who trusted in an unfailing God. Not a single person in Hebrews 11 lived a sinless life. Some, in fact, had rather notorious times of failure. But God, in His grace, chose to look beyond their sins, because people who trust Him bring pleasure to His heart. It is because these people were believers that they are enrolled in the hall of faith.

Also, Hebrews is not populated by those whose lives were risk-free. Faith isn't about "playing it safe," but about choices that are calculated risks on the character and promises of God. Of course, it is never really a risk to trust in the faithful, reliable, good, and gracious God. But often it feels like one! Yet, as someone has said, "You've got to go out on a limb sometimes, because that's where the fruit is." If we never go out on the limb spiritually, if we never step out in faith, we will never lay hold of the fruit that the Lord wants us to enjoy.

The life story of Moses is the story of faith choices made in life-and-death circumstances. Those choices did not begin with Moses but with his parents, and ultimately those choices led him down a trail of faith.

By faith Moses' parents hid him for three months after he was born, because they saw he was no ordinary child, and they were not afraid of the king's edict.

By faith Moses, when he had grown up, refused to be known as the son of Pharaoh's daughter. He chose to be mistreated along with the people of God rather than to enjoy the pleasures of sin for a short time. He regarded disgrace for the sake of Christ as of greater value than the treasures of Egypt, because he was looking ahead to his reward. By faith he left Egypt, not fearing the king's anger; he persevered because he saw him who is invisible. By faith he kept the Passover and the sprinkling of blood, so that the destroyer of the firstborn would not touch the firstborn of Israel.

By faith the people passed through the Red Sea as on dry land; but when the Egyptians tried to do so, they were drowned.

By faith the walls of Jericho fell, after the people had marched around them for seven days.

By faith the prostitute Rahab, because she welcomed the spies, was not killed with those who were disobedient. (Hebrews 11:23–31)

Every day we make choices and decisions. Most of them are routine and relatively insignificant. Some are important. But a few rise to the level of being life-shaping. They determine not only what we will do but also who we will become. I am told that business leaders believe that 95 percent of their future is determined by 5 percent of their decisions. Therefore, wise executives delegate most decisions but realize that they must retain control of the key ones.

Life is the same. There are certain choices that we alone can and must make. We cannot avoid these decisions. Not to decide is itself a decision. Moses' life of faith is all about such choices, decisions that shaped his life and the life of a nation. One of the most significant choices was made not by Moses but by his parents. It was a life-and-death choice that was forced upon them by the sinful decisions of others. Moses' parents were thrust into circumstances that would arouse fear in the bravest of people, circumstances that threatened what was most precious to them and that were beyond their control. They were followers of the Christ long before they knew specifically who He would be.

BY FAITH, CHRIST-FOLLOWERS CONFRONT AND OVERCOME THEIR FEARS

To insulate His people from the moral corruption of Canaan, God, in His sovereign plan, provided a refuge for them in the land of Egypt. They had gone down to Egypt under the protection of Joseph, a family group of seventy-two people. But over a period of approximately four hundred years they had flourished and become a thriving ethnic group of about two million people. This was God at work, fulfilling His promise to Abraham, Isaac, and Jacob.

Suddenly the situation changed dramatically—for the worse. We cannot be sure of all the details, but it seems that an invasion of another ethnic group, the Hyksos, had disrupted Egyptian politics, causing fear and suspicion of foreigners in general and of the Israelites in particular. It threatened the political establishment to have a growing and identifiable ethnic group within the nation, posing a potential military threat. Politicians have always been quick to exploit ethnic differences when it suits their purposes, as they do today. "A new king, who did not know about Joseph, came to power in Egypt" (Exodus 1:8). Appealing to the worst fears and instincts of his fellow Egyptians, this ruler launched a ruthless campaign of oppression and abuse. The first stage was forced labor, a program that resulted in the degradation and virtual enslavement of the Israelites. When that failed, he instituted a plan of slow genocide, demanding that every newborn Hebrew male be executed at the time of delivery. Girls could be used for breeding, but potential warriors must be eliminated. When that plan also failed, because of the subversive and courageous activities of the Hebrew midwives, Pharaoh demanded infanticide, ordering the Egyptian people to join him in ethnic cleansing by throwing any Hebrew boy into the Nile to drown. There is sadistic irony in this, for the Egyptians revered the Nile as a life-giving force. Now they were using it as a life-taking instrument of terror.

In the midst of this reign of terror, an obscure couple who traced their ancestry to Jacob's son Levi found themselves expecting a child. Amram and Jochebed were not people of status or importance. In fact, their names are withheld from us until Exodus 6:20. What is remarkable about them is their faith. "By faith Moses' parents hid him for three months after he was born, because they saw he was no ordinary child, and they were not afraid of the king's edict." Moses was born with a death sentence hanging over his head, and his parents would undoubtedly suffer the same fate for not carrying it out. But they refused to harm their baby, even though they already had two children, whom they were putting at risk by sparing their infant son.

Every normal parent can understand why Amram and Jochebed did what they did. But there was more at work here than normal parental affection. The phrase that the New International Version renders "he was no ordinary child" means that this baby boy was beautiful or pleasing. This is the word the Greek translators used to translate the Hebrew text of Exodus 2:1, which tells us that Jochebed saw that her son was a "good" child. I have had three children and two grandchildren. Each of them was instantly "good" and "no ordinary child" in my eyes. Yet this seems to go beyond that. Somehow, by faith, Moses' parents recognized that he was a special child who would have an unusual role in God's purposes for His people. Acts 7:20 tells us that he was "beautiful or pleasing to God" (literal translation). He was a child of destiny, whom God would use in a unique way. These parents made a life-and-death decision, not only for the baby but also for themselves. Trusting God, they chose life, the life of a newborn child, and therefore risked death at the hand of a tyrannical ruler.

Their faith saved Moses. They hid him in their home for three months, until something forced them to take the desperate measure of placing their little one in a pitch-covered basket and setting him among the lush growth of reeds in the Nile River. Again we see an irony: the place intended for Moses' death became the means of his deliverance. We have no idea why they could no longer keep him at home. Some have suggested that his crying had become too loud to hide. All that indicates is that such scholars haven't had the privilege of baby-sitting a crying newborn recently. And we need to be careful not to misread the words: they did not fear the king's edict. If they had had no fear, they would not have hidden the child. The phrase does not mean that they felt no fear; it means that they acted despite fear, with boldness and courage. Faith is following God's clear leading, despite the dangers and with confidence in God.

We should also know that while faith may be risky, it is not reckless. Moses' parents defied Pharaoh, but they acted wisely.

When Hudson Taylor, at twenty-one-years of age, sailed to China to begin his ministry, he sailed on a small three-masted clipper called the *Dumfries*. The journey would take six months, but only a few days out, they encountered a terrible storm on the Irish Sea, one the captain called the worst he had ever seen. It seemed certain that they would be driven onto the rocks of northern Wales, and no one could hope to survive in such a sea. Still, Taylor refused to put on a lifejacket. That would, he felt, show a lack of trust in God. The ship miraculously survived, but later a more mature Taylor looked back on that event with chagrin. Faith in God does not mean ignoring normal safety measures. Faith has the boldness to take the gospel to areas where there may be severe medical danger, but wisdom makes sure that the one who goes is properly prepared by taking inoculations. Faith may lead us to venture into a dangerous ghetto in a Third-World country; wisdom tells us to go in daylight, with companions. Faith trusts God but hides the baby.

The faith of Moses' parents made a lifelong impact on their son. Amram and Jochebed would have the privilege of being his caregivers for only a few short years, but what Moses saw and heard during that time marked him deeply. Even as an adult reared in the court of Pharaoh, Moses could not forget who he was. He had seen his parents act with the conviction that God was to be obeyed and that God was at work even in apparently disastrous circumstances. This is the essence of faith: to trust God even where His hand cannot be clearly seen.

Peter Enns has these helpful comments on Pharaoh's edict to kill the Hebrew boys:

> It was not as if the Lord "reacted" to the decree and thought, "What am I going to do now?" Rather, it is precisely by means of this decree that God brings deliverance to his people. God is in full control both of Moses' birth and of the external circumstances that threaten to undo it. God does not remove Moses from the situation, nor does he strike down Pharaoh who dares to oppose him, both of which he certainly could have done. Instead, God places Moses in the same Nile that Pharaoh intends for the boy's harm, brings the boy right to Pharaoh's doorstep, and has him raised in Pharaoh's house. Why? To defeat the enemy decisively at his own game, at the very heart of his own strength.[5]

That is a God who can be trusted!

Moses' parents chose to trust God and not to be controlled by their fears. But there came a time when Moses had to make his own choices— just as we do. Moses had not chosen to be born of Hebrew parents or to be reared in the court of Pharaoh. But when those two worlds came into conflict, he had to decide which kingdom he would live for. He made his choice awkwardly and carried it out foolishly, but beneath his blundering ways, we can see the vision of faith.

BY FAITH, CHRIST-FOLLOWERS MAKE KINGDOM CHOICES

Forty years had passed. Moses might have been an Israelite by race, but he was an Egyptian by status, lifestyle, and training. "He was educated in all the wisdom of the Egyptians and was powerful in speech and action" (Acts 7:22). There was no external reason for him to make any changes. Pharaoh was not forcing him to choose. Moses was an Egyptian, and there was no reason not to stay that way—except for the seeds of faith his parents had planted in his heart. Even his name, given him by his adoptive mother, "Moses" (meaning "drawn out"), was a reminder of his unique origins. Suddenly a forty-year-old man found himself facing a life-changing choice. This was not a teenager struggling for his identity. This was a forty-year-old man pondering a decision that had huge consequences.

Moses faced a choice between social status and prestige or social mistreatment and marginalization. This was the Nineteenth Dynasty in Egypt, a period of great luxury and prosperity for the aristocracy. Egypt was a society organized to ensure the comfort and privilege of the royal family, and Moses was entitled to the best his nation had to offer. He was Egyptian by adoption, Egyptian by status, and Egyptian by culture. Yet he could choose to live in slavery and destitution, suffering harassment and mistreatment. This was not a temporary choice. He couldn't try slavery to see whether he would like it, then move back to the palace. And he had nothing in common with the Hebrews except the accident of his birth. He had spent all his life in a world totally unlike theirs.

Moses had a choice between Egyptian identity with its material privilege and personal luxury or Israelite identity with its personal destitution and hard, unfulfilling labor. But here the choice was not what it seemed. Only one of those two groups was the people of God, and it wasn't the Egyptians. If the promise made to Abraham was true, Moses faced a choice between this world and the city whose builder and maker was God. And while Moses knew all about the gods of Egypt, he knew that only Yahweh, the God of his birth parents, was the true God. It was a choice between a lifestyle of personal pleasure and self-indulgence or one of deprivation. Even today, in our affluent world, people line up to catch a glimpse of the treasures of Egypt. On the basis of sight, the choice was obvious. Moses was losing nothing and gaining everything by continuing to be called "the son of Pharaoh's daughter." But the eyes of faith see reality differently. To choose Egypt was to lose the person of God, the promises of God, and the people of God.

Moses made his choice. Exodus 2:11 simply says that Moses "went out to . . . his own people." But his method of making the transition was not well chosen. Seeing an Egyptian beating an Israelite slave, Moses was moved to indignation and deliberately killed the Egyptian to protect the Israelite. He must have known his actions would not remain secret; the man he saved was bound to tell someone. But he probably thought his kinsmen would be grateful and would see him as their champion. Any such illusions vanished almost instantly. The next day, when Moses chose to intervene in a dispute between two Hebrews, he was the recipient of bitter and harsh words. Immediately he realized that his previous act was widely known and was being described in a way that left him defenseless. He had sided with the Israelites in a way that Pharaoh could not tolerate, but the Israelites were not ready to rally to him. So Moses fled into the desert to save his life.

The writer of Hebrews does not defend Moses' methods, but he does understand the force that drove them. Moses was not a victim of circumstances; he was a man of faith acting on principle. "By faith Moses, when he had grown up, refused to be known as the son of Pharaoh's daughter. He chose to be mistreated along with the people of God rather than to enjoy the pleasures of sin for a short time. He regarded disgrace for the sake of Christ as of greater value than the treasures of Egypt, because he was looking ahead to his reward." He refused, he chose, he regarded—these are words of faith.

First, Moses chose the person of God. He renounced Egypt to become part of the people of God. This was not so much a rejection of Pharaoh's daughter, the woman who had saved his life and bestowed on him great kindness, as it was a choice of the living and true God. He owed a great debt personally to his adoptive mother. But this wasn't a choice between his adoptive mother and his birth mother. Nor was the choice an ethnic one, between the powerful Egyptians and the oppressed Israelites. This was a spiritual choice: to follow the one true God who had revealed himself to a favored people, the people of Israel. Somehow, Moses had come to an overwhelming sense of the greatness and goodness of the God of Israel.

Second, Moses chose the will of God. Egypt represented the pleasures of sin. This obviously involved culturally approved practices that violated the standards of God. But the pleasures of sin also refer to things that, neutral in themselves, become evil when they lure us away from God. Moses' position, power, and prestige were not sinful in themselves. After all, Joseph had held similar privileges in Egypt. But these very things now threatened to lure Moses away from the call of God on his life. Such things, whatever they are, become the pleasures of sin, and, enticing as they are, they are only temporary. "But he who does the will of God lives forever" (1 John 2:17). Faith lives for the lasting and the eternal.

Third, Moses chose the treasures of God. Faith has a strange accounting system. The treasures of Egypt are obvious. You can hold them in your hand and see them with your eyes. But Moses said by his choice that such things were of less value than "disgrace for the sake of Christ." I doubt that Moses at this stage of his life had much understanding of God's great messianic program that will culminate in the return of the Lord Jesus in power and glory. But when Moses stepped out and identified with God's people, a people living in disgrace and slavery, he knew that Pharaoh would not and could not tolerate his behavior. In the short run, his choice meant suffering, ostracism, danger, and perhaps even death. But Moses was looking beyond the instant gratification of the pleasures of sin, and even beyond the immediate experience of the disgrace of being associated with the people of God, to the eternal reward of the better city and the better country that people of faith seek. What others saw as a treasure to be pursued—the treasures of Egypt—Moses saw as a distraction to be discarded. What others saw as an experience to be avoided—the disgrace of Christ—Moses saw as a treasure to be cherished. Faith sees everything in terms of its *true* value, because it sees things in the light of eternity.

Moses' choice was a kingdom choice. As the Lord Jesus commanded, "Seek first his kingdom and his righteousness, and all these things will be given to you as well" (Matthew 6:33). Moses rejected immediate wealth and status in Pharaoh's kingdom and chose another kingdom and another reward. I remember a far less momentous choice in my own life, as a fifteen-year-old battling with the disgrace that came from being committed to Christ, a choice that was anything but cool in my high school. I can vividly recall a lunch hour when I walked home, carrying

my Bible, debating whether I would deposit it in the garbage can—
and my Christian life with it. The pleasures of sin and the treasures of
Egypt were powerfully attractive. But I knew that there was a city whose
builder and maker was God and that the Lord Jesus had risen from the
dead to give undeniable proof that He was God incarnate. There was no
other reasonable choice. The disgrace of Christ might be temporarily
difficult, but it was eternally worthwhile. No one has said it better than
Jim Elliot: "He is no fool who gives what he cannot keep to gain what he
cannot lose."

Like many of us, even at the high point of faith, Moses did the right
thing the wrong way. He chose to identify with the people of God, but
he hardly needed to do it by killing an Egyptian. Stephen tells us that
Moses naively "thought that his own people would realize that God was
using him to rescue them" (Acts 7:25). They didn't. Instead, Moses found
his actions thrown in his face by an ungrateful Israelite, realized that
Pharaoh would find out what he had done, and so fled before Pharaoh
could kill him. But even here the writer of Hebrews sees evidences of
faith: "By faith he left Egypt, not fearing the king's anger; he persevered
because he saw him who is invisible." At first glance, it seems that our
writer has got it wrong. How could he say that Moses didn't fear the
king's anger, when Exodus tells us that "when Pharaoh heard of this,
he tried to kill Moses, but Moses fled from Pharaoh and went to live in
Midian" (Exodus 2:15)? We have here something similar to the statement that Moses' parents hid him, not fearing the king. Did they fear
Pharaoh? In one sense, yes. They knew what he wanted to do to their
precious son. But did they fear the king? No, they defied him, and saved
their son. Did Moses fear Pharaoh? Well, he did leave the scene so that
the ruler could not kill him. But if Moses really feared Pharaoh, he would
not have sided with his Hebrew family. He acted as he did not out of fear
of the king but out of faith in the call of God. He was not fear-driven but

faith-driven. Because Moses had a sense of God's call on his life, he left, recognizing that this was not the time to do what he apparently already knew God had called him to do.

By Faith, Christ-Followers Stay the Course And Obey God's Instructions

I'm sure Moses didn't expect that it would be forty years before he would return to Egypt to carry out the will of God. It must have seemed like an enormous waste of time—forty years of chasing sheep around the back side of the desert. But God never wastes time; He invests it. Moses had spent the first forty years of his life in the palace, learning about leadership and government from the inside. Now he would spend forty years learning to survive in the desert, forty years of enduring a barren, unproductive land. He would become a shepherd, learning the ways of sheep and how to lead and care for a flock. What Moses could not know was that for the final forty years of his life he would combine the two roles: leading and governing a nation, shepherding a nation through a desert. But confused as he must have been, in the meantime he persevered.

Moses did not obey because he understood; he obeyed because he believed. Which brings us to a basic message of Hebrews 11. Remember the writer's introductory challenge in Hebrews 10? "Do not throw away your confidence . . . . You need to persevere" (Hebrews 10:35–36). The message of Moses' life is that true faith has staying power. Faith doesn't pack it in when the first difficulty comes. Faith doesn't quit when God has us on the back side of the desert. Faith doesn't bail out when suffering comes. Faith sees the reality of God and "sees him who is invisible." Moses paid more attention to the invisible King of the universe than to the very visible king of Egypt, and so must we.

In Hebrews the final comment about Moses, the man of faith, is that "by faith he kept the Passover and the sprinkling of blood, so that the destroyer of the firstborn would not touch the firstborn of Israel." The Lord had promised to deliver His people from Egypt, but before He did, He gave Moses an elaborate ritual to carry out. It involved the careful examination of a lamb, the preparation of food, the sacrificing of the lamb, the sprinkling of blood, and an unusual eating of a meal—in haste and dressed for travel. And Moses was to establish this as a permanent ritual, "for generations to come."

The instructions were detailed, the ritual was unprecedented, and the demands were high. It required faith on the part of Moses to pass on such detailed directions. It required faith on the part of the people to celebrate in advance an event that had not yet occurred. It would be like the founders of the United States celebrating their independence before the revolution. Everyone knows that's not the way it's done. You win the victory before you celebrate it! But that's not what God directed. Moses and the Israelites were to celebrate the victory before they had experienced it.

By Faith, Christ-Followers Rely on God's Intervention

As this part of the story comes to an end, we are presented with three events that describe people of faith acting in such a way that they are dependent on God's intervention. The first event occurred at the Red Sea when the Israelites confronted an impossible obstacle. Pharaoh's army was rapidly closing from the rear, and before them was an impassable body of water. As the people panicked, Moses declared, "Do not be afraid. Stand firm and you will see the deliverance the LORD will bring you today" (Exodus 14:13). Faith called them to walk toward a body of water, trusting that God would do as He had promised. "By faith the people passed through the Red Sea as on dry land; but when the Egyptians tried to do so, they were drowned." Faith relies on God's word.

The second event is one of the most famous incidents in the Bible, one in which the Lord commanded His people to do not only the unusual but the seemingly illogical. There were many ways to attack a walled city like Jericho, but marching around the city for seven days and shouting and blowing trumpets was not on anybody's list. Yet those were God's instructions, and Joshua led the people in obedience. "By faith the walls of Jericho fell, after the people had marched around them for seven days." Faith follows God's instructions.

The third event involved a prostitute in the city of Jericho, hardly an expected candidate for the hall of faith. Yet the God of heaven was at work in her heart. When the Hebrew spies showed up in her city, she revealed that she had a heart sensitive to God. "I know that the LORD has given this land to you," she said. "We have heard what the LORD [has done for you] . . . for the LORD your God is God in heaven above and on the earth below" (see Joshua 2:8–13). Rahab risked her life to save the lives of the spies and declared her confidence in people who were her natural enemies. Why? Because she saw in them something of the living God. "By faith the prostitute Rahab, because she welcomed the spies, was not killed with those who were disobedient." It is remarkable enough that God's grace spared Rahab; it is even more remarkable that she was accepted into the community of Israel, despite her sinful past; and most remarkable of all is that her name is found on the first page of the New Testament in the genealogy of the Lord Jesus. Faith risks all, relying completely on God's intervention.

Our lives are a series of defining moments. And defining moments are occasions that do three things: they expose our true values, test our deepest commitments, and, by our response, shape our character. Defining moments come in all shapes and sizes. Some are as profound as a forty-year-old man deciding whether he will live as an Egyptian prince or a Hebrew outcast. Others seem relatively minor, such as where a grandfather places his hands when he blesses his grandchildren. But when those choices are made in faith, they shape us into people of faith. They also open a trail for others to follow.

In such defining moments, Moses chose by faith, and as a result the adopted son of an Egyptian princess became one of faith's great heroes. More than any other figure in the Old Testament, Moses was a trailblazer. His trail of faith led his people out of Egypt, through the Red Sea, to Mount Sinai, where they met the living God and entered into a special covenant with Him. Then the trail of Moses' faith led through the wilderness to the borders of the Promised Land. He had seen faith in the choices of his parents. In turn he had made choices that were not only life-shaping but also history-making. And at the end of his life, Moses passed the torch of faith to the next generation, to Joshua and his generation, who were to make their own trail of faith around the walls of Jericho.

In Hebrews 13:7–8, we are given a great exhortation: "Remember your leaders, who spoke the Word of God to you. Consider the outcome of their way of life and imitate their faith. Jesus Christ is the same yesterday and today and forever." Faith never loses its validity because it rests on the unchanging, faithful Lord Jesus Christ. But the phrase that strikes me here is "imitate their faith." We are not called to imitate the practices or traditions of those who have led the way before us, valuable as those things might be. Practices change, and traditions become cold. We are to imitate their faith. That means that I need to be sure that the people I am following are men and women of faith, and that I, in turn, am laying down a trail of faith so that others can safely follow where I am leading.

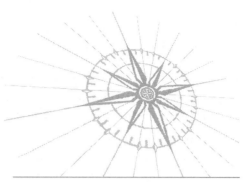

Chapter Fifteen

TRUSTING A SOVEREIGN GOD

Y ears ago my imagination was fired by the description of an advertisement that had appeared in newspapers in London in 1914:

> Men wanted for hazardous journey. Small wages, bitter cold, long months of complete darkness, constant danger. Safe return doubtful. Honor and recognition in case of success.

The account went on to say that this had been the most successful want ad in history. Thousands of men had responded because it bore the signature of a man already famous and respected as an Antarctic explorer: Sir Ernest Shackleton.[1]

Unfortunately, this wording of Shackleton's ad is apparently advertising legend. At least, no copy of such an ad has thus far been discovered. What is true is that on December 29, 1913, Ernest Shackleton did announce in the *London Times* that he was returning to the South Pole, leading an expedition that would be the first to attempt to cross the continent from one side to the other. And it is also true that he was deluged with five thousand responses from men who were, quite literally, willing to go to the ends of the earth with Sir Ernest Shackleton.

Shackleton had already been to the Antarctic twice, trying to be the first to reach the South Pole. In 1901, he had sailed with the famous explorer Robert Scott, and he was one of three men who reached further south than any previous group; but they were forced to turn back without reaching the Pole. In 1907, he led an expedition that had to turn back a heartbreaking ninety-seven nautical miles from the Pole. This was, however, the expedition that established Shackleton's reputation as a courageous and self-sacrificing leader.

On December 16, 1911, the Norwegian Roald Amundsen became the first to reach the South Pole with his dog teams. A month later, Robert Scott and his team achieved the same goal, only to perish on the return journey. Now there remained only one major goal: to cross Antarctica from sea to sea.

In 1914, Shackleton announced his intention to lead an expedition to do just that. It would be a fifteen-hundred-mile journey under brutal conditions, a difficult mix of high danger and extreme discomfort. Yet five thousand men were willing to put themselves under the leadership of Sir Ernest Shackleton to attempt the task. Why? A major part of the reason lies in the character of Shackleton himself. Francis Priestly, a member of his 1907 expedition, wrote this evaluation:

> For scientific discovery, give me Scott; for speed and efficient travel, give me Amundsen. But when you are in a hopeless situation, when you are seeing no way out, get down on your knees and pray for Shackleton. Incomparable in adversity, he was the miracle worker who would save your lives against all odds long

after your number was up. The greatest leader that ever came on
God's earth bar none.[2]

Shackleton never realized his goal. In fact, the crossing of Antarctica
would not take place for another forty years, under very different circumstances and with much less primitive conditions. As I have described
in chapter 2, Shackleton's ship became frozen in the ice, and the mission suddenly became the survival and eventual rescue of his men rather
than the crossing of Antarctica. Shackleton succeeded in a remarkable
and truly heroic manner, which set a model of leadership that is being
increasingly studied almost a century later. Sir Edmund Hillary, the first
to climb Mount Everest and a noted Antarctic adventurer in his own
right, described Shackleton as one of his heroes:

> Of all of the explorers I would like to have known, Shackleton
> was the most admirable. . . . It is as a leader of men and as an
> overcomer of appalling obstacles that Shackleton really excelled.
> Not for him an easy task and a quick success—he was at his
> best when the going was toughest. The enormous affection and
> respect he engendered in his expedition members (often mighty
> men themselves) shines through in their diaries and writings.[3]

It is the description "he was at his best when the going was toughest"
that captures my attention. If you are going to put your life in the hands
of someone, you need to be sure that you can trust that person, whatever
the circumstances. That is what gives a Christian such confidence in following the Lord Jesus. Throughout the centuries He has proven himself
to be completely reliable and trustworthy in the lives of His people. We
are sailing into uncharted waters. We need a captain we can trust and
follow without reservation, and our Lord and Savior is clearly that kind

of leader. He not only models reliability; He inspires and empowers reliability and trustworthiness in those who follow Him most closely. People of faith are not fair-weather followers. They are at their best when the going is toughest.

Hebrews 11 ends with a remarkable record of faith. The writer doesn't give the kind of detail that he has used to describe the lives of Abraham and Moses. But the list of names he gives is designed to stimulate the memory. He also directs us to the experiences of anonymous men and women whose journey of faith not only led them to great exploits but also into great pain and suffering. This gives us an indispensable perspective on the life of faith. Too often modern Christians labor under the illusion that the life of faith is a life of continual victory that exempts us from trouble and suffering. Such a view is both false *and* dangerous. It has been well said that illusion is the mother of disillusion. If we live with illusions about the immediate outcome of the life of faith, we are setting ourselves up for disillusionment and discouragement. The final verses of Hebrews are a powerful antidote to a naïve view of the life of faith.

And what more shall I say? I do not have time to tell about Gideon, Barak, Samson, Jephthah, David, Samuel and the prophets, who through faith conquered kingdoms, administered justice, and gained what was promised; who shut the mouths of lions, quenched the fury of the flames, and escaped the edge of the sword; whose weakness was turned to strength; and who became powerful in battle and routed foreign armies. Women received back their dead, raised to life again. Others were tortured and refused to be released, so that they might gain a better resurrection. Some faced jeers and flogging, while still others were chained and put in prison. They were stoned; they were sawed in two; they were put to death by the sword. They went about in sheepskins and goatskins, destitute, persecuted and mistreated—the world was not worthy of them. They wandered in deserts and mountains, and in caves and holes in the ground.

These were all commended for their faith, yet none of them received what had been promised. God had planned something better for us so that only together with us would they be made perfect. (Hebrews 11:32–39)

As we have moved through Hebrews 11, we have become used to the repeated refrain "by faith." It has occurred eighteen times to emphasize the central message of Hebrews 11:6: "Without faith, it is impossible to please God." The writer does not use this expression, "by faith," in these final nine verses of the chapter, but the idea of faith underlies all that is written. In Hebrews 11:33, we read that these very diverse people did what they did "through faith." We are also specifically told in Hebrews 11:39 that "these were all commended for their faith." This is a crucial insight. Although the visible outcomes will be radically different, the people described are all men and women of faith.

GOD OFTEN EMPOWERS PEOPLE OF FAITH FOR REMARKABLE ACTS OF DELIVERANCE

Having focused on Abraham and Moses, the writer of Hebrews now gives us a random sampling of people of faith from the early years of Israel's life in the Promised Land, the period of the judges, and the early monarchy. Interestingly, each of these remarkable men of faith was marked by significant failure. Yet, weak as they were at times, they were people who knew what it was to trust God.

Gideon was a man who found it difficult to trust God. He lived in a time when discouragement and defeatism had settled deeply into the hearts of God's people. Gideon was no exception. His complaint to God's messenger was, "The LORD has abandoned us" (Judges 6:13). Faced with God's clear promise that He would be with Gideon and use him to destroy the Midianites, Gideon responded with a series of conditions that showed his weakness and doubt. But the Lord, in grace and goodness, brought Gideon to the place where he was willing to lead 300 Israelites against 135,000 Midianites, an act of no little courage. That moment when Gideon stood with his men on the hills overlooking the Midianite camp, armed only with a torch and a clay pot, is one of the great moments of faith in Scripture. The Lord responded to Gideon's faith by giving His people an amazing victory.

If Gideon's is a story of faith overcoming weakness, Barak's is a story of faith overcoming reluctance. Commissioned by God through the prophet Deborah to lead God's people into battle against the Canaanite king Jabin, and promised victory, Barak demurred. He said to Deborah, "If you go with me, I will go; but if you don't go with me, I won't go" (Judges 4:8). Deborah did go with him, and Barak led his men into battle against a much larger and better-equipped army. Again, God gave a remarkable victory.

Gideon and Barak shared a God-given commission to go to battle against a vastly superior enemy force. Neither responded with initial trust, but both were brought to the obedience of faith by a patient, gracious God. Their experiences show us that faith is not about where we begin the process but where we allow God to take us.

The next pair that the writer of Hebrews presents is two men battling with their pasts. Samson had a past full of failure. Uniquely gifted by God, he squandered his strength with immorality. But in the supreme opportunity of his life, he trusted God to strengthen him one last time, knowing that it would be at the cost of his life. Jephthah had to overcome the sordid circumstances of his past. The illegitimate son of a prostitute, he became the leader of what was no more than an outlaw gang. But when God called him to lead His people against the Ammonites, Jephthah led by his trust in God. He confronted the Ammonite king with the declaration, "Let the LORD, the Judge, decide the dispute this day between the Israelites and the Ammonites" (Judges 11:27). Empowered by the Spirit, Jephthah led God's people to victory. You could not find two more unlikely candidates for the hall of faith. But the Lord saw beyond their pasts to their present faith in Him.

Historically, the final two men of faith, Samuel and David, were bound together in many ways. But what unites them in this context is that they were two men who modeled faith in God in the midst of massive national failure and unbelief. The note of faith sounds strongly through David's life from the time when, as a teenager, he confronted Goliath, the gigantic Philistine who intimidated King Saul and all the grown men of his nation. Throughout his life, David trusted his God, evidenced in his leadership and celebrated in his songs. Samuel, who anointed David as king, also showed faith as a young boy, and God used him to rally his people to trust God and to inspire them to victory against the Philistines (1 Samuel 7).

Gideon, Barak, Samson, Jephthah, David, and Samuel—these six men were all different and greatly flawed. They were not always the best and the brightest. Much in their lives puzzles and even repels us. But they did know what it was to trust God. "These were all commended for their faith."

People of faith come in remarkable variety and experience stunning victories. In the following verses, the writer of Hebrews moves away from specific names and individuals to descriptions that cause us to think of many different events. *Faith inspires acts of leadership,* says the writer. "Through faith [some] conquered kingdoms" reminds us of kings like David and Jehoshaphat who trusted God as they led the nation to victory.

"[Others] administered justice" reminds us of the actions of a Samuel, a David, or a Solomon who led the nation to set up government structures that protected the poor, controlled the powerful, and dispensed justice in the courts. "[Some] gained what was promised" probably refers, in a context that has emphasized God's promises to Abraham, to the extension of Israel's kingdom through military victories over its enemies. When God's people trusted Him, when Israel's leaders acted in faith, the nation became strong and stable—a nation to be reckoned with in the midst of its enemies. Faith inspired leaders to lead as God intended.

Faith also inspires personal heroism. It is impossible to read that "[some] shut the mouths of lions" without thinking of Daniel's courageous loyalty to God, which did not waver, even when, in his old age, he was thrown into the den of lions.[4] And God miraculously intervened to shut the lions' mouths and to spare Daniel. "[Others] quenched the fury of the flames" points us to Shadrach, Meshach, and Abednego. By faith they refused to bow before the idol of the king with the defiant declaration, "If we are thrown into the blazing furnace, the God we serve is able to save us from it, and he will rescue us from your hand, O king. But even if he does not, we want you to know, O king, that we will not serve your gods or worship the image of gold you have set up" (Daniel 3:17–18). The three were thrown into the fire, but God quenched its effect upon them, and when they came out, "the fire had not harmed their bodies, nor was a hair of their head singed; their robes were not scorched, and there was no smell of smoke upon them" (Daniel 3:27). It is less clear what specific events the writer has in mind when he says, "[some] escaped the edge of the sword." David was pursued by angry Saul, Elijah by a determined Jezebel, and Elisha by the king of Syria. In each of these cases, and in many more, an apparently defenseless people experienced God's gracious intervention, delivering them from apparently hopeless situations because they trusted Him.

Faith overcomes and overwhelms human weakness. The heroes of faith were not so much strong people made stronger by God as weak people made strong through and for Him. Some were people "whose weakness was turned to strength." One thinks of Gideon's tiny band or a shepherd boy advancing before an armor-covered giant, armed only with a sling. Others "became powerful in battle and routed foreign armies." Such kings as David, Asaph, and Jehoshaphat come quickly to mind. "Women received back their dead, raised to life again" reminds us of the miracles God brought about through Elijah and Elisha (1 Kings 17; 2 Kings 4).

These are remarkable and inspiring stories of God doing the most unexpected and inexplicable things because people chose to trust Him. God honors faith, sometimes in the most amazing ways. He is a God who will do the miraculous on behalf of His people. And that is no less true today. The basis of these stunning interventions by God wasn't the skill or character or circumstances of those involved. It was the sovereign, gracious, uncoerced response of God to faith. And He has not changed in His response to people who trust Him. God honors faith.

But the life of faith is not simple, and the writer of Hebrews makes that clear. It is true that God often empowers people of faith for stunning acts of deliverance. But deliverance is not the only way God works. For even if we have experienced stunning victories, we may now find ourselves in the midst of staggering defeats.

God Sustains People of Faith in Difficult Times

Hebrews 11:35 is a remarkable verse. And there is an amazing shift in the middle of this verse that has enormous implications for an understanding of how God works in the lives of His people. If you think you have figured out how God works and have reduced it to a formula—"If I trust God, He will help me overcome any circumstance I confront"—you will be shocked when you run smack into Hebrews 11:35. "Women received back their dead, raised to life again. Others were tortured and refused to be released." Both phrases refer to people of faith. As Hebrews 11:39 tells us, "These were all commended for their faith." Although there is no difference in their faith, there is an enormous difference in their experience. It is tempting to say that if the latter had only trusted God more, the outcome would have been different. It is tempting, but it is also wrong, and the writer of Hebrews makes us face head-on the mystery of faith.

I must confess that I like the descriptions of the results of faith up until the middle of Hebrews 11:35 more than the ones that follow: "Through faith . . . women received back their dead" thrills me. I love stories in which desperate people call out to God and experience His remarkable deliverance. But there are many who, this side of heaven, do not find release from suffering and trouble. In earthly terms, they experience crushing defeat, and in this way they follow the Lord Jesus, whose cup of suffering did not pass away from Him. There is an ecstasy of faith, but there is also an agony. Faith does not bring immunity from humiliation, opposition, persecution, or even martyrdom. But faith does bring courage and an awareness of God's presence in the face of death.

"Others were tortured and refused their release" describes, in this case, old covenant saints who remained loyal in the face of brutal mistreatment. Centuries of Christian history multiply their number, and even as you read these words, somewhere in the world brothers and sisters in Christ are experiencing torture and imprisonment. The fact is that millions more have found themselves in the last part of Hebrews 11:35 than in the first half. The specific term used for "torture" reminds us how intensely some suffer for their faith. The word is *tympanizo*, a word obviously linked to our term *tympani*, a large drum. The Greek word describes the process by which a person was stretched on a rack and then beaten (like a drum) to death. Believers were threatened with horrifyingly painful deaths but were promised release if they would only renounce their God and follow the prevailing culture. They refused the easy way, and as a consequence, they paid the price. Here were people who, rather than being delivered by faith, suffered because of it.

Our writer may have in mind some incidents that come from the time of the Maccabees, a group of Jewish patriots who rose in rebellion against the wicked demands of the Syrian king Antiochus Epiphanes. Antiochus was determined to impose Greek culture and religion on the Jewish people and to stamp out every vestige of Jewish worship. In the midst of his reign of terror, his soldiers tried to force a ninety-year-old scribe named Eleazar to eat pork. The story is told in the book of 2 Maccabees, which, although not part of inspired Scripture, does have stories of faith that move us with their accounts of costly loyalty to God. We are simply told that Eleazar, facing the choice of death or compromise, "welcoming death with honor rather than life with pollution, went up to the rack of his own accord" (2 Maccabees 6:19). There he was beaten to death, after having given an eloquent declaration of his trust in God. The same books tell the story of a family of a mother and seven sons who "were being compelled by the king, under torture with whips and cords, to partake of unlawful swine's flesh" (2 Maccabees 7:1). When one of the sons declared his willingness to die rather than break God's laws, Antiochus reacted in fury. He had the man's tongue cut out, his hands and feet cut off, and the man roasted to death in the fire, before his mother and brothers. One after the other, the brothers were skinned, scalped, and burned, and finally their mother, who urged her sons to stay loyal to their Lord, was also tortured and killed. It is at once horrifying and moving to hear the words of the brothers as they refuse release "so that they might gain a better resurrection." As one of them said to the king with his dying breath, "You accursed wretch, you dismiss us from this present life, but the King of the universe will raise us up to eternal life, because we have died for his laws" (2 Maccabees 7:9).

Their motivation of "a better resurrection" reminds us of the writer's earlier description of the "better country" and the "better city" for which people of faith long and look (Hebrews 11:16). They believed in resurrection, not just resuscitation. They lived for the eternal, not the temporary. Everything about the Christian faith is "better." We have a better High Priest, a better hope (Hebrews 7:19), a better covenant (Hebrews 7:22), better promises (Hebrews 8:6), a better sacrifice (Hebrews 9:23), better and lasting possessions (Hebrews 10:34), a better country (Hebrews 11:16), and a better resurrection (Hebrews 11:35). This is the crucial insight of faith, whether then or now. Faith tells us that what God has for us is better than anything we can experience now. Therefore, if He even calls us to difficulty rather than deliverance, we know something better awaits us. As Paul puts it, "Our light and momentary trials are achieving for us an eternal glory that far outweighs them all" (2 Corinthians 4:17).

In the context of the political rights and freedoms of the Western world, these words have the feel of something long ago and far away. But for many of the first readers of this letter to the Hebrews, these trials were not abstract possibilities. Under the terror launched by the Roman emperor Nero, many of them faced death and martyrdom. And these words are not theoretical for large numbers of our fellow Christ-followers in the world today. One of the results of the revolution in information technology is that news is now readily available immediately and universally. Not a week goes by that news does not come from somewhere in the world of Christ-followers being persecuted, attacked, or even killed.

Faith not only gives courage in the face of death. It also sustains endurance under suffering. At times people of faith suffer such horrors precisely because they are people of faith. Faith is not a magic elixir that prevents suffering. And sometimes it is a lightning rod that draws suffering.

The writer probably had specific things in mind as he built his catalogue of suffering. We can only guess at what they were. "Some faced jeers and floggings" could refer to a multitude of occasions on which believers were subject to public humiliation. "Others were chained and put in prison" may refer to the experience of God's righteous prophet Micaiah at the hands of wicked King Ahab (2 Chronicles 18:25–26) or perhaps Jeremiah, victimized by wicked King Zedekiah because of his refusal to twist God's message into words acceptable to the king (Jeremiah 38). "They were stoned" may describe the God-inspired priest Zechariah, who rebuked King Joash for leading his nation into idolatry and was stoned to death in the temple for his faithfulness to God. What makes the story even more poignant is that Zechariah's father, Jehoiada, had saved King Joash's life when he was a baby and reared him as his own son (2 Chronicles 24:20–21). "They were sawn in two" probably refers to the great prophet Isaiah who, a well-established tradition suggests, was sawn in two with a wooden saw in the time of Manasseh. "They were put to death by the sword" perhaps refers to the prophets of God executed by Jezebel (1 Kings 19:10) and to the prophet Uriah, a contemporary of Jeremiah, who was hunted down in Egypt and brought back to Jerusalem to be executed in the presence of King Jehoiakim (Jeremiah 26:20–23). "They went about in sheepskins and goatskins, destitute, persecuted, and mistreated" describes men like Elijah and Elisha and perhaps embraces the Maccabean rebels as well. "They wandered in deserts and mountains, and in caves and holes in the ground" describes a great many who found themselves driven from home and family because of their loyalty to their God.

This is not just a journey into history; it is a profoundly important insight into the life of faith. Faith doesn't guarantee comfort, prosperity, escape from adversity, victory over one's enemies, or even one's physical survival. Although it is not the issue here, faith does not guarantee physical health or exemption from what we call accidents. Faith does, however, guarantee the presence and empowerment of God the Spirit in whatever the sovereign Lord calls us to endure. Faith does guarantee sufficient grace. We can trust God's purpose and God's timing, even though we may not understand His ways.

There are important lessons here, and the first is that *people of faith receive God's approval, regardless of present outcomes.* "These all were commended for their faith." You cannot judge the value of faith by present outcomes. True faith can produce different results, as we have seen. By faith, some escape. They know remarkable deliverances and dramatic answers to prayer. By faith, others endure. They call on God out of a pure heart of faith, and yet they are not delivered or healed or spared. But by faith, all receive divine approval. Peter and James, the brother of John, were imprisoned by Herod, according to Acts 12. James was executed, while Peter was miraculously delivered. Yet there is no suggestion that Peter had a level of faith that James did not. God is sovereign in His purposes, and He has not chosen to tell us why He does what He does and allows what He allows.

In an age that loves immediate results and is enticed by the teaching that health, wealth, and prosperity are God's purpose for every "child of the King," this is a message we must carefully ponder. If you lack these things, many say, it is because you lack faith. But that is not the perspective of God's Word. It is not true that if you trust God you will recover from every illness. It is not true that if you trust God your business will finish in the black every year. It is not true that if you love and follow God people will love you and you will never experience persecution. It was not true in Old Testament times; it was not true in New Testament times; and it is not true now.

I am grateful for those who can share stories of great deliverance, but I have learned far more from people who have lived lives of great endurance. Ron Dunn offers this helpful and healthy correction to the shallowness of much modern thinking:

I have an idea that for most of us the problem is not that we lack sufficient faith to be healed—we lack sufficient faith to remain sick if that be God's will. It requires greater faith to endure than to escape, I imagine, and it is easier to believe that *God is* when it looks as though He is than to believe *He is* when it looks as though He isn't and that is the kind of faith that pleases God.[5]

The second message of this passage is that *people of faith trust God's purposes*. The heroes of faith were people of whom "the world was not worthy," yet they did not receive what God had promised. The reason was not the quality or quantity of their faith but the purpose of their God. The Lord may stretch our faith and call us to trust Him. Hebrews 11 is full of people who were called to trust God, to live with a vision of the future that inspired them to great exploits and led to great kingdom triumphs. We need men and women who will follow God's clear leading down paths discernible only to the eyes of faith and who will attempt great things for God. As our culture falls faster and deeper into biblical and spiritual illiteracy, we need people of faith who will hear and follow the Lord Jesus. But the Lord may also choose to sustain our faith, to call us to trust Him through trial and challenge. It is His sovereign right to determine whether He will stretch our faith or sustain our faith. Our call is simply to trust Him.

The third great message of these verses is that *people of faith await God's reward*. "None of them received what had been promised. God had planned something better for us so that only together with us would they be made perfect." The heroes of faith had to wait. Abraham had to wait; Moses had to wait. Not because of lack of faith but because of God's sovereign purpose. God has a program that is bigger than any individual. God's fulfillment of His covenant with Abraham awaited the coming of the Lord Jesus. So Abraham—and others—became models, not just of waiting but also of waiting in faith. These heroes of faith longed to see the immediate fulfillment of God's promises, but that was not to be. So, until then, they had to trust God's past promises, obey God's present commands, and anticipate God's future blessing. They staked everything on God's promised future.

We already have the completion of the promises of God in Christ. We are forgiven, born into God's forever family, and indwelt by His Holy Spirit. We are heirs of God and fellow-heirs of Christ. Our position in Christ is complete and perfect. But we are not yet home. The Lord Jesus has not returned to take us into His presence. Our redemption is certain, but it is not yet complete. One day the Lord will come for us, and we will enter into the fullness of all that He has promised. We will see the completion of God's program and be with Him forever. But here and now, God has a program that is greater than my individual life. He has a program, and He has a people that He is calling to His Son. He invites us as people of faith to join Him in what He is doing. People of faith trust God's past promises given in His Word. People of faith obey God's present will. People of faith anticipate God's future blessing.

Faith is not a convenient set of beliefs. It is not a set of positive-thinking mottoes. It is not a magic ticket to prosperity. It is a heart-deep confidence in the God who loved us and gave His Son for us. A more recent hero of faith, George Muller, put it like this:

> No one ever knew Jehovah without being able to exercise faith in him. It is when God is not known that difficulty comes. The great point, therefore, is to acquaint ourselves with God, to know God as he has revealed himself in the Scriptures.

No one who truly knows God has trouble trusting Him. The central question then is how well I know Him.

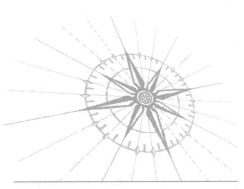

Chapter Sixteen

STAYING THE COURSE

On October 21, 1520, off the coast of South America, Ferdinand Magellan spotted a narrow bay off to starboard.[1] More than a year earlier, he had set out from Spain with 237 sailors in five barely seaworthy ships with a mandate to reach an opening to the west. The pope had divided the New World between Spain and Portugal, and even though Magellan himself was Portuguese, he had disowned loyalty to Portugal and was sailing under the flag of Spain. Anything he discovered to the west would belong to the Spanish. His goal was to be the first to sail west around South America into a part of the world yet to be explored by Europeans, and on to the Spice Islands. Magellan and his men had already experienced a shipwreck, a mutiny, a winter marked by bitter weather, and terrible storms. He had sent out various parties to probe for an opening to the ocean, but each attempt had been thwarted. This was an unknown part of the world, so there were no maps, charts, or oral instructions. They were in unfamiliar territory, finding their own way, and they also were getting perilously low on supplies. Still, Magellan refused to consider turning back: "Though we have nothing to eat but the leather wrappings from our masts, we will go on."[2]

Magellan had no way of knowing, when he pointed his ship westward into the bay he had just seen, that he was entering the body of water that later would bear his name, the Straits of Magellan. Daniel Boorstin calls it "the narrowest, most devious, most circuitous of all the straits connecting two great bodies of water . . . a meandering narrow maze."[3] Magellan found himself facing treacherous currents, powerful winds, dangerous rocks, and continual dead ends. Navigating this passage is difficult enough in modern times, with complete charts and modern ships. For Magellan and his men, it meant continually putting their lives at risk. One of the ships turned around and headed back to Spain, and Magellan's crew began to beg him to do the same. Magellan refused. Finally, after thirty-eight days of high danger and difficulty, his ships broke out into the open sea. Magellan wept for joy, and cried out, "We are about to stand into an ocean where no ship has ever sailed before," and he called it Mar Pacifico, the peaceful ocean.

On nearly all the lists of the most important people in the second millennium after Christ, Magellan stands near the top. His voyage opened up a huge area of the globe for adventurers to explore. Magellan is credited with being the first person to sail around the world, although he did not complete his epic journey. He was killed by a group of natives in the Philippines, and eighteen of his men were left to complete the journey.

Magellan is rightly credited with the journey, however, because his determination made it possible. One of his sailors said, "Among the virtues which he possessed, he was always the most constant in greatest adversity. . . . No other had so much talent, nor the ardor to learn how to go around the world, which he alone did."[4] Magellan endured. He had staying power. In the face of the greatest difficulty, he kept on keeping on.

As we began our journey through Hebrews 11, we noted that the writer of Hebrews opened his account of faith with an appeal to his beleaguered readers: "Do not throw away your confidence. . . . You need to persevere" (Hebrews 10:35–36). At the core of faith lie the qualities of hope and perseverance. The great heroes of faith followed the clear leading of the Lord not because they could see the outcome, but because they trusted God for the outcome. Because their eyes were fixed on the future—hope—they stayed the course—perseverance. They refused to turn back or abandon their goal.

It is impossible to overstate the importance of perseverance. The nature of faith is that, empowered by God's Spirit, it keeps on keeping on. Faith is far more than positive thinking, an optimistic attitude, sheer determination, or a stubborn refusal to quit. It is a robust confidence in God and a delight in His promises that keeps us moving forward. And our supreme example is not one—or all—of the great heroes of faith but the Lord Jesus himself. The former may inspire us, but He empowers us. So our journey ends with a marvelous call to fix our gaze on our Lord and Savior.

> Therefore, since we are surrounded by such a great cloud of witnesses, let us throw off everything that hinders and the sin that so easily entangles, and let us run with perseverance the race marked out for us.
>
> Let us fix our eyes on Jesus, the author and perfecter of our faith, who for the joy set before him endured the cross, scorning its shame, and sat down at the right hand of the throne of God. Consider him who endured such opposition from sinful men, so that you will not grow weary and lose heart. (Hebrews 12:1–3)

A literal translation of this passage helps us see even more clearly the emphasis of the writer: "Therefore, since we are surrounded by such a great cloud of witnesses, throwing off everything that hinders and the sin that so easily entangles, *let us run with perseverance the race marked out for us,* fixing our eyes on Jesus, who . . . endured the cross." The central appeal is, "Run with perseverance. Run with endurance."

The greatest temptation these Hebrew Christians faced, and the greatest one we face, is to take what looks like an easier way or a short-cut. James makes an interesting comment in his epistle: "We consider blessed those who have persevered" (James 5:11). The fact is, most of us consider blessed those who haven't had to persevere. But even the Lord Jesus needed to endure to finish the course, and so must we. The biggest test in every race comes not in the first lap but at that point somewhere much later, when early enthusiasm has drained away and the finish line is distressingly far in the distance. The test for Magellan wasn't when he left Spain; it was when he realized that his greatest challenge, despite all he and his men had endured, was still before him. The toughest place for the Christ-follower is when the initial joy of new faith comes face to face with the ongoing cost of being a disciple.

CHRIST-FOLLOWERS ARE CALLED TO STAY THE COURSE

We have been using the metaphor of navigating the Christian life. But here the metaphor is a different one. Here we are called to run a race, a specific kind of race. The word is *agon,* the source of our word *agony.* The writer of Hebrews is not describing a morning jog or even a sprint, demanding as those can be. The Christian life must be seen as a long-distance race, a cross-country race, a steeplechase, or a marathon. Such races are grueling and exhausting, calling for every bit of energy a runner may possess. You cannot run a marathon casually. It requires disciplined preparation and maximum exertion. I know from my friends who have run marathons that, long before race day, the race dominates large parts of their lives. It determines how they eat and what they do with their time. They run the race in their imagination, planning their pace and toughening their attitude. They prepare themselves mentally as well as physically. And then, during the race, they struggle through the moment when they hit the wall and everything within them wants to quit. A marathon runner also has to run according to the rules. No shortcuts are allowed. A marathon has a set distance of slightly more than twenty-six miles, and the required course is marked out for the competitors.

A long-distance run offers many important parallels to what it means to live as a follower of Christ, here and now. Our spiritual life is not a walk in the park or a workout that makes us feel better. Neither is it a short sprint to a nearby finish line. God has called us to a long-distance race that is draining and demanding and will require everything we have. And the race is "marked out for us." We don't get to choose what we will meet along the way.

Our spiritual race differs from a physical race in two ways. First, there is an individual course for every believer. Abraham did not run the same course as Moses, and Abel did not encounter what Jacob did. I will not run the same course as you. God sovereignly marks out the conditions and circumstances of my journey, and it is a course suited for what He wants to do in and through me. I need to allow the Lord to be as creative and as personal with me as He is with others. I also need to trust the wisdom of the course He has set. The second distinctive of our spiritual race is that we are not in competition with anyone else. I am not running to beat or better others but to please God. Every course, individual though it is, leads to the same finish line, and there we will be rewarded by a gracious God on the basis of how well we have run His course set for us—not on the basis of how well someone else might have run it.

The indispensable quality required in all of this is endurance. In each of these three verses we meet the word: "run with endurance"; "he endured the cross"; "consider him who endured such opposition." To understand what is meant by this, it helps to see that the Greek word here is a word picture. It means "to remain under," which is a picture of someone who is under challenge, under difficulty, under trial, under suffering—someone who chooses not to get out but to go on. Endurance is the capacity to stay in circumstances of trouble and difficulty, resisting the temptation to take an easy way out, and to keep moving relentlessly toward the goal. It is the refusal to cave in under difficulty or discomfort, and it is a choice to keep on keeping on. Endurance has nothing to do with fatalism or resignation or passivity. It is the determination to remain rather than escape, to meet difficulties head-on and to overcome them in the power of Christ. It is the commitment to be what God calls me to be, where God calls me to be, to the glory of God.

We live in a society that perpetually takes what it believes is the easy way. Faced with an unwanted pregnancy, we kill the unborn. Faced with marital challenges and conflicts, we terminate the marriage. Confronted with a ministry that costs more than we thought, we resign. Meeting a situation that goes against our preferences, we change churches. Feeling a need that we are sure must be met, we violate God's standards. Overwhelmed by a temptation that we cannot avoid, we give in.

True godliness does the opposite. It has staying power. It does not welcome hardships, but it is not surprised by them. It knows that life calls for endurance. It also knows that the goal of pleasing and honoring God is always worth the price, whatever that may be. *Endurance* is the word that describes a soldier who chooses to remain in the heat of the battle, to serve his King. I have been helped by this insightful description by William Barclay:

[Perseverance] is not the patience which can sit down and bow the head and let things descend upon it and passively endure until the storm is passed. . . . It is the spirit which can bear things not simply with resignation, but with blazing hope; it is not the spirit which sits statically enduring in the one place, but the spirit which bears things because it knows that these things are leading to a goal of glory; it is not the patience which grimly hopes for the end, but the patience which radiantly hopes for the dawn. It has been called a "masculine constancy under trial". . . . It is the quality which keeps a man on his feet with face to the wind. It is the virtue which can transmute the hardest trial into glory because beyond the pain, it sees the goal.[5]

One of the first rules distance runners learn is that the race is run in the mind before it is run with the feet. A runner who has not thought through what it will take to run the race has little chance of finishing. Ignorance is not a blessing. A runner who has not counted the cost of running will be overcome by problems that should have been obvious, had he taken the time to inform himself properly. That is also very true of the Christian life. If I do not take seriously the fact that it is an endurance race, I will be discouraged with and defeated by things that the Bible clearly teaches me to expect.

James Fixx was one of the gurus of the exercise revolution of the 1970s, the author of a best seller entitled *The Complete Book of Running*. His passion for running and fitness inspired thousands of others to join in the quest. In his book, he describes his experience of learning to run with endurance:

When we race, strange things happen to our minds. The stress of fatigue sometimes makes us forget why we wanted to run in the first place. In one of my early marathons I found myself unable to think of a single reason for continuing. Physically and mentally exhausted, I dropped out of the race. Now I won't enter a marathon unless I truly want to finish. If during the race I can't remember why I wanted to run in it, I tell myself, "Maybe I can't remember now, but I know I had a good reason when I started." I've finally learned how to fight back when my brain starts using tricky arguments.[6]

Good words for a Christ-follower to apply to his or her race!

CHRIST-FOLLOWERS DETERMINE AND PREPARE TO STAY THE COURSE

A race that requires endurance is a constant battle against discouragement. There is always the danger of growing weary and losing heart, as Hebrews 12:3 indicates. And there is the double danger of inward exhaustion and personal discouragement. The second phrase, "losing heart," is a graphic one. Those who have been there know this feeling of soul weariness, a sense that one's resources have been thoroughly depleted and there is nothing left to go another step. Some of that exhaustion comes from a sense of our own weakness, a feeling of being overwhelmed by our shortcomings and failures. Here, however, the writer has in mind "the opposition of sinful [people]," such as the Lord Jesus encountered. Even the sinless Son of God experienced the active and determined opposition of others, and He warned that we would experience the same: "In this world you will have trouble. But take heart! I have overcome the world" (John 16:33). "Blessed are you when people insult you, persecute you and falsely say all kinds of evil against you because of me" (Matthew 5:11). Peter writes with typical bluntness: "Dear friends, do not be surprised at the painful trial you are suffering, as though something strange were happening to you" (1 Peter 4:12). John, the beloved disciple, adds, "Do not be surprised, my brothers, if the world hates you" (1 John 3:13). The fact that we are surprised only shows us that we have drifted from biblical perspectives. In our society, the hostility is sometimes overt and direct when we meet those who despise and oppose our loyalty to King Jesus. More commonly, though, it is disguised as cultural values that undermine and oppose biblical values. We should not be caught off-guard when we encounter opposition, overt or covert, to our allegiance to the Lord Jesus.

In such circumstances, we should look to the inspiring models of those who have run the race with endurance, amidst opposition. That, the writer says, is exactly what we have: "We are surrounded by such a great cloud of witnesses." In the Bible the word *witness* is never used to mean a spectator. Rather, a witness is someone who sees something and says something. This "great cloud of witnesses" is not a group of spectators who watch us as we run, but witness bearers who have gone before and show us how to run. This "great cloud" is the group of champions of faith described in Hebrews 11 who show us what it means to live by faith. They are witnesses to the nature of faith and to the life of faith, with all of its ups and downs. They give credence to the possibility of faith in times of uncertainty and to the power of faith in times of distress. If they are spectators, it is as relay runners who, having run their leg to the best of their ability, have passed the baton to us and now cheer us on to the finish line.

One of the great weaknesses of the modern church is that we have so many celebrities and so few heroes. Our Christian bookstores are full of the stories of people who are well known but who have not necessarily lived well. They impress us, but they have little capacity to instruct us or inspire us, because theirs are not lives of deep godliness and spiritual authenticity lived out over years of faithfulness. One of the lessons of Hebrews 11 is that we need to know well the lives of the heroes of faith in God's Word. We also do well to learn the life stories of more recent followers of the Lord, people who have lived wisely and well, often under circumstances of deep difficulty. Such individuals show me that if they lived by faith, so can I.

We become like the heroes we admire. So we need to see the cloud of witnesses, biblical and nonbiblical, who show us how to run with endurance, despite the pull of discouragement.

A second danger in the race is distraction. We need to "throw off everything that hinders." The picture here is of an athlete about to get in the starting blocks, setting aside anything that might keep him from running at his best. He has toned his body and laid aside unnecessary weight. He takes off not only his normal clothing but also his warm-up suit. He takes off normal street shoes and puts on running shoes carefully chosen to maximize performance. The point is that none of the things he "throws off" are illegal. But they are unnecessary. Not only that, they are hindering. All of us know what it is to be dressed for one thing and then discover that there is work to be done or a game to be played. Our first response is to change our clothes. Our present dress may be fine for shopping or attending church, but when we need to run, street clothes get in the way. They weigh us down and eventually help to wear us down.

There are things in my life that may not be sin, in and of themselves, but which hinder me in my race. They keep me from maximizing my performance. The list is surprisingly personal. Things that may not hinder you may for me be like carrying an anchor. At times in my life I have had to realize that there were people, nice and good people, who distracted and delayed me in my spiritual race. There have been relationships I have had to change, things I have had to decline, activities I have had to avoid, and practices I have had to abandon because they were hindering me. Abraham had to set aside a life of wealth in Ur; Moses had to leave a life of prestige in Egypt; Daniel had to abandon a position of power in Babylon. None of these things was wrong, until it interfered with following the clear leading of God. We need to be honest enough with ourselves to recognize that there are things that weigh us down in the race. Our choice is never about what others can do; it is about what we need to do to "run with perseverance the race marked out for us." Even good things can become hindrances if they keep us from the best things. The old adage is true: The good is often the enemy of the best.

A third danger in the race is disqualification. By that I do not mean that a true believer can lose his or her salvation. We are kept by the power of God to salvation, as Peter tells us (1 Peter 1:5). But Paul also tells us, "I beat my body and make it my slave so that after I have preached to others, I myself will not be disqualified for the prize" (1 Corinthians 9:27). The writer of Hebrews speaks of "the sin that so easily entangles." It is unlikely that he means that one particular sin more than any other distracts and ensnares God's people. Middle Eastern people in New Testament times customarily wore long robes that needed to be gathered up and tucked into a belt to free the legs. If they didn't, their feet would easily become entangled, and they would find themselves flat on their faces. Sin, of whatever kind, has a way of tripping us up. Probably each of us is particularly prone to a certain set of sins. We cannot and must not excuse them or accept them. They will halt our progress and cause a humiliating and painful fall.

I am a Canadian, and that means that the 1988 Summer Olympics in Seoul, Korea, hold a particularly painful memory. On September 24, Ben Johnson ran one of the great races of history. He blew away the field to win the 100–meter race and set a new world record in the process. When he stood on the podium to receive his gold medal, and as we heard "Oh Canada," there was an enormous surge of national pride across a country that is normally pretty reserved. Not only had our man won; he had beaten our neighbor to the south, Carl Lewis! But only two days later, everything changed. Word came that Johnson had tested positive for steroids. He was stripped of his medal and his world record, and he returned home to Toronto in disgrace. The sin of ambition had entangled him, and he had broken the rules. He wasn't stripped of his citizenship, but he lost his honor, his reputation, and his reward.

Because sin so easily entangles us, we need to deal ruthlessly with sin in our lives. We need the wisdom to avoid things that entice us and not play with them. We also need to repent of sin when we fall prey to it and discipline ourselves to avoid repeating the foolishness of sin. We have seen many prominent Christians fall to entangling sin in recent times. The one thing we can be sure of is that none of them fell suddenly. All had played with sin rather than dealing with it decisively. They imagined that they could keep running, even as they allowed sin to tangle itself around their legs.

People who run well have to defeat or beware of discouragement, distractions, and disqualifying entanglements. If they don't, they will never finish well. The same is true for us.

CHRIST-FOLLOWERS FOCUS ON JESUS TO STAY THE COURSE

"Let us run with endurance, fixing our eyes on Jesus. . . . Consider him who endured." As we look at our Lord Jesus, we see Him as our enablement and our example in the race. He is the object of our faith and trust. He is the goal to which we run, and He is the judge for whom we run. The picture that comes to my mind is of a race of toddlers at a church picnic. The mother kneels next to her child at the starting line while the father stands at the finish line. "There's Daddy. Look at Daddy," the mother says to the child. "When I tell you to, run to Daddy as fast as you can! Don't look around. Run to Daddy." The instructions usually don't do much good, but the child who follows them is almost certain to win.

The writer of Hebrews first wants us to see that the Lord Jesus is our enablement for staying the course. We are told to "fix our eyes" on Him. This is a call to look away from other things, to lock our eyes on Jesus in such a way that we are not distracted by things around us. Looking to Jesus directs us.

When I keep my eyes fixed on Him, I remember why I am running, for whom I am running, and where I am going. I learned this lesson when I was very young. In 1954, the British Empire Games (now called the Commonwealth Games) were held in my home city, Vancouver, British Columbia. The British Commonwealth was still at its strongest, and because of that the British Empire Games had a prestige only slightly behind the Olympic Games. But these games of 1954 were also special because they brought together the first two men to break the four-minute mile, a feat once thought improbable if not impossible. That summer, Roger Bannister of England had made headlines around the world when he showed that the barrier was mental, not physical. A few weeks later, John Landy of Australia bettered his time. The games represented the first meeting of these two men in a race that was being called the Miracle Mile before it was even run. Landy quickly jumped out to the lead and led nearly the whole way. As he rounded the last curve, he turned his head to locate Bannister. As he did, two things happened: he broke stride slightly, and Bannister, who had his eyes locked on the finish line, swept by on his other shoulder to break the tape first. I remember listening to that race on the radio and seeing it rerun on television. But most of all I remember seeing, outside the stadium where it occurred, a statue depicting that moment. Every time I passed that statue on the way into a football game I was reminded of the message: Keep your eyes on the prize! "But one thing I do," wrote Paul. "Forgetting what is behind and straining toward what is ahead, I press on toward the goal to win the prize for which God has called me heavenward in Christ Jesus" (Philippians 3:13–14).

We are called to fix our eyes on Jesus. The simple name *Jesus* points us to the earthly life of our Lord. The writer is not suggesting that we do not look at the heavenly glory of our risen Lord, but here his attention is on the life of our Lord on earth. We are to look at His life, listen to His teachings, watch His choices, observe His lifestyle, examine His character and conduct under adversity. Most of all, we are to look at Him experiencing opposition, enduring humiliation, and suffering crucifixion. We are to remember that He knows all about a race of endurance.

We are also to "consider him." This word describes a process of reflection and comparison. We are to fill our minds with Him, even as we fix our eyes on Him. Looking at and considering Jesus not only directs us; it empowers us. Observing the heroes of faith inspires me; looking at Jesus empowers me. As we focus on the Lord Jesus, the Holy Spirit changes us. People who spend time in the presence of Christ increasingly become like Him. There is a wonderful picture in the experience of Peter on Lake Galilee. As he fixed his eyes on Jesus, he stepped out of the boat and began to walk on water. But then he began to look around, he felt the wind and saw the waves, and immediately he began to sink. As long as his eyes were on Jesus, he was empowered. We don't need to walk on water, but we do need to run the race, and Jesus empowers us to run with endurance.

Jesus is not only our enablement for staying the course; He is our model for finishing the race. First, He is our model of faith. He trusted His Father and relied completely upon Him, so that He is called "the author and perfecter of our faith." Both of these words are difficult to translate into English. The first word says far more than our word *author* says. It is used of the originator or source of something, and since an author is the source of a book, that is an appropriate rendering. But the word also is used of a trailblazer, a pioneer, a founder, one who establishes something new or who opens a new way. It is also used of a champion, and perhaps in this instance this is the main idea. Jesus is the champion of faith, the one who more than any other shows what faith is like. The other term, "perfecter," looks at the completer, the finisher, the one who reaches the goal. Jesus not only opens the way of faith but brings it to completion. He brings the people of faith all the way home.

One of Ernest Shackleton's men evaluated the man who had led him through such arduous circumstances in these terms:

> It was certain that a man of such heroic mind and self-sacrificing nature as Shackleton would undertake the most difficult and dangerous task himself. He was, in fact, unable by nature to do otherwise. Being a born leader, he had to lead in the position of most danger, difficulty and responsibility. I have seen him turn pale, and yet force himself into the post of greatest peril. That was his type of courage; he would do the job that he was most afraid of.[7]

Ernest Shackleton's example is a great one, but we have one even greater. The Lord Jesus models completely and perfectly what He asks of His followers. As the champion and completer of faith, He is our perfect model for running with endurance. "For the joy set before him, he endured the cross, scorning its shame, and sat down at the right hand of the throne of God." We can hardly imagine how deep the shame of the cross was. It was a brutal death—horrific enough in itself. But to Romans, the cross was also a scandal, a punishment meted out only to slaves and social outcasts, the ultimate punishment for crimes of high treason. They called it "the tree of shame."

"Death on the cross was the penalty for slaves, as everyone knew; as such, it symbolized extreme humiliation, shame and torture."[8] For Jews, it was the supreme evidence that a person was under God's judgment, for "cursed is everyone who is hung on a tree" (Galatians 3:13). To ordinary human beings, it was shameful beyond words. As Martin Hengel notes, "By the public display of a naked victim at a prominent place—at a crossroads, in the theater, on high ground, at the place of his crime—crucifixion also represented his uttermost humiliation."[9] Jesus hated the shame of the cross. It violated all that He was as true God and sinless man. He knew all that it involved. Yet He endured it, in full measure.

He also endured "such opposition from sinful men." Mockery, brutality, contempt, cruelty—the list is endless. Jesus endured the petty complaints of weak men, the evil machinations of cruel men, the pious posturing of evil men, and the multiplied abuses of violent men. He was no helpless victim. With a word He could have ended their opposition and terminated their existence. But He endured, to the point of death.

Why? For the joy set before Him. The joy of "bringing many sons to glory" (Hebrews 2:10). Endurance is the product of anticipated joy. We put up with the difficulties of the present because of our anticipation of the future. This was true of our Savior. His was the joyful anticipation of redemption accomplished, of heaven opened for the people of faith. It was the joyful certainty of having fully done the Father's will and rejoicing in the eternal city with the bride He had purchased at such a terrible cost. He was sustained by the certainty that what God had promised would come to pass, despite all that seemed true at the present. This is the way of faith. We have seen Abraham living as a pilgrim because of the joy of the heavenly city that was set before him. We have seen Moses enduring the loss of Egypt's treasures because "he was looking ahead to the reward" (Hebrews 11:26). Now, most of all, we see in our Lord, the champion and completer of faith, a robust confidence that God keeps

His word and fulfills His promise. Faith endures because of the joy set before us.

Jesus is also our model of final victory. At His Father's time and in His Father's way, He "sat down at the right hand of the throne of God." He has no need to fight for the throne. He has been exalted by the Father to the highest place, and all that heaven affords is rightly His. The Father's reward is certain, and the Lord's exaltation is the promise and proof to Christ-followers that we will know life with Him in the city whose builder and maker is God. We run with endurance now, but one day the race will be finished and we will receive the prize.

In 1968, the Summer Olympics were held in Mexico City. An hour after the winner of the marathon crossed the finish line, one man was still on the course, John Stephen Akhwari of Tanzania. Not many people were in the stadium when he finally reached it, but those who were could immediately see that something had happened along the way. Akhwari was limping badly, with a bloody, crude bandage wrapped around his leg. He had obviously fallen and injured himself rather severely. The crowd greeted him with polite applause. But as they watched him making his slow, painful circle of the track, something happened. His determination and courage were contagious. The spectators moved as close to the track as they could and began to cheer and yell encouragement to this determined man. Finally, as their response built to a roar, he crossed the line. Later, when he was asked what kept him going, he made this marvelous reply: "My country didn't send me here to *start* the race; my country sent me here to *finish* it."

The same is true of us. Our Lord didn't send us here to start our race but to finish it. So keep on keeping on! And if you've fallen, get up and keep going!

CONCLUSION

On August 25, 1768, with James Cook at the helm, the *Endeavour* set sail from England on a journey that would take it around the world. Once he rounded South America, Cook would enter uncharted waters and places unknown to Europeans. "I had ambition not only to go farther than any one had ever been before me," Cook wrote in his journal, "but as far as I think it possible to go."[1]

His ambition would take Cook, in the course of three epochal voyages, to the edges of Antarctica, to New Zealand and the eastern shore of Australia, to nearly every major island group in the Pacific, to the west coast of British Columbia and Alaska, and would finally lead to his death in the Hawaiian Islands. Travel anywhere in the Pacific and you will find traces of Cook. His legacy has inspired the imagination of succeeding generations, from Captain Hook of *Peter Pan* to Captain Kirk of *Star Trek*, whose mission in the starship *Enterprise* is clearly borrowed from Cook: "to boldly go where no man has gone before." But Cook's influence isn't only found in the realm of fiction. NASA borrowed from the name of his first ship, *Enterprise*, for Apollo 15 in 1971 and the space shuttle in 1992.

Cook's voyages achieved great things, but they were also unbelievably costly, as Martin Dugard describes in memorable fashion:

> Whether by shipwrecks, fire, cannibals, mutiny, shipboard fighting, scurvy, suicide, or just plain accidental drowning, death occurred to at least a few members of every crew on every long voyage. . . .
>
> Most of the sailors would die at sea, so they drank as if there were no tomorrow. Because of risk and mortality, 60 percent of all sailors were under the age of thirty, with the average age being twenty-seven. . . . At sea, they faced not just storms, but lightning, freezing temperatures, fire (the seaman's greatest fear on board wooden ships), and sudden death from a crashing mast or amputation from a snapped rope.[2]

Cook spent much of his time sailing off the map. In fact, he was creating the maps and charts others would use to follow his path. Even when he knew where he was headed, the task was anything but simple. One of the major reasons for his first voyage was a scientific one. Astronomers had announced that on June 3, 1769, Venus would cross the face of the sun. If they could observe this "transit of Venus" from different places on the earth, they would be able to calculate precisely Earth's distance from the sun, a discovery with great scientific value for mapping the heavens. Cook was sent to carry out such observations in the South Pacific on the island of Tahiti.

It was one thing to know his destination; it was another to find it, because at that time it was still impossible to determine exact longitude.

While Cook was an accomplished navigator with a cartographer's knowledge of geography and had a thirty-three-year-old astronomer . . . to guide him through the more complex celestial-navigational computations, there was a great deal of luck involved in finding Tahiti. The breadth of the Pacific and the small size of the South Pacific islands (though these twenty-five thousand islands are scattered across millions of square miles of ocean, their combined mass is only roughly the size of America's west coast) demanded precision navigation, good weather, and benevolent winds. Finding Tahiti in that watery mass was a literal search for a needle in a haystack. At just thirty-three miles long and sixteen miles wide, Tahiti was the sort of landmass a ship could easily bypass in the night.[3]

But James Cook didn't miss it. He is the epitome of the navigator, the man of adventure who follows a burning ambition to "go as far as I think it possible to go."

We began our journey in this book on the quiet shores of Lake Galilee. No one seeing the Lord Jesus interact with a few fishermen in a boat could have imagined where following Him would take them. Their adventure with Jesus makes Cook's pale into insignificance. They were people who boldly went where none had gone before. They had no maps to guide them. But they did have the navigational tools and skills that the Lord Jesus had given them. They relied on His Word, depended upon His Spirit, followed His example, dialogued with Him through prayer, forged godly character, cultivated sensitive consciences, partnered with one another, and walked in the steps of the people of faith who had gone before. Their lives were lived off the maps, often in the midst of terrific storms. But they reached their destination, having done the will of God in their generation, as they looked to Jesus, the champion and completer of faith.

Our world is very different from theirs. If any one of the apostles were suddenly transplanted into our time and place, they would be utterly mystified. But the same navigational truths that guided them can and will guide us. We do not need updated navigational technology. The ones we have can never be improved upon, because they are not the products of human invention but of divine grace. The maps have changed; the navigational realities haven't. We are not called to imitate the apostles' journey; we are called to imitate their faith. Until the Lord Jesus comes, we need to keep our bearings on "true north," using the tools the Lord has given.

In our generation, we are called to go further than we think it is possible to go, because we are following in the way of faith. When navigators in the thirteenth century began to use the compass, they changed the world. Perhaps as we discover anew the everlasting navigational tools the Lord has given, we will change ours.

Sail on!

Notes

Introduction

1. Cited in William Bennett, *The Broken Hearth: Reversing the Moral Collapse of the American Family* (New York: Doubleday, 2001), 1.
2. Amir D. Azcel, *The Riddle of the Compass: The Invention that Changed the World* (New York: Harcourt, 2001), xii.

Chapter One: Ocean Bound

1. Simon Winchester, "After Dire Straits, An Agonizing Haul Across the Pacific," *Smithsonian* (April 1991), 84–95, at http://marauder.millersv.edu/~columbus/data/art/WINCHE01.ART.
2. Daniel J. Boorstin, *The Discoverers* (New York: Vintage Books, 1985), 263. A further account of Magellan's passage through the straits is found in chapter 16 of this book.
3. Boorstin, 265.
4. Ibid.
5. Winchester, 6, 7 (website version).

6. "The Heart of the Matter," *Fast Company* (July/August, 1999), 16.

Chapter Two: Finding True North

1. The story of the Shackleton expedition has captured the attention of many writers, many of them in recent years. The most accessible account is by Carolyn Alexander, *The Endurance: Shackleton's Legendary Antarctic Expedition* (New York: Alfred A. Knopf, 1999). A moving firsthand account is found in Frank Worsley, *Shackleton's Boat Journey* (New York: W.W. Norton, 1977).

2. Worsley, *Shackleton's Boat Journey*, 115.

3. Warren W. Wiersbe, *Why Us? When Bad Things Happen to God's People* (Old Tappan, NJ: Fleming H. Revell, 1984), 41.

Chapter Three: "Don't Leave Home Without It"

1. Dava Sobel, *Longitude* (New York: Penguin, 1996), 13.

2. Sobel, 6, 13, 14.

3. Matthew 4:1–11 reverses the order of the second and third temptations. Most commentators believe that Matthew's order is original and that Luke has changed the order to highlight his theme of the climax of events in Jerusalem. The message of the temptation is not affected by the order in which the events occurred.

4. John Stott, *Evangelical Truth* (Downers Grove, IL: InterVarsity Press, 1999), 56.

Chapter Four: Spiritual Ballast

1. Gordon MacDonald, *The Life God Blesses* (Nashville: Thomas Nelson, 1994), 2.

2. C. Samuel Storms, *Reaching God's Ear* (Wheaton: Tyndale, 1988), 84.

3. Walter Lord, *The Night Lives On* (New York: William Morrow and Company, 1986), 32, 33.

Chapter Five: God's Compass

1. "On the top of the country, Jackson reconciles career, family," *USA Today*, September 1, 1998, 1D.

2. Malcolm Muggeridge, *A Twentieth Century Testimony* (Nashville: Thomas Nelson, 1978).

3. J. I. Packer, *Rediscovering Holiness* (Ann Arbor, MI: Servant Publications, 1992), 151.

Chapter Six: Load Limits

1. "How Much Is Enough?" *Fast Company* (July/August, 1999): 110.

2. Ibid., 114, 116.

3. Philip H. Towner, *1–2 Timothy & Titus* (Downers Grove, IL: InterVarsity Press, 1994), 139.

4. James Hope Moulton and George Milligan, *The Vocabulary of the Greek New Testament* (London; Hodder and Stoughton, 1930), 445.

5. Warren W. Wiersbe, *On Being a Servant of God* (Grand Rapids: Baker, 1993), 142.

6. Adapted from John Piper, *Desiring God* (Portland, OR: Multnomah, 1986), 156.

7. Roger Lowenstein, *Buffet: the Making of an American Capitalist* (New York: Random House, 1995), 416.

Chapter Seven: Money Matters

1. *People*, June 12, 2000, 62.

2. Charles Colson, in the foreword, "The Least of These, the Rest of Us," in Ronald J. Sider, *Just Generosity* (Grand Rapids: Baker, 1999), 9.

3. Susan Pulliam and Scott Thurm, "Echelon of ex-millionaires sees stakes plunge as net craze fades," *Wall Street Journal*, from PreachingToday.com.

4. Fred Smith, "A Holy Boldness Towards Money," *Leadership* II: 2 (Spring, 1981), 48.

5. John and Sylvia Ronsvalle, *Behind the Stained Glass Windows* (Grand Rapids: Baker, 1996), 202.

Chapter Eight: Character Counts

1. The story of the Stefannson expedition is told with great skill by Jennifer Niven, *The Ice Master: The Doomed 1913 Voyage of the Karluk* (New York: Hyperion, 2000).
2. The contrast is effectively drawn in terms of secular leadership methods by Dennis N. T. Perkins, *Leading at the Edge* (New York: Amacom, 2000). Shackleton is discussed again in chapter 15 of this book.
3. William Laird McKinlay, *Karluk: The Great Untold Story of Arctic Exploration* (New York: St. Martin's Press, 1977), 99.
4. Michael Josephson and Wes Hanson, eds., *The Power of Character* (San Francisco: Jossey–Bass, 1998), 1.
5. I have chosen the New American Standard Version here primarily because of its more literal rendering "flesh," rather than the New International Version's rendering, "the sinful nature." The flesh represents all that we are outside of Christ.
6. John Stott, *The Contemporary Christian* (Downers Grove, IL: InterVarsity Press, 1992), 148.
7. William Morrice, *Joy in the New Testament* (Grand Rapids: Eerdmans, 1984), 85, 86
8. The story of Lilias Trotter is told by Miriam Huffman Rockness, *A Passion for the Impossible* (Grand Rapids: Discovery House, 2003). I have lost the reference for the Algerian's quote, but it is not found in the Rockness book.
9. Gordon Fee, *Paul, the Spirit, and the People of God* (Peabody, MA: Hendricksen, 1996), 120, 121.
10. Daniel Goleman, "What Can We Do About Emotional Illiteracy?" in Josephson and Hanson, *The Power of Character*, 318.
11. Source unknown.

Chapter Nine: Staying Power

1. Eli Cohen and Noel Tichy, "Operation Leadership," *Fast Company* 27 (September, 1999): 280.
2. Cohen and Tichy, 286.
3. Dawson Trotman, *The Need of the Hour* (Colorado Springs: NavPress, 1975).

Chapter Ten: By Faith Alone

1. Tracey Stewart and Ken Abraham, *Payne Stewart* (Nashville: Broadman and Holman, 2000), 299.
2. Steward, *Payne Stewart*, 308.
3. Bart Kosko, "The Problem with Faith-based Programs Is Faith Itself," *Los Angeles Times*, February 19, 2001, B7.

Chapter Eleven: Travel Guides

1. Anna Muoio, "We're All Explorers," *Fast Company* 17 (September, 1988): 160.
2. Richard Halverson, source unknown
3. Adapted from Marshall Broomhall, *Hudson Taylor's Legacy* (London: Hodder and Stoughton, 1974), 59, 60.

Chapter Twelve: Homeward Bound

1. James Lovell and Jeffrey Kluger, *Lost Moon* (Boston: Houghton and Miflin, 1994), 284.
2. C. S. Lewis, *Mere Christianity* (New York: Macmillan, 1960), 118.
3. Miriam and Stuart Bundy, *Restoring the Soul* (Chicago: Moody Press, 1999).
4. Bundy, 30, 31.
5. Malcolm Muggeridge, *Jesus Rediscovered* (New York; Doubleday, 1979), 48.
6. A. W. Tozer, *Whatever Happened to Worship?* (Camp Hill, PA: Christian Publications, 1985), 30, 31.
7. Tozer, 13.

Chapter Thirteen: Stress Test

1. Sean McNeill, "Young America Taking Stock," Quokka Sports, November 9, 1999, available at www.americascup.org/news.

2. "The Fine Line," Quokka Sports, November 9, 1999, available at www.americascup.org/news. The quote is adapted from an interview with Chris Todter.

3. Larry Edwards, "Looking Back," Quokka Sports, November 9, 1999, available at www. americascup.org/news. The quote is adapted from a statement by Ian Burns.

Chapter Fourteen: Choices

1. Table of Contents, "Into the Unknown," *New York Times Magazine*, June 6, 1999, at www.nytimes.com/library/magazine/millennium/m3/index .html.

2. Nicholas D. Kristof, "1492: The Prequel," *New York Times Magazine*, June 6, 1999, at www.nytimes.com/library/magazine/millennium/m3/kristof .html.

3. Ibid., 7.

4. Ibid., 8, 9.

5. Peter Enns, *Exodus: The NIV Application Commentary* (Grand Rapids: Zondervan, 2000), 73.

Chapter Fifteen: Trusting a Sovereign God

1. Chapter 2 contained a description of the last stages of this expedition, Shackleton's dramatic journey from Antarctica to South Georgia Island. See the sources cited there.

2. This quotation is cited often, but I have been unable to locate its original source.

3. Sir Edmund Hillary, "Introduction," in F. A. Worsley, *Shackleton's Boat Journey* (New York: W.W. Norton and Company, 1977), 12.

4. It is often overlooked that Daniel must have been at least eighty years old when the events recorded in Daniel 6 took place.

5. Ron Dunn, *Don't Just Sit There . . . Have Faith!* (Amersham-on-the-Hill, England: Alpha, 1994), 120.

Chapter Sixteen: Staying the Course

1. The story of Magellan is also considered in chapter 1 of this book.

2. Simon Winchester, "After Dire Straits, An Agonizing Haul Across the Pacific," *Smithsonian* (April 1991): 84–95, at http://marauder.millerv.edu/~columbus/data/art/WINCHE01.ART.

3. Daniel J. Boorstin, *The Discoverers* (New York: Vintage Books, 1985), 263.

4. Ibid., 261.

5. William Barclay, *New Testament Words* (London: SCM Press, 1964), 144–45.

6. James Fixx, *The Complete Book of Running* (New York: Random House, 1977), 92.

7. F. A. Worsley, *Shackleton's Boat Journey* (New York: W.W. Norton, 1977), 95, 96.

8. Martin Hengel, *Crucifixion* (Philadelphia: Fortress Press, 1977), 62.

9. Hengel, 87.

Conclusion

1. Cook's story is told expertly by Martin Dugard, *Farther Than Any Man: The Rise and Fall of Captain James Cook* (New York: Pocket Books, 2001).

2. Ibid., 10, 21.

3. Ibid., 90.

NOTE TO THE READER